SEARCH
AND
RESCUE

Lorna Siggins is a journalist working in print and on radio, and a former *Irish Times* western and marine correspondent. She is the author of *Everest Calling* (1994 and 2013), on the first Irish ascent of Everest and subsequent expeditions; *Mary Robinson: The Woman Who Took Power in the Park* (1997); *Mayday! Mayday!* (2004); and *Once Upon a Time in the West: The Corrib Gas Controversy* (2010). She is co-producer with Sarah Blake of RTÉ's Documentary on One, *Miracle on Galway Bay* (2021).

SEARCH

AND

RESCUE

TRUE STORIES OF IRISH AIR-SEA RESCUES
AND THE LOSS OF R116

LORNA SIGGINS

MERRION
PRESS

First published in 2022 by
Merrion Press
10 George's Street
Newbridge
Co. Kildare
Ireland
www.merrionpress.ie

978 1 78537 357 2 (Paper)
978 1 78537 358 9 (Ebook)

A CIP catalogue record for this book
is available from the British Library.

Typeset in Minion Pro 11/15 pt

Cover images courtesy of Pat Flynn, Ennis, Co. Clare.
Cover design by: riverdesignbooks.com

Merrion Press is a member of Publishing Ireland

CONTENTS

LIST OF ABBREVIATIONS

AAIU	Air Accident Investigation Unit
AIS	Automatic Identification System
Armn	Airman
CFT	Comhairle Fo-Thuinn
CHC	Canadian Helicopter Corporation
Cmdt	Commandant
Cpl	Corporal
CUAG	Coastal Unit Advisory Group
DSM	Distinguished Service Medal
EAS	Emergency Aeromedical Service
EGPWS	Enhanced Ground Proximity Warning System
EPIRB	Emergency Position Indicating Radio Beacon
FLIR	Forward-looking Infrared
HSA	Health and Safety Authority
IAA	Irish Aviation Authority
IALPA	Irish Airline Pilots' Association
ICAO	International Civil Aviation Organisation
ICRR	Irish Community Rapid Response
IMES	Irish Marine Emergency Service (later the Irish Coast Guard)
MCA	Maritime and Coastguard Agency
MCIB	Marine Casualty Investigation Board

MRCC	Marine Rescue Co-ordination Centre
NAS	National Ambulance Service
PFD	Personal Flotation Device
PLB	Personal Locator Beacon
RAF	Royal Air Force
RDS	Royal Dublin Society
RIB	Rigid Inflatable Boat
RNLI	Royal National Lifeboat Association
ROV	Remotely Operated Vehicle
SARDA	Search and Rescue Dog Association
Sgt	Sergeant

ACKNOWLEDGEMENTS

This is a snapshot of air-sea search and rescue off the Irish coastline, rather than a chronological history, and there have been many individual acts of courage and bravery which are not included here but have been recognised by bodies such as Water Safety Ireland and the RNLI.

I would like to thank the many people serving with the Irish Coast Guard, the Air Corps, Naval Service and RNLI who gave interviews for the book, some of which were conducted during my time as a journalist with *The Irish Times*.

Dermot Somers and Bernadette O'Sullivan read drafts and gave invaluable feedback, and I would like to acknowledge assistance from Ross Classon; Maria O'Flaherty; Niamh Fitzpatrick and the Fitzpatrick, Duffy, Feeney, Glynn, Oliver, Ormsby and Smith families; Darina Clancy and the Zanon family;Eamon Dixon of the Erris Fishermen's Association; Bernard Lucas and Davy Spillane; former Irish Coast Guard director Chris Reynolds; Greencastle Coast Guard officer-in-charge (OIC) Charlie Cavanagh; retired Chief Superintendent Tony Healy; Saorla Begley and Sadbh Quinn of the Department of Transport; Defence Forces press officer Commandant Gemma Fagan; Air Corps press officer Commandant Stephen Byrne; RNLI Ireland press officer Niamh Stephenson; retired Baltimore RNLI coxswain Kieran Cotter; RNLI Dunmore East crew members Brendan Dunne and Neville Murphy; RNLI Lough Swilly lifeboat press officer Joe Joyce; RNLI Arranmore lifeboat press officer Nora Flanagan; Water Safety Ireland chief executive John Leech, and Roger Sweeney; Dr Joan

O'Doherty; solicitor Joseph Chambers; RTÉ Documentary on
One producer Sarah Blake and series producer Liam O'Brien;
Met Éireann head of forecasting Evelyn Cusack, climatologist Liz
Gavin and operations manager Hugh Daly; RNLI Galway lifeboat
crew Olivia Byrne; Aine Ryan; and photographers Pat Browne, Pat
Flynn, Nigel Millard, Cpl David O'Dowd of the Irish Air Corps
Press Office, Joe O'Shaughnessy and Fergus Sweeney.

My thanks to literary agent Jonathan Williams; the Merrion
Press team of Conor Graham, Wendy Logue and Patrick
O'Donoghue; marine journalist Arthur Reynolds; and Cian
Siggins and Rua for their patience.

INTRODUCTION

It might be a piece of music, an Instagram posting, a diary note. Such prompts frame certain events in our lives – and then there are the events which need no frame at all.

It might be the first time you heard about a pandemic and were told it was just a mild flu. It might be the moment you heard that two young women missing on paddle boards in Galway Bay had been found, and were alive.

Or it might be the morning you turned on RTÉ Radio 1's *Morning Ireland* and heard that a helicopter was missing off the north Mayo coast.

During the long days and weeks of the search for the missing Rescue 116 winch crew, Paul Ormsby and Ciarán Smith, a chat with the Smith family in the community hall in Eachléim, near Blacksod, led to this book being written. I had interviewed Ciarán Smith for an earlier book on Irish air-sea rescue, entitled *Mayday! Mayday!*, some years ago, and he spoke with both humour and modesty about some epic rescues he had been involved in when with the Air Corps.

Since 2004, when that first book was published, there has been much change and development in the area of air-sea rescue, including the state's leasing of Sikorsky S-92 helicopters for the Irish Coast Guard as part of a 500-million-euro, ten-year contract. State-trained paramedics can now administer many types of medicine while treating casualties on board aircraft before they reach hospital. Hundreds of successful rescues have been recorded over the past seventeen years off the Irish coastline.

Although the Air Corps was withdrawn from search and rescue duties in 2004, in 2021 it marked almost ten years in providing an invaluable emergency air medical service. It is backed up by the privately funded Irish Community Air Ambulance based in County Cork. Like the Irish Coast Guard, as well as the many volunteers crewing RNLI lifeboats, emergency medical flights have made the difference between life and death in many situations across this island.

In July 2021, former UKIP leader Nigel Farage, who championed Brexit, gave rescue at sea an unexpected boost when he posted a photo on Twitter of the Ramsgate RNLI lifeboat carrying refugees it had plucked from the English Channel. He accused the 'wonderful RNLI in Kent' of becoming 'a taxi service for illegal immigration'. The charity defended its actions, stating it was incredibly proud of the humanitarian work its volunteer lifeboat crews did to rescue vulnerable people in distress. The public voted with their credit cards, resulting in a substantial increase in donations to the RNLI in Britain. While migrants are not making perilous sea journeys to reach this island, my proceeds from this book will go to the RNLI in Ireland for a similar reason.

Many memorable figures have helped to develop search and rescue in this country. Among those who feature here are the Air Corps pilot Barney McMahon; the campaigner Dr Joan O'Doherty (McGinley), who campaigned successfully for the formation of a west coast search and rescue service from her kitchen table; the late Dr John de Courcy Ireland; Irish Coast Guard officers in charge, including Charlie Cavanagh in Greencastle, County Donegal; RNLI coxswains, including the recently retired Kieran Cotter in Baltimore, west Cork; campaigning lawyer Michael Kingston; the four aircrew who lost their lives off Tramore in 1999; Caitríona Lucas, the Irish Coast Guard's first volunteer to die on duty; divers Michael Heffernan and Billy O'Connor, who lost their lives on sea searches; and the four crew of Rescue 116.

All shared one belief. Rescue at sea should always be for humanitarian reasons, without judgement as to how or why anyone has to call for help.

PART 1

A Black Year:
Lives Lost Off Clare's Kilkee
and Mayo's Blacksod

1
A DARK DAY

Bernard Lucas couldn't stay at home. The County Clare farmer was well used to dropping everything to respond to a vessel in trouble off the coast. As an experienced volunteer with the Irish Coast Guard unit at Doolin, he had done so many times before.

When his pager went off on 12 September 2016, details were sketchy. A boat had capsized off Kilkee, farther north up the coast, and he was initially asked to drive up there to assist. He was en route to Kilkee in his car, close to Miltown Malbay, when he was asked if he could turn around and go back to Doolin to provide crew for his unit. He did so and found officer-in-charge Mattie Shannon and colleagues waiting for him with the unit's D-class rigid inflatable boat (RIB).

Bernard and fellow Doolin volunteers Conor McGrath and Davy Spillane launched, and he was on the VHF radio and close to Kilkee when advised to head directly for the pier. Bernard was puzzled and checked to confirm this over the radio. He thought they should be heading straight for the capsize.

As they approached, two gardaí were standing at the foot of the pier steps; they asked if Bernard was on board. Spillane remembered feeling a distinct sense of disquiet as his friend and colleague was escorted ashore and into a Coast Guard vehicle.

Bernard barely remembered being driven to a nearby clifftop. Only a few hours before, his wife, Caitríona (41), had left home for Kilkee to assist in a search for a missing man. She had anticipated she would be walking the shore with members of Kilkee Coast Guard. Now, just several hours later, Bernard could see paramedics working to stabilise a casualty before they were all airlifted by the Rescue 115 Shannon helicopter to hospital.

The casualty was his wife.

***

Spillane and McGrath stood off Kilkee pier in the Doolin RIB, listening to the VHF radio. They knew from the terminology, and a reference to 'vital signs', that something was seriously wrong. Their first confirmation of this was when the RNLI Aran all-weather lifeboat approached them. The lifeboat crew lined up on deck to offer their sympathies to the two Doolin men.

By then, Bernard had been flown with his wife to hospital in Limerick. Caitríona was pronounced dead several hours later. As news of the fatality filtered out, those who knew the Lucas couple and their work with the Irish Coast Guard were lost for words. Caitríona had been one of the most respected and competent volunteers with her unit in County Clare. Her qualifications ranged from coxswain and navigation to climbing, first aid and emergency response, along with suicide-prevention training. She was also national secretary and an active member of the Search and Rescue Dog Association (SARDA). Some striking photos of her, which appeared subsequently in the press and on social media, reflected a woman who loved her family and her dogs, the people around her and the great outdoors. One SARDA volunteer recalled later how her calming presence had helped trained search and rescue dogs to cope with the roaring engines of a helicopter.

Caitríona Lucas was the first Coast Guard volunteer to die while on active service.

***

The Doolin unit to which the Lucas couple were attached had earned a reputation as one of the top Coast Guard teams around the coast. Led by Mattie Shannon, it was also one of the busiest, meeting a diverse and challenging range of call-outs – from vessels in trouble at sea to climbers and walkers in difficulty, and people reported missing off the Cliffs of Moher.

School teaching advisor David McMahon from Lissycasey had been missing for the best part of a week when Caitríona had travelled to Kilkee to help with the search. Both the Civil Defence and Kilkee Coast Guard had been tasked with finding the missing man. However, the Kilkee unit was having difficulty mustering volunteers due to internal tensions.

Some traced these tensions back to 2013, when a 30-year-old community marine rescue service founded by Manuel Di Lucia was incorporated into the Coast Guard. The community had initially favoured the state takeover, since it was finding it difficult to raise funds and Coast Guard involvement would guarantee its future and equipment. However, the transition did not run smoothly.

As the Independent Clare TD Dr Michael Harty subsequently told the Dáil on 15 February 2018, many Kilkee volunteers with experience and local knowledge were not accepted on the new roster. Harty also noted that a plaque commemorating the activities of the former community service was removed, and the number of people involved had dropped from twenty-six to twelve. This loss of valuable experience included qualified coxswains. Di Lucia later said he tried repeatedly to highlight the issues which arose, and noted that there were several public demonstrations.

Coast Guard management had appointed Doolin Coast Guard unit member Martony Vaughan as officer-in-charge at Kilkee in 2013, initially for six months. It was felt that a skilled outsider could best deal with any issues arising during the transition. However, Vaughan had a direct management style that did not always sit well with volunteers. Despite this, he continued in the position for the next few years. On 24 March 2016, Coast Guard manager Michael

O'Toole was formally alerted to problems when four members of the Kilkee unit forwarded him a memo after several informal contacts. The memo referred to problems with communication, lack of clear definition of roles and responsibilities, and inadequate supervision of training. It also referred to an 'air of distrust' over the use of CCTV to 'monitor people' and identified a need for head office training for new officer roles, along with familiarisation of policies, procedures and protocols. It said there should be full debriefings with all crew in relation to incidents and occurrences, and 'no more one-on-one chats'.[1]

The memo continued, 'While we are acutely aware that we are an emergency service which requires a professional, safe and efficient response ... the social aspect of the unit no longer exists.' It suggested that 'an active training plan and more openness within the entire team' would 'help in rectifying this issue'. It also said, 'Morale and enthusiasm are at an all-time low within the unit, and there is a danger of a significant number of people exiting the unit which could severely hamper our ability to respond to taskings.'

Coast Guard management held a meeting with the Kilkee volunteers in July 2016 to discuss the issues raised. At another meeting, on Friday 9 September, Kilkee volunteers were told that Vaughan was stepping aside and, from Monday 12 September, taking up another position. The unit's deputy, Orla Hassett, would be appointed interim officer-in-charge until a permanent replacement was found. That Friday also, a search for the missing man was initiated.

There were several search launchings over the weekend of 10–11 September, which Vaughan co-ordinated, and on the Sunday evening he asked volunteers to be at the station early on Monday, when Hassett was due to take over. Launching involves a 'triple lock' system of approval by a Coast Guard rescue co-ordination centre, along with the unit's officer-in-charge and the coxswain. As there was a shortage of available qualified boat crew, Valentia Coast Guard was asked to request assistance for Kilkee from the Doolin unit.

A small craft warning had been issued for Monday and specified that southerly winds would reach force 6 or 7 on coasts from Donegal to Dublin and on southerly coasts to Roche's Point off Cork. However, its forecast for the south-west and west coasts was for a less severe westerly force 3, with wind speeds further decreasing in the afternoon.

There was an early launch that day, and then a second at 10.30 a.m. Kilkee coxswains Jenny Caraway and James Lucey, who was on the helm, required one more crew member for their second launch of the Kilkee Delta RIB. Doolin's Caitríona Lucas had the necessary qualifications. She had her own drysuit and helmet but was given a life jacket at Kilkee. The search plan was to head towards Intrinsic Bay and then north of George's Head to Chimney Bay.

The Delta RIB was returning to base when it reported on VHF radio at 1.06 p.m. that it was just off the back of the Pollock Holes, a popular Kilkee swimming spot, and would do 'one search around underneath the shelter', then 'head in'. It entered a small cove northeast of Foohagh Point – a shallow area and potential 'surf zone'. Local knowledge has it that the seabed rises in 'sharp cliff faces', rather than a gradual shelving, and this can cause confused seas, with unexpected sudden uprisings and large swells. The previous Friday, Hassett had been asked by her officer-in-charge to search in this area but had refused, as she believed it was too hazardous. She remembered she was reprimanded for this over the VHF radio.

The Delta RIB was 20 metres from the shoreline on that Monday when a large breaking wave directly to starboard tipped it over, throwing all three crew overboard, before it righted itself again off Knockroe Point. Coxswain Caraway had the only functioning radio, her personal hand-held VHF, and issued a 'Mayday' call on channel 16.

Her broadcast was not picked up by Valentia because of transmission difficulties involving hand-held devices. However, an eyewitness on the shoreline phoned Kilkee station, which in turn contacted Valentia. It tasked the Shannon-based Rescue 115 helicopter, the RNLI Aran Island lifeboat, the Civil Defence and the local fire service to assist.

Martony Vaughan arrived at Kilkee Coast Guard station sometime after noon and began liaising with other agencies and with the Coast Guard helicopter. He then left to go up to the nearest headland, leaving Hassett in the station. Recognising an 'imminent threat to life', she asked the local gardaí to requisition a privately owned RIB, which she joined and took to sea.

Initially, all three of the Delta RIB crew had been able to form a huddle in the water, staying as close as they could to their vessel, which was now upright again. But before they had a chance to try to reboard it, they were separated in the confused seas close to the rocky shoreline. As Caraway was swept towards a cave, she saw Lucey trying to reach Lucas, but without success. By now, all three had lost their helmets in the turmoil.

Lucey, who had now also been swept towards the cave, managed to haul himself up onto a ledge near its mouth. Meanwhile, Caraway, an experienced diver, was being pounded off the cliff face and knew she had to try to swim out to sea. Her best chance of doing so was to keep her life jacket deflated. Civil Defence drone video footage recorded Lucas trying to hold onto the port bow section of the RIB, with the waves repeatedly breaking her grip. After three minutes, she lost her grip entirely and was next seen lying face down in the water. Her life jacket was not inflated. She was unconscious when airlifted from the water by the Irish Coast Guard's Rescue 115.

At this point, the Doolin RIB, with Spillane and McGrath on board, was standing off the cave, with dozens of rescue agency personnel watching from the clifftop above. Gary Kiely and Adrian Kenny of Kilkee Marine Rescue, who were both experienced in using jet skis for surfing, were asked by Vaughan to try to gain access to the cave. They tried twice, at great personal risk, losing gear in the white breakers. Spillane remembered putting a space blanket around one of the two men after these attempts to protect him against hypothermia.

Caraway was at the base of a cliff face and still trying to swim out when Hassett spotted her. When there was a break in the waves, she managed to reach the RIB and Hassett pulled her on board. She had ingested a lot of water and required hospital treatment.

It would take more than four hours to rescue Lucey from his precarious position, after another team from Lahinch, including Dave Ainsworth and Steve Thomas, had been asked to attempt to swim into the cave. Doolin Coast Guard and Kilrush Fire Service cliff teams eventually managed to get Lucey a line and he was winched to safety by the Rescue 117 helicopter from Waterford.

It was dusk when Spillane and McGrath in the Doolin RIB headed back south for home, in a gathering Atlantic swell. There had been issues with their boat taking water throughout the day and it was not handling well as they passed under the Cliffs of Moher. They stopped the engine and raised the outboard to check the propeller, but nothing was found – the boat was taking water underneath. After they berthed, Spillane remembered there was no debriefing, 'hot' or 'cold', as would be normal procedure in such an incident. It effectively meant that the crew who had boarded the RIB many hours before were left in a type of limbo.

***

'Don't put things off. Do them now. Life is short; life is very precious,' Bernard Lucas said at his wife's funeral, before reading a poem in her honour.[2]

Parish priest Fr Denis Crosby told the packed congregation in Liscannor church that the thousands of people who had attended the night before 'were able to convey something that words can't do – respect and thanks'. 'Caitríona Lucas lived as if she was the light. She carried the light wonderfully into our world. She was a light in our world that is very often dark and careless,' Fr Crosby said. She 'gave her life, all her life, and she knew that living was giving,' he continued, recalling her work in the local library and how she had set up a Lego club for youngsters. In joining the Coast Guard, she had overcome a fear of heights to undertake rigorous coast and cliff rescue training, he noted.

'She was particularly blessed in life to have Bernard; they were perfectly matched: they were both cracked, they were crazy people and the primary craziness they had was that they were crazy about one another,' Fr Crosby said. He recalled how they had shared journeys, travelled widely, and their greatest achievements were their two wonderful children, Ben (20) and Emma (18).

Ben recalled a mother who was an exceptional, honest, kind and caring person, and his hero, while Emma read from the Gospel of St John on how 'there is no greater love than to lay down one's life for one's friends'. Symbols of Caitríona's life brought to the altar included her climbing helmet, a painting by her of a Coast Guard helicopter and the Doolin RIB, and a replica she had made of the same craft.

One such helicopter – Rescue 115 from Shannon – flew in over Liscannor Bay and dipped its nose in tribute, as hundreds of people, including many from the search and rescue community, accompanied her coffin draped in a tricolour to Kilmacreehy cemetery. She was buried in her native Clare soil to the haunting strains of 'Roisín Dubh', played by Davy Spillane and Blackie O'Connell.

***

When it came, the debriefing for the Doolin and Kilkee units was far from ideal. Both units were invited to meet at the Doolin station – a fraught situation given the fact that a volunteer had died. The meeting was attended by two senior Coast Guard officers – against normal practice, as this could constrain people from speaking their minds on a confidential basis.

Shortly afterwards, a survival at sea exercise was organised off Doolin pier by its commander, Mattie Shannon. Senior Coast

Guard management were present. In an interview with me afterwards, Spillane recalled:

> During that exercise, my drysuit started filling with water up to my thigh, which was alarming. It failed in the sea, with water up to my groin. I got out of the water and approached management to tell them ... Mattie checked the seal at my neck, and told me I had put the suit on incorrectly and to resume the exercise. I refused to do that and went straight back to the station.
>
> As I was taking my suit off to shower, my drysuit neck-seal then failed catastrophically and completely separated from my suit. I got dressed, went to the operations room where there was a formal safety meeting in session, run by the unit safety officer. At that meeting, I formally stated on the record in my capacity as a qualified coxswain to the safety officer that the personal protection equipment was not fit for purpose. I asked that this be recorded.
>
> I specified then that the helmet, drysuit and life jacket were not fit for purpose and asked that each of these details were recorded in the minutes – which they were. There were a number of unit volunteers present in the room at the time.

Two investigations were initiated into Lucas's death – one by the state's Marine Casualty Investigation Board (MCIB) and one by the Health and Safety Authority (HSA). Spillane informed investigators he had retrieved a helmet from the water. He recalled that the helmet had its buckle fully fastened – suggesting it was properly worn but had failed to stay on because of an impact.[3]

Independently, the Coast Guard was alerted a few weeks later to an issue with the Rescue 400 life jackets used by its volunteers. The unit which raised the alarm was told there was no issue. However, later events would confirm its concerns.

2
A PICTURE OF
FRICTION AND STRAIN

More than two years after Caitríona Lucas's death off the Clare coast, the final report by the MCIB was released on 7 December 2018. The printed report was in two parts, as it included lengthy appendices with comments by notified parties, including Bernard Lucas, the survivors and the Coast Guard.

It began by identifying a catalogue of safety defects and lack of regulatory compliance, and it criticised the Coast Guard for failing to have in place an effective safety management system. Although its role was not to apportion blame, the MCIB investigation stated that the Kilkee unit's Delta RIB had critical deficiencies. It also said the RIB was out beyond its operational limits, that it should have had a passenger boat licence and that its coxswain should have had the necessary certification for this.

The Delta RIB had been broken up by the surf at the base of the cliff over a twenty-four-hour period, which hampered a proper survey for investigation purposes. However, the report noted that before its first launch on 12 September 2016, the radar was not operational, the glass reinforced plastic (GRP) hull was taking in water 'during operations', and there was air leaking from the air suspension in the starboard aft seat, which was taped off and not in use. The coxswain had reported two additional faults on return from that first launch – the echo sounder was not operational and one fixed VHF radio transceiver was not working. The report also said that the Delta RIB was not equipped with an emergency position indicating radio beacon (EPIRB), which could have pinpointed the location of an incident if activated. It said that none of the personal locator beacons (PLBs) worn by the three crew had been activated – in fact, none of these had been found.[1]

According to the report, the RIB's operations should be limited to a significant wave height of 2 metres, and it was not permitted to operate in surf. It referred back to an incident where a Coast Guard RIB had capsized in a shallow 'surf zone' off Dingle, County Kerry, in 2014. The Dingle RIB was trying to 'outrun a breaking wave' and was stern-to and ahead of it when the wave broached and capsized the vessel. An internal inquiry into the Dingle incident had made twenty recommendations in February 2015, relating to 'communication difficulties', damage to one drysuit, detachment of helmets and difficulties encountered by three volunteers in operating the inflation mechanism on their personal flotation devices (PFDs), but the MCIB report noted that the recommendations had not been fully acted upon. That internal inquiry had also noted that the 'management and administrative responsibilities placed upon the local volunteer officer-in-charge' were considered to be 'excessive'.

The MCIB's report into Caitríona Lucas's death was less con-clusive on why the equipment she was wearing had not saved her. In her published comment on this, Jenny Caraway said that 'none of the team' – i.e., her Kilkee unit, as distinct from the Doolin unit with which Caitríona Lucas served – had 'ever' been provided with 'proper instruction in relation to the wearing and the operation maintenance' of helmets.[2]

A post-mortem identified a trauma to the side of Lucas's head at a point where it should have been protected by her helmet. She had 'expended a lot of energy holding on to the boat, would have ingested water', the MCIB report said, and probably had sustained an impact to her head when she was submerged. The investigation recorded that two of the three PFDs examined afterwards did inflate, but it observed that the three crew either had difficulty in finding the activation toggle or decided not to use it. 'A fully inflated life jacket can reduce swimming and manoeuvrability and may have been a factor' in this, it said. Volunteers knew it could be virtually impossible to board a RIB from the sea unaided if one was wearing a fully inflated life jacket.

The investigation made no reference to tests undertaken in late September 2016 by a community rescue unit based in Mallow, County Cork, which had shown that the toggle used to inflate the jackets was very difficult to reach. The Mallow unit had notified Water Safety Ireland, which trains and administers the community rescue boat fleet, and it in turn informed the Irish Coast Guard.[3]

In a lengthy response to the draft MCIB report, the Coast Guard described the findings as 'flawed' and 'misleading'. It said that more than a million 'man hours' had been spent on more than 30,000 rescue missions since 1991 and this was its first fatality. It also argued against passenger boat legislation – on the basis that rescue RIBs are not ferries – and defended the Kilkee unit's decision to launch. The Coast Guard also defended its safety-management system and contended that it represented a 'significant leap' for the MCIB to suggest that a 'tragic accident in one instance in one Coast Guard unit is representative of a whole organisation'.[4]

Another criticism of the MCIB Kilkee report concerned GPS co-ordinates. It said that three different sets of co-ordinates were recorded for the capsize location, all within the general area, but claimed the most accurate was recorded by an eyewitness. However, the latitude and longitude were queried by Caraway, Lucey and Hassett when the draft was circulated for comment. In spite of this, the position was not corrected in the final report – giving the impression that the boat had capsized in deeper water, clear of any surf zone.

Had the boat been fitted with an EPIRB, or had the crew activated their own PLBs, the rescue response would have been almost immediate, as the beacons would have directly alerted the emergency services. Bernard Lucas made this point in his comments on the draft document, which were included in the final report.[5] He also raised a number of issues relating to faulty equipment that the investigation had identified but had not adequately explored, including whether life jackets and helmets were operating properly, and poor maintenance of the Delta RIB radios.

Bernard noted that there appeared to be contradictions in the report as to whether the coxswain was qualified or not, and 'confusion' about 'who was in charge during and after' the accident. He claimed faulty co-ordinates for the location of the incident had been given to the Shannon Rescue 115 helicopter. Lucas also stated that he believed 'bullying and harassment' at Kilkee in the preceding couple of years was 'a contributing factor in this accident'. Kilkee had 'lost an awful lot of experience' and 'morale within the team was very bad', he said.[6]

Orla Hassett of Kilkee Coast Guard addressed certain problems in more detail in her comments on the draft. She highlighted the inaccuracy of the location given and noted that weather information for the area on the day indicated that a launch was within operational limits – a point also made by the Coast Guard. Hassett noted that the final document had failed to include sufficient chart information and clarification on whether the Kilkee Delta RIB entered a surf zone and whether this was the cause of the capsize. She also said the report failed to address the adequate training of Coast Guard crews in a surf zone.

Like Lucas, Hassett believed that neither the draft nor final MCIB reports adequately examined equipment failure. Volunteers understood that the type of life jacket used by the Coast Guard had sufficient buoyancy to keep a head above water in a situation where the wearer was unconscious – as Caitríona Lucas was latterly. 'The report does not suggest whether these jackets are fit for purpose,' she said. She pointed out the report's failure to deal with the helmet issue, and why all three had come off. She said that she had been instructed 'on numerous occasions' not to inflate the bladder of the helmet. And she recorded how another crew member's neck seal had been incorrectly fitted and had to be repaired before the boat was launched. Had this not been noticed, the neck seal would have failed if the crew member was thrown in the water, causing her drysuit to fill with water. Hassett expressed her disappointment that this had not been adequately explored by the investigation. This was 'surprising', given the 'massive potential' for this to recur, she said.

'The report also fails to mention that Coast Guard management were made aware six months prior to the accident of issues within the unit that could compromise the unit's ability to respond to taskings effectively and safely,' Hassett concluded.[7]

Minister for Transport Shane Ross issued a statement on the MCIB findings after publication of the final report in December 2018, in which he outlined three actions he had taken as an 'immediate response'. He had decided to 'broaden' a review already underway into the national search and rescue framework, initiated after the Rescue 116 helicopter crash over a year and a half earlier. He had instructed the Coast Guard to accelerate its work on an independently accredited ISO safety management system that would be 'robust and fit for purpose'.[8] And he had asked the Coast Guard and Marine Survey Office to take the 'necessary and pragmatic steps to ensure that any issues which could impact on vessel or crew safety are addressed as a matter of urgency'.

'Caitríona Lucas was an extraordinary woman – brave, committed, supremely generous – and her death was an appalling tragedy,' Ross said in his press statement. 'Her life will be remembered by the actions of all those involved in search and rescue activities. I know the Irish Coast Guard, including its 900 volunteers, are committed to honouring her memory. We will ensure volunteer safety remains at the heart of search and rescue operations.'

Two new Irish postal stamps paying tribute to the work of the Coast Guard, issued in 2019, featured artwork by Caitríona.

**

In an interview for *The Irish Times*, published a couple of weeks after the final MCIB report was released in December 2018, Bernard Lucas expressed his severe disappointment in a service to which both he and his wife had dedicated their lives. He said he believed the Coast Guard's management system allowed no recourse for volunteers who might have concerns that could lead to differences with an officer-in-charge. His colleague and friend Davy Spillane concurred.

'If you questioned issues, you were told by your senior "this was not a democracy", and were pointed to the door,' Spillane said.[9]

Bernard also recalled another key low moment, when he learned in late 2017 that Martony Vaughan, former officer-in-charge at Kilkee, was transferring to the Doolin unit. 'I wasn't suggesting any blame – it was just that it was so insensitive. I asked the Coast Guard to defer it until at least the official reports were completed,' Bernard says. 'That didn't happen.'

'The Coast Guard was my life, it was what I did, and I felt protected by my comrades. That was all blown apart when I heard about this,' he said. 'It made it impossible for me to be there and prevented me from grieving. I needed the Coast Guard. I was clinging on by my fingernails ...'[10]

Bernard Lucas took a step back from the Doolin station from January 2018 to February of the following year. During that time, there was no contact from his station, not even an invitation to the Christmas party, he said later. In mid-2019, when his legal action against the state over his wife's death had been filed, he spoke of his continuing isolation from the Coast Guard and his disappointment over a response he had received from Minister for Transport Shane Ross about handling issues raised by volunteers. In this, Ross had referred to a structure known as the Coastal Unit Advisory Group (CUAG), which had been in place for over twenty years to represent the concerns of volunteers. Bernard pointed out that the CUAG comprised officers-in-charge, had no volunteers on its panel and lacked transparency. Ross's letter did say that the structure was 'under review' to ensure it remained 'fit for purpose'.

Speaking to me afterwards, Davy Spillane believed that Bernard had been effectively abandoned by headquarters at a time when he needed support. Fellow volunteers from both Doolin and Kilkee were also left in limbo with the failure to debrief adequately.

County Clare solicitor Joe Chambers, acting for Orla Hassett and two other clients, said the care provided to the volunteers 'post incident' by the Irish Coast Guard was 'late and limited', and the trauma was in some cases 'compounded' by its actions. He said his three clients continued to receive private help at their own expense.

The Coast Guard replied to these criticisms by stating it offered both critical incident stress management and confidential counselling for volunteers in the aftermath of stressful incidents.[11] It said a human resources company had verified that its code of practice in relation to handling grievances represented 'good practice for the type of operation involved'. It further noted that training has been and 'continues to be' provided by sectoral managers, officers-in-charge and deputies on 'grievance management and other HR supports', and an offer of counselling support was offered to an 'individual' in February 2018.

Furthermore, the organisation stressed that its equipment was maintained to a very high standard. It explained that while no certified life jacket can be guaranteed to 'self-right' an unconscious user – and this is stated in a manufacturer's warning panel – 'the buoyancy provided should ensure they will in the great majority of cases'. It also said it had conducted independent testing of its life jackets in Britain and found them to be 'fully compliant' for use in Atlantic waters.[12]

*　*　*

In late 2019 – three years after Caitríona's death and the concerns raised shortly thereafter about life jackets – the Coast Guard said it had begun an investigation into 'recent malfunctioning' of the equipment. In an email to its unit officers-in-charge on 15 November 2019, the Coast Guard said that 'specifically, the 275N section of the [Rescue 400] life jacket failed to fully function when activated', and it was suspending boat operations with immediate effect at twenty-three of its forty-four stations around the coast. The Department of Transport said safety concerns over the life jackets was a separate issue to the problems that contributed to the death of Caitríona Lucas.[13]

In January 2020, Bernard trekked to the Arctic Circle with supporters of the Caitríona Lucas Challenge, a trust set up to fundraise for charity. Later, in the summer of that year, he was informed that the Director of Public Prosecutions had decided no criminal charges should be brought in relation to the incident, after a report was forwarded to it by the HSA.

That same summer, the MCIB's authority was questioned in a European Court of Justice judgment, which found it was not independent as its board included the Department of Transport secretary general, or his or her deputy, and the Marine Survey Office chief surveyor. These two postholders subsequently stood down.

An analysis of the MCIB by a former state marine surveyor, Captain Neil Forde, was submitted to an Oireachtas (parliamentary) committee, claiming it was 'not fit for purpose'. The analysis had been commissioned by maritime lawyer Michael Kingston, who lost his father in the *Betelgeuse* Whiddy Island explosion in

1979. It claimed the MCIB failed to investigate incidents it had a statutory duty to inquire about, questioned its resources and independence, and claimed the inquiry into Caitríona Lucas's death was 'riddled with inaccuracies' – starting with the wrong location for the incident. These inaccuracies were not corrected because MCIB investigators 'simply have not had the resources required to do the job properly', Mr Kingston stated in a presentation to the Oireachtas Transport and Communications Networks committee.[14]

Captain Forde also questioned why the MCIB did not investigate a previous incident which occurred in similar circumstances to that of Caitríona Lucas's death, where an Irish Coast Guard Dingle unit RIB capsized off Inch, County Kerry, in August 2014. Although there were no fatalities, the failure to investigate it was a breach of the Merchant Shipping (Investigation of Marine Casualties) Act, 2000, he said.

Bernard Lucas said he was shocked by Forde's analysis and called for a reinvestigation into his wife's death: 'We have a fully staffed Air Accident Investigation Unit and a Railway Accident Investigation Unit, but a part-time body investigating marine accidents that is poorly resourced and, therefore, compromised. When it can't even get the location where Caitríona died right, the MCIB report raises more questions than it answers. We need a reinvestigation.'[15]

Minister for Transport Eamon Ryan told the Oireachtas committee on 29 January 2021 that he planned a 'fundamental review' of the structures in place for marine accident investigation.[16] This was welcomed by the committee, which expressed its own concern at the issues raised by stakeholders at its hearing.

In response to Forde's analysis, the MCIB said it did not comment on published reports issued on the conclusion of investigations, and that it was not the purpose of an investigation to attribute blame or fault, but to avoid other casualties occurring.[17]

Irish Coast Guard director Chris Reynolds had been seconded to the EU's capacity-building mission in Somalia in July 2016. In several interviews in 2021, he spoke publicly of strains between the Irish Coast Guard and the Department of Transport. He said that after he had used social media to question a decision in March 2021 to suspend seventeen Irish Coast Guard coast and cliff rescue teams for 'safety reasons', his social media posts were tracked and downloaded by the department, which he described as 'scary'. 'If they do that to the director, then volunteers have a problem,' he told *The Times* (Ireland edition).[18]

In August 2021, Reynolds confirmed his departure from the Irish Coast Guard to continue his work in Somalia, stating the department had turned down his request for an extended leave of absence. In a wide-ranging interview with the *Irish Independent* that month, he elaborated further on difficulties he had encountered while in the role. He said the Coast Guard must be separated from the Department of Transport and established as an independent agency with adequate state resources. He also said he had approached Tánaiste Simon Coveney about merging the Coast Guard with the Naval Service. 'I felt that the Irish Coast Guard was a tiny organisation with huge responsibility and it would work better if it was taken in under the wing of the Naval Service or Customs Maritime Unit,' he told the newspaper.[19]

In October 2021, Michael Kingston called for a public inquiry into issues which had arisen in the Coast Guard. That same month, a new Coast Guard volunteers' representative association was formed among present and past members with a remit to seek an urgent meeting with the Minister for Transport. The first meeting, in Kilkee, County Clare, remembered Caitríona Lucas, with her daughter, Emma, placing a wreath on the cliff top above the Atlantic where she lost her life.[20]

The Irish Times reported a picture of 'friction and strain within the Coast Guard, in particular over disciplinary actions taken against volunteers, and also criticism that the organisation's management has become too risk averse'. It conducted interviews with more than a dozen serving and former senior volunteers, including Jim Griffin, award-winning former officer in charge of the Dunmore East unit and a Sinn Féin councillor in Waterford since 2014. The newspaper reported that the Coast Guard has spent nearly €140,000 on consultants over the preceding three years to assist in training, conflict resolution and meditation support, in part arising from the disciplinary actions. The sums paid to the consultancy firm Graphite HRM Ltd between 2018 and 2020 were released to the newspaper under the Freedom of Information Act.[21]

Later that month, a report issued by the Comptroller and Auditor General, the state's spending watchdog, criticised the Coast Guard's purchase of vans for cliff rescue teams due to a number of 'anomalies' in how the contract was awarded.[22]

Acting Coast Guard director Eugene Clonan, who spent eighteen years in the Naval Service, told *The Irish Times* he rejected claims that volunteers had been targeted, or subjected to unfair disciplinary inquiries, and said there was an appeals process for any volunteer who felt they had been subject to unfair disciplinary process. 'If you're going to sign up and do what we want you to do, and give your time for the community and search and rescue, there's certain things you need to abide by,' Clonan said. 'That doesn't mean you can get into a boat without personal protective equipment and feck off, that doesn't mean you can take a boat and go wherever you want. We are not about best mates here, we're about trying to run an organisation ...'[23]

With so many more people drawn to the water, the Irish Coast Guard recorded a 12 per cent increase in call-outs in 2021. However, it struggled to tackle fundamental issues within its organisation, identified by Kingston and Fianna Fáil TD for Clare Cathal Crowe who called for an independent inquiry into the Coast Guard, claiming it was in a 'state of organisational rot' with 'deep problems running from the higher echelons of management right down to each station'.[24]

After six resignations in Doolin in November 2021 over reported 'interpersonal issues', the unit, which had been one of the busiest and most experienced on the west coast, was stood down by the Coast Guard. Instead of a minister stepping in to look at the broader picture, mediator Kieran Mulvey was appointed by the Department of Transport to examine what could be done. He produced a report which concluded that no form of mediation would resolve matters of dispute at Doolin. His main recommendation – to reconstitute the Doolin unit – was accepted by Minister of State for Transport Hildegarde Naughton, who pledged to initiate this. For those seasoned observers of search and rescue who knew fundamental reform was paramount, it was an opportunity missed.

3
'IT'S 116 – WE CAN'T GET HER'

Fergus Sweeney had almost dozed off when he heard his cousin Simon calling his name. Time to go back to the lighthouse, no doubt, where his uncle, Blacksod lightkeeper Vincent Sweeney, would be listening out on the VHF radio for a pilot's voice.

Several hours before, the cousins had driven from home, close to Blacksod lighthouse at the southernmost tip of north Mayo's Mullet peninsula, to the nearest takeaway for food. At about 10 p.m. they were on the way back from the town of Belmullet, and not far from Blacksod again, when they spotted the floodlighting. It was the familiar signal that a helicopter was expected for refuelling at the lighthouse helipad.

The night was misty and wet, with poor visibility. The cousins were hungry – appetites whetted by the hot meal in the car – but they decided to head to the lighthouse to check if Vincent might need help.

Sure enough, Vincent had received a call from Malin Head Coast Guard, one of three marine rescue co-ordination centres run by the Irish Coast Guard. A medical evacuation or 'medevac' was underway, and Rescue 118, a Sikorsky S-92 helicopter based in Sligo in the north-west, was en route and would refuel at Blacksod.

A crewman on board a Scottish fishing vessel hunting for blue whiting had injured his hand and required medical help, but the precise details of the call-out were scant. The location was some 141 nautical miles west of Mayo's Eagle Island, out in the

Atlantic. A second aircraft had been asked to provide 'top cover' or communication support, which was the practice for long-distance missions.

***

'Delta Hotel 245, this is Blacksod. *Tá fáilte romhat.*'

The familiar welcoming words of lightkeeper Vincent Sweeney, issuing the latest wind direction, and speed and visibility details, would be picked up on radio by helicopters approaching the Mullet peninsula lighthouse to top up on fuel before heading farther west. Using waypoints as 'stepping stones', rescue aircraft could select one of several approaches to Blacksod, at the head of a short pier and facing out into the Atlantic, with Achill Head, Saddle Head and Achill's Slievemore to points south.

Former Coast Guard chief pilot at Shannon David Courtney wrote a memoir of his years flying search and rescue, which is now regarded as an invaluable historical record of the early years of the Irish Coast Guard, as it is now constituted, and a time when rescue agencies worked closely together. He described how he and his crew would use 'every piece of on-board equipment, every ounce of their experience and wisdom, to slide like a slalom skier between the islands, climbing slightly in case you had drifted and were close to one island or another, knowing that the black shape to the south was Achill, its northern cliffs at Croaghan standing at 2,192 feet.'[1]

On a clear night, Blacksod's sweeping lighthouse beam can be seen for miles into the Atlantic. Twelve nautical miles to be precise, as it rotates like a compass needle, flashing white and red every seven and a half seconds. It has been a constant guide since 1865, on a treacherous part of the north Mayo coast formed from some of Ireland's oldest rocks. Strong tides and currents, islands and reefs have claimed many ships over the centuries.

Blacksod's sister light, built of granite blocks, lies 9 nautical miles to the west on an inhospitable outcrop known as Blackrock

Island. The circular tower was built to a height of almost 17 metres (55 feet) in the early 1860s, making it the second highest of all Irish lighthouses at 86 metres (282 feet) above sea level. Both beams sweep constantly over the Atlantic and over a natural amphitheatre framed by the Mullet peninsula and, to the south, Achill Island. To the north there lies a scattering of islands – home to grey seals, migrant barnacle geese, whooper swans and Manx shearwaters – including the Inishkeas, Duvillaun Mór and Beag, and Inis Glora, mythical home of the Children of Lir.

Vincent Sweeney had taken over from his father as keeper at Blacksod in 1981. He grew up in the draughty lighthouse living quarters with only open fires for heat and the squat building exposed to the full force of prevailing westerly winds – so strong that in 2014 the gales snapped the bolt on one of the lighthouse doors.

Blacksod Bay's deep water was used as a frequent anchorage by the British navy during the Second World War. Vincent's mother, Maureen, had communicated a vital forecast in June 1944, as she watched the barometer fall, averting military catastrophe by delaying the D-Day landings for thirty-six hours. She was just 21 years old, unaware that her readings were the first to signal an impending storm, which would lead to the postponement of Operation Overlord and point also to the short weather window that General Dwight D. Eisenhower required for the Normandy invasion, which changed the path of the conflict.

Over the years, as lighthouses were gradually automated, Vincent was retained as an attendant, with a vital role in refuelling helicopters for both the Commissioners of Irish Lights and for search and rescue. Initially, the aircrews he assisted had British accents, as the British Royal Air Force (RAF) and Royal Navy provided long distance air-sea rescue cover for decades until the Irish state expanded its own capability.

Sweeney's ears were always tuned to the VHF radio and the international distress frequency, channel 16. Even after many years of refuelling search and rescue helicopters, he could never quite relax – on tenterhooks when crews were out 150 to 200 nautical miles west, and only able to breathe fully again when they were landing a casualty at a hospital, or back at base.[2]

Crew returning from missions would sometimes have to do a second refuel. They might have time to shut down and sip tea served up by the keeper or one of his children in the sparse lighthouse kitchen, with its framed photos on the walls presented by several bases. Sometimes there might even be time for a big fry-up. Among the more recent images on the walls was one taken by Vincent's nephew, Fergus, of a Sikorsky S-61 from the Coast Guard's Sligo base dropping off a Christmas card and a bottle of whiskey to say thanks.

On the night of 13 March 2017, Vincent had already prepared the high-pressure refuelling system for the helicopter by the time Simon and Fergus arrived. This involved deploying a line into a standby position just off the helipad and pulling a light earthing cable from its drum. The earthing cable would remove any static charge that the helicopter might develop in flight and would be attached to the body of the aircraft before refuelling started. Carrying a hand-held VHF radio, he then walked the circumference of the fully lit helipad to check for debris.

The wind was south-westerly and the drizzle was turning into torrential rain as the three men sat chatting in the living room, before the two cousins headed home to eat. Once there, Simon checked a marine traffic 'app' on his smartphone, which gave automatic identification system tracking details for both vessels at sea and Irish Coast Guard helicopters. Normally, the support aircraft for a medical evacuation would be a fixed-wing plane flown by the Air Corps, part of Ireland's Defence Forces. However, that night the Air Corps was not in a position to respond, so a second helicopter had been sent instead. The Sikorsky S-92, with call sign Rescue 116, had been dispatched by the Irish Coast Guard from Dublin. It was also expected to refuel at Blacksod before heading farther west, and Simon noted that it was over Longford, while Rescue 118's arrival was imminent. He decided to head back to help his dad.

Fergus told Simon he would follow him in a while. His teenage daughter, Eva, was asleep, although his dog, Biscuit, was very much awake. He had acquired a new camera and wanted to shoot some footage to test it, but he also wanted to wait for the rain to ease. He put on the kettle, returned to some editing work on his computer, then opened the guest-room window and lit a cigarette. As he finished his smoke, he could hear the noise of an aircraft moving south of the house in the direction of Blacksod. That would be Rescue 118, the Sligo helicopter, topping up on fuel before its long run out over the Atlantic.

The helicopter was on the ground for a bare seven minutes. Fergus could only hear its engine as it moved upwind. He knew it was late and he closed the window, then slung himself onto the bed for a few moments.

What seemed like just minutes later, he recognised the distinctive sound of his cousin's van. He wondered why Simon was driving so fast, but continued dozing on the bed, still in his clothes. He was woken from his half-sleep by his cousin calling his name.

The hill behind the lighthouse, known as Deirbhile's Twist after a stone circle created on its summit by sculptor Michael Boffin, was a good point for checking conditions before a helicopter would arrive. Simon had been up there in the dark, scanning the skies all around him with a hand-held VHF.

'It's 116 ... we can't get her,' Simon was now telling Fergus. 'Nothing on the radio ... she might be gone down ...'

***

Several hours earlier, on that Monday night, a Coast Guard helicopter crew employed by CHC Ireland was discussing weather and charts at its Dublin Airport base. Captain Dara Fitzpatrick (45) had received the phone call at home from Dublin's Marine

Rescue Co-ordination Centre (MRCC), with a request to provide 'top cover' or communication and operational backup, for a medical evacuation.

On duty with her were Captain Mark Duffy (51) and the winch team of Paul Ormsby (53) and Ciarán Smith (38). Fitzpatrick, from south Dublin, had been flying rescue for over two decades. She had started with the Irish Coast Guard at Shannon, one of its four air-sea rescue bases and the longest established of the network, dating back some thirty years. Duffy, from County Louth, was known as a 'natural' pilot by colleagues, having worked abroad before securing what he described as his 'dream job' with CHC Ireland in 2001. Smith, from Swords, north Dublin, and his winch colleague Ormsby, from Ballyfermot, south Dublin, had both trained with the Air Corps before moving to the company contracted to fly for the Coast Guard.

'Yes, four persons on board,' Duffy told Dublin's ground air traffic control as he sought clearance to fly a short time later. 'Our departure from the field westbound either to Sligo or Blacksod – we're not sure at the moment – with the possibility we might need to use runway 28 for departure; we'll keep you advised,' he confirmed.

The crew was directed to runway 16 and given instructions about its westerly route. After a successful take-off, the Dublin pilots picked up Shannon air traffic control around County Meath.

'Shannon, good morning, [this is] Rescue 116 with you,' Fitzpatrick said.

'Rescue 116, Shannon information, good evening,' Shannon replied, gently correcting her.

'Shannon, good evening, Rescue 116 is just 10 miles outside of Kells … proceeding to Blacksod,' Fitzpatrick said, confirming 'we're at 3,000 feet and will be climbing to 4,000 feet in about 20 miles.'

'Just confirming you're bypassing Sligo and going straight to Blacksod,' Shannon said.

'Rescue 116, direct Blacksod now,' she replied.

'Rescue 116, roger,' Shannon confirmed. 'Rescue 118 is just headed off the west coast now, no contact with me, so if you're talking to him, just ask him to give me a call please.'

Shannon air traffic control picked up Rescue 118's location when it was 110 miles west of Blacksod Bay and spoke to the aircraft. The Sligo helicopter crew estimated it would be on location at the fishing vessel in forty-seven minutes.

Shannon copied this: 'You'll probably get out of our range of our transmitters at that stage, and I believe Rescue 116 is on the way out, following behind you.'

It was after midnight when Rescue 116 was over the west coast and preparing for a descent from 4,000 feet to refuel at Blacksod. The co-pilot, Duffy, spoke to Shannon air traffic control at 12.34 a.m.

'Okay, that's copied,' Shannon replied. 'You can report airborne again.'

Shannon's last radar return for the helicopter was twelve minutes later, at 12.46 a.m.

'Rescue 116, Shannon,' the air traffic controller called.

No response. Shannon tried again, twice more.

'Rescue 116, Shannon, how do you read?'

Rescue 118 responded, airborne out west in the Atlantic.

'Thank you, sir,' Shannon replied. 'Have you had any contact with Rescue 116?'

'That's a negative,' Rescue 118 replied.

'Okay, have you had any updates on 116 in the last while?' Shannon asked the Sligo pilots.

'That's a negative,' Rescue 118 replied.

'No position reports whatsoever?' Shannon asked.

'Negative,' Rescue 118 replied.

At 1.13 a.m., Malin Coast Guard issued a 'Mayday' alert.

4

TOP COVER

Dara Fitzpatrick's passion for flying had begun at 18, when she was taken up in a helicopter and was 'immediately sold on it'.

'If someone had told me when I was quite young that I'd be doing this for a living, I'd have thought they were nuts,' she said in an interview in 2009.[1] She recounted how she had initially considered studying business and economics but didn't get the necessary Leaving Certificate points. A radio advertisement which led to a short flight on a helicopter had her hooked. She began learning to fly in 1990, securing her private pilot's licence that December and training with Island Helicopters in Knocksedan, Dublin. She had secured her commercial pilot's licence by March 1992.

She was hired by CHC Ireland, formerly Irish Helicopters and then Bond, which had been awarded the search and rescue helicopter contract for the Irish Marine Emergency Service – as the Irish Coast Guard was known up to 2000. To gear up for search and rescue, Fitzpatrick spent much of 1994 on secondment, flying Sikorsky S-61 helicopters on transport runs to and from rigs in the North Sea, based in Aberdeen, Scotland.

Shannon was the only state helicopter search and rescue base when she was first employed there as an all-weather search and rescue pilot. After the Coast Guard's search and rescue network expanded to four bases, she moved to Waterford in 2002, where she was appointed chief pilot. She became a familiar face on television when RTÉ broadcast a series on the work of the Rescue

SEARCH AND RESCUE

117 base in 2010. The RTÉ Cork film crew spent six months at the south-east helicopter base, and the series profiled eighteen different rescues, in operations ranging from airlifts from ships on the high seas to mountain rescues and medical evacuations.[2]

One of those rescues earned Fitzpatrick, co-pilot Ronan Flanagan and the winch team of Neville Murphy and Keith Devaney, along with their engineers Martin Dennehy and Colm McCloughry, a 'Best of Irish' award. On 11 August 2009, John O'Shaughnessy had to ditch his two-seater, single-engine aircraft in the Irish Sea. Fortunately, he was spotted close to the Tuskar Rock lighthouse off the Wexford coast by the crew of *British Orchid*, a rowing boat circumnavigating Britain, and they raised the alarm. The S-61 helicopter was returning from a training exercise, refuelled, and reached O'Shaughnessy within ten minutes. He was standing on the wing of the aircraft when Devaney was lowered down to winch him up.

'It was a very controlled landing; he was very skilled. When we heard that there was someone standing on the wing, we knew that he was okay,' Fitzpatrick said afterwards. 'It's always nice to have someone alive. It's terrible to say but it doesn't happen that often,' she added.[3]

In 2013, Fitzpatrick flew the Irish Coast Guard's first ever all-female mission alongside her co-pilot, Captain Carmel Kirby, undertaking two medical evacuations. That same year, she transferred to the Irish Coast Guard's Dublin base for family reasons and in 2014 she adopted her baby son, Fionn, who became 'the light of her life'.

***

Rescue 116 helicopter flight captain Mark Duffy (51), a father of two from Blackrock, County Louth, had landed what he had described as his 'dream job' with the Irish Coast Guard in 2001. Birthday and Christmas gifts were model aircraft; visiting his grandparents' home in Newry from a young age, he would often watch British army helicopters coming and going from the military base at Bessbrook, 5 kilometres away in Armagh.

He had paid for his first flying lesson at the age of 16 with money he had earned on a part-time summer job in Dundalk, securing a helicopter flight with a former US army combat pilot, John O'Sullivan, who lived near him in Termonfeckin, County Louth. When he finished school, Duffy applied to the then state-owned airline Aer Lingus for fixed-wing training, but was turned down as he hadn't met the stipulated 'honours' Leaving Certificate exam mark in Irish. He was driving plant machinery when he decided to borrow money from his mother and the local credit union for private flying lessons with Westair Aviation.

He worked in the US in the late 1980s and came home in 1992. He began flying helicopters in 1996, securing a private pilot's licence that October and a commercial licence for helicopters in the US in 1998. He took up a job in December 1999, flying a Bell 206 Jet Ranger for businessman Declan Ganley. Ganley described him as a friend, 'a brilliant pilot' and an 'absolute pro' and said he had been so proud of him when he 'wanted to leave flying for me and go to the Irish Coast Guard'.[4]

Duffy trained up for multi-engine and instrument rating with a British company in 2001, also flying in Norway on a Sikorsky S-61. He was recruited by CHC Ireland to become a Coast Guard pilot at its Dublin base the year after he and his wife, Hermione, married. The couple had settled in his County Louth home village of Blackrock; their daughter, Esmé, was born in 2002 and their son, Fionn, in 2004. In December 2007, he was assigned as a captain at the Dublin base.

Much of his work over his sixteen years in search and rescue took him to the Wicklow mountains and the Irish Sea, and across the border to the Mourne mountains in County Down. Training drills in the Irish Sea and over his home county of Louth were common, and neighbours would quip that 'there's Mark saying a wee "hi" to Hermione'.

He was flying with Ciarán Smith and winchman Richard Desay when they undertook a particularly challenging rescue of a woman who had fallen and was stuck on a cliff in Balscadden, Howth, north Dublin, in May 2016. Desay was lifting her up in the strop, or sling, when the woman slipped, and he had to grip her with all his might while Duffy manoeuvred the aircraft to higher ground.

'When you make a difference, there is no better feeling than that ... it's priceless,' Duffy said of his job in an interview with County Louth radio station LMFM in December 2013. He described how training prepared one for 'whatever emergency might be thrown at you' and noted that, statistically, helicopters had saved more lives than they had taken.

'I love what I do,' he said, adding that making the difference was what counted. Having undertaken many medical evacuations and emergency flights, Duffy was also passionate about organ donation, and always encouraged people to carry organ donor cards and to donate blood.

His wife, Hermione, would later recall how much he loved his job, how his passion for flying was such that he would often run through checklists at home with her, and how he had given her strict instructions not to travel to the scene if he was ever involved in an accident during a mission.

'Don't come and don't take the kids,' he had advised her. 'I don't want you to see that. You are to stay at home, and I will come home to you ...'⁵

***

Paul Ormsby (53) had been one of an Air Corps' elite Dauphin search and rescue crew in challenging years, when night search and rescue was evolving in Ireland. As a former colleague recalled, 'his wit and humour belied a steely calmness and determination which had marked him out as one of the Air Corps' best'.

After he moved to the Irish Coast Guard, he earned a national commendation for his role in a joint Shannon–Dublin mission, which saved seventeen Spanish and Portuguese crew from a burning fishing vessel in the Atlantic in January 2000.[6]

Paul was born and reared in Ballyfermot, south Dublin. One of his three older brothers, Thomas, died when he was 21, and his father, also Thomas, passed away a year later, at the age of 54. Kathleen Ormsby was left to rear four young children on her own. Paul took a course in painting and decorating in Bolton Street College, Dublin (now Dublin Institute of Technology) after leaving school, but he always had a hankering to join the army. He realised his ambition in his late twenties, then transferred into the Air Corps, where he trained to become part of the winch crew in search and rescue, flying in Alouette III and Dauphin helicopters.

After CHC Ireland secured the Coast Guard search and rescue contract, he transferred over – along with a number of Defence Force colleagues – in 1998 and was assigned to the Dublin search and rescue base as a dual-rated winch operator and winchman. He was also a qualified paramedic. The death of one of his close Air Corps friends, Sergeant Paddy Mooney, in the Dauphin helicopter crash in Tramore, County Waterford, in July 1999, hit him hard.

Paul lived with his mother, caring for her after she retired from her job as a school cleaner. He was also close to his sister, Angela, her husband, Dave, and their two children, David and Jennifer, and would go walking and hiking with his brother-in-law, and swimming at the Forty Foot in Sandycove. He was never short of a joke, finding humour in every situation; the BBC's *Dad's Army* series was one of his favourite television programmes.

During one tasking in 2014, there was a serendipitous outcome to a quip Paul made as he scanned the FLIR (Forward-looking Infra-red) camera in the back of the helicopter. His Dublin crew had been called out on the night of 1 July, following a report that three men had not returned from a walk near the coast at Malahide.

'That looks like Jedward!' Ormsby had remarked as he scanned the outlines on screen, referring to Dublin-born identical twins John and Edward Grimes, who had developed their musical career on the back of a trademark hair style. Initially parodied for having more enthusiasm than musical ability and described as 'not very good' by former British prime minister Gordon Brown – who then had to apologise – the pair had represented Ireland in the Eurovision song contest on two occasions and recorded a series for BBC's children's television entitled *Jedward's Big Adventure*.

That night in July 2014, they had their own 'big adventure'. Ormsby had, indeed, seen Jedward on his screen. They had gone walking with their cousin at Donabate beach and had become disoriented when darkness fell on a rising tide. Their mother had called the emergency services.

Skerries Coast Guard unit volunteers waded into the sea after Ormsby spotted them on screen. The helicopter lit up the area from overhead and the three young men were escorted ashore near the Malahide estuary at around 1 a.m. The twins later thanked the Irish Coast Guard for the rescue, recording their shock at how quickly a stranding could occur and warning people to be wary of the sea.[7]

***

Ciarán Smith (38), or 'Smithy', as he was known to colleagues, was a father of three, a keen cyclist and Wild Geese GAA player, as well as the holder of several awards for his rescue work, including one for the difficult rescue of a swimmer off County Derry in May 2003.[8] He had joined the army apprentice school at the age of 16, passing out with a 'best soldier' award, training as an army electrician and serving in the Lebanon for six months. When he transferred to the Air Corps, he quickly moved into search and rescue, and was in training in Alouette III and Dauphin helicopters when four of the defence wing's crew were killed in a Dauphin helicopter crash on the Waterford coast in July 1999. It was the one time his mother, Teresa, and his father, Michael, asked if he might consider another career, but he loved it too much.

In 2004 he joined CHC and was assigned to the Dublin base. Like Ormsby, he was also a paramedic. A keen athlete, he had taken part in ultra-challenge cycle racing, raising more than €20,000 for numerous charities in the Race Around Ireland Ultra Endurance Challenge. He had also travelled several times to South Africa as a volunteer with the Niall Mellon Trust, initially on his own as an electrician, but latterly with CHC colleagues Ed Shivnen and Derek Everitt.

He poured similar energy into the home that he built with his wife, Martina, in Oldtown on the Dublin–Meath border. He was devoted to his daughters, Caitlin, Shannon and Finlay. 'Happiness is when you realise that your children have turned out to be good people,' he had observed on social media.

***

'I won't be seeing out of those at night,' Captain Dara Fitzpatrick remarked to winchman Paul Ormsby, as she fetched a stepladder to clean the streaks off the windscreen and side windows of her helicopter.[9] The crew were preparing to depart on their top cover mission that fateful March evening.

The mood at base had been somewhat subdued that day, due to sadness over the passing of a close colleague. Daithí Ó Cearbhalláin, an experienced search and rescue helicopter airman and a committed family man, had died in County Clare the week before, at the young age of 53, after a short illness.

Originally from Dublin, Ó Cearbhalláin had a passion for music and the Irish language, which he developed when he moved with his family to Clare. He was on the very first search and rescue mission carried out by the Air Corps from the state's new search and rescue base at Shannon Airport. His passing occurred on the twenty-seventh anniversary of a rescue mission for which he received a Distinguished Service Medal (DSM), when a 19-metre (65-foot) fishing vessel, the *Locative*, with four crew on board, lost engine power in March 1990 and was taking in water in treacherous seas off Arranmore Island, County Donegal. He received another award for a different mission the following year, when he was part of an Air Corps crew that worked with the British RAF to assist a French-registered fish factory ship that had run aground in Galway Bay.[10]

Ó Cearbhalláin moved from the Defence Forces to the Coast Guard in 2002, working for CHC Ireland and becoming chief crewman. He had been instrumental in training many Irish Coast Guard colleagues for a regime that involved being airborne within fifteen minutes of an emergency request or 'tasking' during daylight, and forty-five minutes at night. Although he was very popular, taking on a management job like this could be challenging when working with contemporaries.

The first call for a tasking would come from a marine rescue co-ordination centre to a helicopter base phone – nicknamed the 'Bat phone' in Dublin. The co-ordination centre would also alert the crew on the TETRA radio – the communication system used by all emergency services. Crews were on twenty-four-hour shifts – the only emergency service in Ireland to have this long shift pattern – but had the option of sleeping at home if living within twenty minutes of the base.

Dara Fitzpatrick was able to avail of this option. Her shift on 13 March had begun as normal – she had been up since shortly after 6 a.m. to leave her two-and-a-half-year-old son, Fionn, to his crèche. She started work at the Dublin base at 1 p.m. It was a quiet enough afternoon, but there was always training and administration to catch up on. She opted to sleep at home that night, arriving around 9.25 p.m. at the house she shared with Fionn and her sister Emer.

She was barely half an hour in bed, and had been reading her book, when her phone rang. Back downstairs at 10.15 p.m., she told Emer that she had to head to work.

She was on the phone as she drove to Dublin airport, contacting the Sligo base which had received the initial tasking and speaking to the winch operator on duty. He told her that his two pilots were out at the helicopter, preparing for start-up, and he was about to join them. The Rescue 118 crew planned to head out west and he assumed Rescue 116 would head out behind them to provide support.

Dara's colleague, Captain Mark Duffy, had attended a service earlier that day for Ó Cearbhalláin, having spent the morning checking work emails, meeting a friend for coffee and doing some household jobs. He drove from the service to work to begin his shift and opted to stay at the base that night. He spoke with his wife, Hermione, by phone at around 9.15 p.m.

Winchman Ciarán Smith had been able to attend Ó Cearbhalláin's funeral in Clare that Saturday. On Monday, he had started work at 1 p.m. and his wife, Martina, and three daughters collected him at 9 p.m. so he could sleep at home. He was still awake when his TETRA radio activated with the tasking and he left home again for the Dublin base. He sent a text message to Martina later, saying that they were headed to Sligo for fuel, then following the Sligo helicopter R118 out towards a fishing vessel, and that he would sleep at the base after they returned.

Winch operator Paul Ormsby had seemed particularly upset about his former colleague's death and also the fact that he had not been able to attend the funeral. He had opted to spend the evening part of the shift at home and was reading in bed when the TETRA radio sprang into life.

***

'Just giving you direct to Sligo there, we'll put everything in en route,' Dara Fitzpatrick told her colleague, Mark Duffy, as the crew went through a checklist before take-off. Duffy advised air traffic control at 10.53 p.m. that the Sikorsky S-92 would be westbound, 'either to Sligo or Blacksod, we're not sure at the moment'. The Sikorsky S-92 left Dublin airport at 11.03 p.m., and established contact with its Sligo counterpart, Rescue 118, three minutes later, via the TETRA radio. The Sligo crew were just landing in Blacksod and promised to contact them after refuelling.

'Oh great, thanks, you might just find out what the conditions are like there as well,' Fitzpatrick said.

Once airborne and cruising at 3,000 feet, Fitzpatrick asked Duffy to calculate a fuel quantity and time for a flight to Sligo to refuel and onwards. At that point, they were estimating that it would take over three hours to reach the fishing vessel.

Paul Ormsby tried to make contact with Rescue 118 again to get details on the weather at Blacksod. He had been on a mission that refuelled at the north Mayo lighthouse a few days before – the only one of the four crew to have been there recently.

The Sligo helicopter's report was recorded by Malin Head Coast Guard, stating that 'conditions at the pad are fine, eh, eh, kind of some low cloud, eh, approximately 500 feet up to the north while we were inbound through Broadhaven Bay, over'.

The Rescue 116 flight crew didn't hear the full transmission, however. The pilots were told that 'conditions are good at Blacksod'.

Cleared to ascend to 4,000 feet, Fitzpatrick handed over controls to Duffy at 11.15 p.m., and began calculating whether Sligo or Blacksod would be best for refuelling. She worked out that opting for Blacksod would save 700 pounds of fuel and thirty minutes' flying time.

'It kinda makes more sense, guys, really, to go to Blacksod,' Fitzpatrick said, and both Duffy and the rear crew agreed. She noted that they were under no time pressure and had plenty of fuel to reach Sligo if they were unable to land in north Mayo. At 11.21 p.m., she advised Dublin air traffic control that they were heading to Blacksod.

As they flew west, an approach route known as 'Blacksod south' was keyed into the flight management system, which involved flying out into the Atlantic beyond Blacksod and looping back in towards the Mullet peninsula, overflying Blackrock Island 9 nautical miles to the west. On the cockpit recorder, both Fitzpatrick and Duffy could be heard to complain about the cockpit lighting. In the back of the aircraft, the winch team were trying to establish two-way communications with Rescue 118 but without success.

'Yeh, no point in us not having comms with 118 … that's what we're here for,' Ormsby noted in frustration.

'God, I'd say I haven't been in Blacksod in about fifteen years,' Fitzpatrick remarked at 11.52 p.m.

'Yeh, it's been a while for me too alright,' winchman Ciarán Smith replied.

'How about you … have you been in recently?' Fitzpatrick asked Duffy.

'No, not recently, been a while,' Duffy said.

There is no record on the cockpit voice recorder of Ormsby commenting he had been there earlier in the week.

Blacksod helipad contacted Rescue 116 on marine channel 16 just after midnight, at 12.08 a.m. Ormsby said they would arrive in twenty minutes, and asked for wind, cloud base and visibility information. He was told the cloud base was 'three, four, five hundred feet' and is 'good enough to come in'.

Five minutes later, at 12.13 a.m., Duffy said he wouldn't mind having a look at the 'map', and Fitzpatrick took over the controls, advising him that everything was an 'overfly waypoint' with the exception of one 'smart turn'. Duffy asked what the 'escape route' was, if they did not 'become visual'. The latter term is used by pilots to describe the point where they have enough visual references outside the aircraft to continue the approach to land. If they do not, then an 'escape route' involves a diversion to an alternative, more suitable landing location.

After further discussion, Duffy offered to 'come back on the sticks' and take over controls, but Fitzpatrick declined, saying she was 'happy enough there if you are actually … I'll stay on it.'

It is customary for the winchman to be called forward to the cockpit for a briefing prior to an approach to land, given that he would be monitoring the FLIR thermal imaging camera in the back of the aircraft. The southern approach route to and from Blacksod helipad involved following a series of seven legs, denoted by waypoints which started with 'BLKMO', the eastern end of Blackrock Island. Duffy went through the plan with Smith, and the winchman noted that high ground was 'obviously in here somewhere', and there would be a strong tailwind on the approach. Fitzpatrick said they would 'keep the speed back' and, if they were not happy on the first pass, 'we'll go back around, we'll couple it up, go back around, and we go back in again, though it's been donkey's years since I've been in here, but we'll stay nice and controlled …'

At 12.27 a.m., Fitzpatrick noted they were abeam of Achill Island, and requested a series of approach checks, including landing gear down, radar on and switching on all external lights. She then briefed the crew for the 'let-down' procedure, where the aircraft would clear all obstacles to a particular position at low height. After the checks were complete, Smith noted that Rescue 118 was just five minutes away from the fishing vessel with the injured crewman. 'Fantastic,' Duffy observed.

The helicopter began its descent from 4,000 feet to approach Blacksod at 200 feet. At 12.36 a.m., an automated voice called 'level off', and two minutes later another synthetic voice called 'minimums, minimums'.

As Duffy called out the height in 100-foot increments, Fitzpatrick requested confirmation that they were clear on radar and on the emergency ground proximity warning system (EGPWS), which is designed to give alerts on terrain awareness. Duffy confirmed they were 'clear ahead on ten-mile range'.

At 12.45 a.m. Duffy noted that there were 'small targets at six miles, 11 o'clock … large out there to the right', and three seconds later an automated voice issued an 'altitude, altitude' caution.

'There's just a small island, that's BLMO itself,' Fitzpatrick said reassuringly. She was believed to be referring to an outcrop of two small rocks, Carrickduff and Carrickad, some 0.65 nautical miles to the west of Blackrock Island.

From the back of the aircraft, Smith informed the commander he was 'looking at an island directly ahead of us now, guys, you wanna come right'.

She asked for confirmation and he replied, 'Twenty degrees right, yeah.'

Fitzpatrick asked Duffy, the co-pilot, to select heading mode and he confirmed that this was done.

Within one second of this acknowledgement, and almost 13 seconds after his first warning, Smith urged the pilot to 'come right now, come right, COME RIGHT'.

A second automated 'altitude, altitude' warning issued 26 seconds after the first, coinciding with a sound believed to be impact with terrain.

The last recorded words were those of Mark Duffy: 'We're gone.'[11]

* * *

The empty helicopter pad was lit as Fergus arrived at the lighthouse. He could hear his uncle, Vincent, repeatedly calling on VHF radio. At 1.08 a.m., Vincent advised Malin Coast Guard that he had no contact with the helicopter. The radio station broadcast the first 'Mayday' on marine radio channel 16 at 1.13 a.m., informing all stations that communications had been lost with Rescue 116 and requesting any vessels with information to contact it.

The RNLI Achill Island and Ballyglass all-weather lifeboats responded to the 'Mayday', as did two Coast Guard helicopters, along with the Coast Guard's shore unit based at Ballyglass in north Mayo. The Air Corps, which had been unable to provide top cover for Rescue 118 three hours earlier, tasked a CASA aircraft to fly west from Casement Aerodrome, its base in Baldonnel, County Dublin, and reached Blacksod before dawn.

First on the scene was the Sligo-based Rescue 118 helicopter. It had been completing its medical evacuation 140 nautical miles west of Mayo's Eagle Island and was out of radio range when the fishing vessel involved received a broadcast from Malin at 1.21 a.m. that stated Rescue 116 'may have ditched' off Blacksod. Malin asked it to advise the Rescue 118 crew.

Rescue 118 climbed away from the fishing vessel with the injured fisherman on board and flew directly to the Mayo coast, checking all the time for any satellite signals from the emergency locator beacons on Rescue 116. It informed Belmullet Coast Guard radio at 1.48 a.m. that it had been unable to pick up any beacon signals.

By 2.10 a.m. Rescue 118 was over Blackrock Island, west of Blacksod, and searching. Its crew spotted strobe lights a minute later, emitted by an immersion suit on the sea's surface. Framed against the dark water by the helicopter's lights overhead, Dara Fitzpatrick appeared lifeless in her fully inflated life jacket – her arms outstretched, no helmet on her head and her long hair flowing with the swell.

The aircraft made several unsuccessful attempts to reach her, hampered by the fact that one of its winch crew had sustained an injury when he fell onto the deck of the fishing vessel during the medical evacuation. The RNLI Achill crew of coxswain Dave Curtis, Declan Corrigan, Seán Ginnelly, Michael O'Hara, Pat Kilbane and Joe Casey, who had been dispatched by Malin Coast Guard at 1.13 a.m., were directed to the area, two miles west of the Duvillaun islands, to assist.

The sea surface was covered in debris, and Rescue 118's searchlights were trained on a location some 1.5 nautical miles south-east of Blackrock lighthouse as the lifeboat approached. Dara Fitzpatrick was taken on board the vessel at 2.37 a.m., unresponsive. Removing her inflated life jacket, the Achill crew cut open the immersion suit to begin immediate cardiopulmonary resuscitation (CPR). Curtis recalled at the preliminary inquest that the conditions were so rough the crew had to hold each other in position on the deck as they tried to revive her. They worked feverishly for twenty-five minutes, while the coxswain communicated with Rescue 118 on the search for the three other helicopter crew.

At about 3 a.m. Curtis joined the lifeboat crew still administering CPR on the afterdeck. There was no pulse, no sign of life. The difficult decision was made to stop resuscitation efforts. The pilot's body was wrapped in a blanket and an ambulance pouch and made secure, while the lifeboat continued the search for the other missing crew, along with Rescue 118.

***

The Shannon-based Rescue 115 helicopter duty crew were airborne by 2.06 a.m. and, like 118, were on the alert for PLB signals. There were none. Nor had the missing helicopter emitted its own EPIRB, which would give an immediate position via satellite on impact with water. A westerly gale was reaching force 7 as the 115 crew, under the command of Mick Meally, with co-pilot Carmel Kirby and winch team Eamonn Ó Broin and Philip Wrenn, joined the search.

The 115 crew were told that Dara Fitzpatrick had been taken on board the Achill lifeboat. A radio call to Rescue 118 confirmed she was 'unresponsive … she is gone'. Meally informed his crew on the internal intercom, but also pointed out that there were still three colleagues out there who could still be alive and they were in the best position to find them as the only aerial asset. At this point, Rescue 118 had left the scene to land its casualty, the injured fisherman, at Blacksod.

Later, as dawn broke, a defined debris field to the south-east of Blackrock Island would become visible, pointing to where the main fuselage had struck. Rescue 115 would locate two fuselage sponsons – designed to separate in the event of high impact – floating on the surface, along with the fuselage belly panels with their distinctive high visibility orange chevrons and even individual kit bags which the winch crew had on board.

However, at this point it was still dark, with a full moon to the west and strong westerly gusts. As the Rescue 115 crew continued their difficult search, they caught sight of the floodlights of approaching fishing vessels, crashing through the swell to join the search. As one of the crew said later, 'it was a real morale lift in our time of need'.

5

THE TOUGHEST CALL

The sound of the doorbell, almost exaggerated in pitch with time, is one that Martina Smith would never forget. Her husband's good friends, CHC Ireland pilots Ed Shivnen and Sid Lawrence, were at the door with difficult news. Ciarán's helicopter was missing. It had been long-time practice among helicopter search and rescue crews to nominate colleagues who would contact their next of kin in the unlikely event of something going wrong.

In County Louth, Hermione Duffy, wife of Mark, was woken by a knock on the door of her home around 5.30 a.m. On the step were Loy McParland, a former CHC pilot and close friend of her husband, and winch operator Derek Everitt. When she heard that the helicopter was missing, Hermione remembered responding that this 'couldn't be happening … it's a calm night … there is no wind'.[1]

Angela Ormsby was always up at 5.30 a.m. On the morning of 14 March 2017, she was in the kitchen of her home in Ballyfermot, Dublin, when she heard her son, David, moving about. He had ordered a set of training weights and was expecting them in the post that day.

'So when the doorbell rang, I thought it was that delivery. I told David to go out and answer it. Paul's colleagues, Blackie [Colm Blackburn] and Christy [Mahady] were standing on the step. Christy called my name and all I heard was the word "helicopter" and I knew something had happened. I ran up the stairs, screaming. My husband had been asleep up till then and didn't know what was going on ...'

It was shortly before 6 a.m. when Dara Fitzpatrick's sister Emer was first contacted. Captain Mark Donnelly, who had been on the previous shift at Dublin, had volunteered to call out to Dara's home with aircraft maintenance engineer Eoin Murphy. Emer called her sister Niamh, who lived just four houses away.

In her own moving account, published over three years later, Niamh Fitzpatrick, a professional psychologist, remembered every small detail of those hours – as if frozen in a series of photographs.[2] She had set her alarm for 6 a.m. She remembered she was sleeping with her face towards the window, and she remembered Emer's first five words when she picked up the phone – 'the heli has gone down'.

Niamh phoned her mother, Mary, and her siblings. Their father, John, had travelled to Britain the day before to attend the Cheltenham racing festival and initially couldn't be reached.

A few minutes later, Emer opened the door to Niamh; Donnelly and Murphy were standing in the kitchen. Dara's young son, Fionn, was still fast asleep upstairs, so they spoke in whispers as the two men explained that communication had been lost with the helicopter.

During that morning, news bulletins reported that a body had been found, but did not mention any more details. Shortly before midday, the Fitzpatricks were told that representatives of CHC Ireland were on their way. They were informed that the body recovered from the water by the RNLI Achill lifeboat had been formally identified.

'There was a sharp intake of breath from everyone in the room, then stifled screams, tears and complete disbelief,' Niamh recorded. 'I can still hear those screams even now, the anguished sounds of sorrow ...'[3]

Life as she and her family knew it had stopped just there and then.

***

'One of the toughest calls I've done in my career,' CHC paramedic Phil Wrenn, who had been part of the search in Rescue 115 that night, said in an interview for a TG4 *Tabú* documentary on the Irish Coast Guard, broadcast three years later. He'd been asked about the impact of the Rescue 116 crash.

'Everybody got just a huge shock that morning to get that phone call, you know, to try and get your head around it,' his winch team colleague Darren Torpey told *Tabú*. 'You always had it at the back of your mind that an aircraft could go down, you know … and it was in the full glare of the media, so you were dealing with the loss of friends, you were dealing with your own grief and you were still searching, you were still flying.'

Wrenn recalled the initial call and the voice on the phone of his colleague, pilot Mick Meally, telling him Rescue 116 was missing. Then came the shock of finding the wreckage. 'You were sitting in an aircraft [the same as] that you're searching for, and you can see the similar bits of your aircraft scattered across the sea,' he said.[4]

All Sikorsky S-92s had been grounded globally in January 2017 after a dramatic tail rotor failure on an oil and gas rig helipad. Though the Coast Guard S-92s had all been inspected to confirm their airworthiness, they were still operating in March 2017 under the strict restriction of a fixed number of flight hours before engineers were required to inspect them again. This restriction determined the time Shannon Rescue 115 could stay on scene, so the Waterford-based Rescue 117 helicopter had relocated overnight to Shannon as a relief aircraft.

At 8.45 a.m., Rescue 115's crew winched the body of Dara Fitzpatrick on board from the Achill lifeboat and flew to Mayo

General Hospital in Castlebar. Recovering the pilot took place in very challenging sea conditions from a small deck. In his mission report, Meally praised the work of winch crew Ó Broin and Wrenn, given the physical conditions and the psychological pressure they were both under.

'I worked with Dara in Waterford, knew Ciarán, knew Mark, worked with them all but … it's an unusual feeling to carry your colleague – take them from the scene and carry them into the hospital,' Wrenn said. 'It's something you can't describe.'

Ó Broin explained at the later preliminary inquest that the Rescue 116 crew were not just workmates, but close friends – he had known Fitzpatrick for twenty-five years. Having to leave the scene, with one of their colleagues now lifeless on board and three still missing at sea, was gut-wrenching for the Rescue 115 crew.

Initially, the Coast Guard wanted Dara Fitzpatrick to be flown to Dublin. However, this would have caused complications under coroners' legislation. When Rescue 115 arrived at Mayo General Hospital, the waiting ambulance crew and garda staff offered to assist in carrying the body from the aircraft. The Rescue 115 crew politely refused their help and carried her to the ambulance as a unit. They stayed with her at the mortuary until the relief crews from the Shannon base arrived to take over from them.

Fitzpatrick was officially pronounced dead in Castlebar and formally identified. The State Pathologist's office then sought an undertaking from the gardaí that all legislation had been complied with, before conducting a post-mortem.

'I think we all kind of knew it can happen, everyone knows it can happen, but I don't think many people thought about being lost at sea,' Rescue 118 winch crew Gavin Playle said in *Tabú*. 'My memory at the time is completely saturated with searching. Most times we left here [Sligo], we were on for four hours … we'd go down and we'd fly a couple of hours, and we'd go into Blacksod. Sometimes we'd refuel and leave straight away, sometimes we'd shut down ... we'd meet the families down there. It was just upsetting talking to the families and seeing how they were.'[5]

'When these things happen, we're gutted, but at the same time it's happened to the families and they feel it from us as well,' Rescue 117 winch crew Neville Murphy, based in Waterford, added. 'I remember my nine-year-old at the time and the questions he was asking that time, you know, and he cried as well ... as we all cried. So it really drove home to me the effect it all has on them.'

***

Ballyglass Coast Guard unit volunteers including Michael Hurst had heard their pagers go off at about 1.30 a.m. The RNLI Ballyglass lifeboat joined the search at sea at 3.20 a.m. They were joined by the fishing vessels which Rescue 115 had seen approaching and which hailed from as far south as Castletownbere in west Cork and as far north as Greencastle in Donegal. The Naval Service also dispatched a patrol ship, the LÉ *Róisín*.

Inshore fisherman Eamon Dixon and a group of twenty colleagues with small vessels began combing the coastline, the first voyage for some of them after being laid up for the winter. Three crab vessels owned by north Mayo fisherman Pat O'Donnell and his sons, Jonathan and Patrick, put to sea from Ballyglass. In October 1997, O'Donnell had been instrumental in locating and rescuing a family of three who were trapped in a cave after a currach capsized. The currach owner and a Mayo diver, Michael Heffernan from the Gráinne Uaíle diving club, lost their lives.[6]

'There was a bit of a rush to get out as we knew they would be wearing immersion suits and there was every chance the helicopter might have ditched and they might still be alive,' Pat O'Donnell recalled.[7]

The fishermen had heard the communications between the Sligo helicopter and the RNLI Achill lifeboat shortly after Fitzpatrick's immersion suit was spotted, and they continued searching. Back on Blacksod pier, Belmullet garda superintendent Tony Healy was establishing a chain of command.

Local gardaí had first learned about the crash from a Coast Guard vehicle on the road and had phoned the state agency to check the details – there had been no formal report to the gardaí at that stage. There were more blue lights on Blacksod pier as ambulances arrived, one of which took the injured fisherman from Rescue 118 to hospital by road. As the hours wore on, however, the waiting vehicles would disperse.

Minutes were now merging into hours, night turning to day as the Sweeneys and the gardaí established a shore base for the search effort, with no time to think of the personal impact. Vincent was on first-name terms with many Coast Guard helicopter crew members, and knew all four who had died in the Dauphin helicopter crash off the south-east coast on 1 July 1999. Captains Dave O'Flaherty and Mick Baker, Sergeant Paddy Mooney and Corporal Niall Byrne had landed at various times to refuel in Blacksod when stationed in south Donegal before they were transferred to Waterford. At the time, the Air Corps was responsible for running two of the four search and rescue helicopter bases, at Finner in Donegal, and latterly at Sligo and Waterford.[8]

Back in Dublin, at an early morning press briefing at the Department of Transport in Leeson Lane, acting Coast Guard director Eugene Clonan outlined what was known of the last moments of Rescue 116. This was a 'very dark day' for emergency services in Ireland, he said, and one crew member who had been recovered from the water was 'critical'. Clonan acknowledged that hope was 'fading that we will find the rest of the crew'.

Fergus Sweeney fielded calls from journalists on radio stations as press began to arrive on Blacksod pier. He and his daughter, Eva, emptied his parents' fridge of food for the search and rescue effort. In the village of Eachléim, several miles north of Blacksod towards Belmullet, a community was already mobilising to transform the local hall into a field kitchen for the emergency services.

There was a brisk south-westerly and bright sunshine when Garry Bohan and John Shevlin berthed at Blacksod pier with some wreckage, including a large panel, from the helicopter. They described a gathering swell and difficult conditions, and told journalists that debris was being carried north to the Inishkea islands.

Even as they spoke, a helicopter landed to refuel and then returned to sea again. An hour later, the Air Corps flew in Naval Service divers, while the Garda Water Unit, with its trained search and recovery sub-aqua team, arrived by road.

Shortly before 2.30 p.m., an ashen-faced Coast Guard operations manager, Gerard O'Flynn, came out to address waiting journalists on the pier. Captain Dara Fitzpatrick, the Coast Guard's most senior pilot, had been confirmed dead, he said. The search was continuing for her three colleagues. He described a sense of complete shock.

'Dara was the most senior pilot and has been with the company for close on 20 years. Outside of her work as a pilot she did an enormous amount of work on water safety and was always available to do school visits and promote water safety,' O'Flynn said. 'For all of us involved in the Coast Guard, and particularly for her family, it has come as a complete shock. And we want to extend our sincere sympathy to all her family and to her flying colleagues in CHC and simply to everybody who knew her.'[9]

He recalled that, just several days earlier, many Coast Guard and RNLI lifeboat crew had been together under very sad circumstances – the funeral of Daithí Ó Cearbhalláin. The rescue community is a 'small, tight family. We all know each other so well,' O'Flynn said.[10]

* * *

In the following days, President Michael D. Higgins and Taoiseach Enda Kenny led the tributes to Fitzpatrick, with Kenny one of

several government ministers who visited Blacksod pier to meet
the families and the search teams. Photographs of the four aircrew
were on every news bulletin, every media platform and in every
print newspaper.

By then, the pilot's father, John, had arrived home from
Cheltenham. The Fitzpatricks were taken to Mayo General
Hospital; en route, they were told that two long-time friends of
Dara, Captain Cathal Oakes and Captain Ciarán Ferguson, had
arrived in Castlebar and that, between them and the crew of
Rescue 118, someone would stay with Dara's body in the hospital
mortuary until her family arrived that night, sometime between
9 and 10 p.m. The family sat with her all through the night, with
blankets over their knees and hot tea supplied by mortuary staff.[11]

John, Mary and Niamh Fitzpatrick were interviewed by Teresa
Mannion for RTÉ Television outside the hospital mortuary the
following day. 'She always told us that if anything ever happened,
she never wanted to be left alone,' Mary Fitzpatrick told Mannion.

Asked where her sister had found the courage and bravery
to do her job, Niamh gestured to her parents, recalling how they
had lost a baby girl on the same date, 14 March, thirty-nine years
earlier. Now they had lost a second daughter.

6

'WE NEED THOSE BOYS HOME'

A faint chirp was picked up at sea the day after the helicopter crash, when three of the four Rescue 116 crew were still missing. A local vessel equipped with a Marine Institute hydrophone detected the sound of the flight recorder on 15 March 2017, in some 40 to 50 metres of water close to the south-east corner of Blackrock Island.

This was a 'hugely significant step', Air Accident Investigation Unit (AAIU) Chief Inspector Jurgen Whyte told reporters at Blacksod pier. However, the possible location was in 'difficult waters' on an exposed rock positioned right in the path of a relentless Atlantic swell close to the edge of the Continental Shelf, he said.

Fishermen along the Mullet peninsula knew just how difficult it was, as did lightkeeping staff who were stationed on Blackrock Island. Such was the ferocity of the weather during the winter of 1942/43 that three lightkeepers were stranded on the island for weeks. Five years before that, on 17 September 1937, keeper Patrick Monaghan (27) descended the very steep steps hewn from the rock to get a pail of water and was swept away by the surging sea. His body was never recovered. His grandson, RTÉ radio presenter Cathal Murray, fulfilled a long-time ambition to visit the rock in June 2010. By then, the lighthouse had been automated for over thirty-five years. In a short documentary Murray made of the visit, his mother, Mamie, told him how his grandfather had been due home on leave, but the sea relief trip was delayed by weather. His last letter home described how he hoped to be back shortly.[1]

Whyte's briefing continued, 'We are very lucky that within less than 36 hours we have picked up what is a signal.' He noted that other investigating authorities had sometimes spent months searching for an aircraft's black box. 'The hope is the recorder is with the wreckage,' he explained. Whyte confirmed that British air accident investigators with additional specialist equipment were due to arrive at Blacksod that evening.

Relatives of the still missing Rescue 116 crew were briefed at Blacksod lighthouse and met Minister for Transport Shane Ross there that same day. The transport minister said he had spoken to the Taoiseach Enda Kenny, and 'we agreed immediately that every single resource available in the State would be made available ... There will be absolutely nothing left ... Everything possible will be done ...'[2]

Yvonne Shields, chief executive of the Irish lighthouse authority, the Commissioners of Irish Lights, also visited Blacksod that day and offered the organisation's sympathies and its continued support, providing its ship *Granuaile* to help in the search effort. This multi-purpose vessel, built to service lighthouses and navigation buoys around the Irish coast, was equipped with lifting equipment, which would be useful for retrieving wreckage. Shields noted that Blackrock lighthouse was fully functioning on the night of the crash – as was the automatic identification system, which could be picked up by aircraft or passing ships.

In a statement, the crew's employer, CHC Ireland, said the company maintained full confidence in the S-92's safety and design, and that the aircraft was in compliance with all airworthiness directives and alert service bulletins. The multinational company, with headquarters in the US, oil and gas operations based in the Aberdeen, and search and rescue in Australia and South America, had been awarded the 500-million-euro, ten-year contract to provide air-sea search and rescue from four Irish bases to the Irish Coast Guard in 2010.

As the multi-agency air and sea search continued, questions were asked in the media as to why the Air Corps had not been able to provide fixed wing top cover for Rescue 118 on the night of 13 March, and, instead, a second helicopter from Dublin was tasked to do so. The Defence Forces' press office stated that the Air Corps was unable to provide the service owing to a 'loss of experienced personnel (both aircrew and air traffic control)'.

***

With the weather deteriorating throughout the week following the crash, a 5- to 6-metre swell around Blackrock hampered efforts to pinpoint the flight recorder's precise location using the hydrophone equipment on a 12-metre locally owned vessel, *An Gearoidín*. Two days after the crash, British and Irish investigators were flown out to Blackrock by the Air Corps. That evening, the team said it had recovered 'significant debris', including a helicopter tailpiece, close to the lighthouse. It said there was no sign of impact on the lighthouse structure itself.[3]

North Mayo fishermen like Eamon Dixon were very familiar with the strong north–south running tides along the Mullet peninsula. They secured the agreement of Superintendent Tony Healy of the Belmullet gardaí to put to sea with nets to see if they could retrieve the three missing crew. However, when they arrived at the pier, they were turned back. They were told the Naval Service patrol ship LÉ *Eithne* had established on-scene command and a 3-mile exclusion zone had been set around the search area.

Torrential rain as the weekend approached reflected the mood, and the St Patrick's Day parade in Belmullet was cancelled as a mark of respect. Over on the east coast, an entire south Dublin village turned out, along with state dignitaries including

President Michael D. Higgins and Taoiseach Enda Kenny, for Dara Fitzpatrick's funeral in Glencullen.

In his tribute, CHC colleague Cathal Oakes noted that it was no coincidence that Dara's helicopter was named *Banríona na Spéire* [Queen of the Sky]. Oakes described her as a 'consummate professional' who 'carried herself with effortless style'. *The Irish Times* recorded how 'the most difficult eulogy was delivered with emotion, aplomb, wit, pride and anger by Captain Fitzpatrick's psychologist sister, Niamh'.[4]

As Dara's coffin was carried out, Coast Guard Rescue 117 emerged from the mist and drizzle to the west and circled overhead. The helicopter then dipped its nose as a mark of respect before flying away over Glencullen village.

***

During long and harrowing search days, there was constant support and sympathy for the families' ordeal at the community hall, Halla Naomh Bhreandáin, in Eachléim, where a team led by Annette Gallagher provided sustenance. An Indian take-away owner based on Achill Island landed in with prepared meals, while another man drove through the night to deliver a mobile cold room. North Dublin chef John Dowd, loaded up with cooking equipment and his white uniform, also headed to north Mayo. 'I used to see the S-92 helicopter pass over my house in Swords, so I just thought I'd get in the car with the trailer on Friday and travel up with food and gear,' he said.[5]

Cards came in from schoolchildren across many counties, including one from 10-year-old Katie Frazer from Castlebar, with some baking. 'It's nothing big, it's only a couple of buns, but I wanted to help in any way possible,' she wrote, reflecting sentiments expressed in many similar messages of support.

Numerous individuals travelled to assist in the Coast Guard shore search, including Bernard Lucas from Clare, who had lost his wife, Caitríona, just six months before. He found one of the pilot's gloves. Also with him was former rescue pilot David Courtney. A fund to support the families was established by John Gallagher, chairman of the local community group.[6] Donations arrived from far and near, including a large cheque from the Aran islands.

The crash had resurrected painful memories of recent and not so recent losses at sea on a part of the coastline where the Atlantic has taken a heavy toll. It was only eighteen months since the community had appealed to the Naval Service for help after 23-year-old Carrowteigue fisherman Daniel Doherty was reported missing. On 11 September 2015, Doherty had gone out to check pots. His boat, *Tara Rose*, was found that night and his body was recovered a fortnight later in Lacken Bay, 32 kilometres away.

Some sixteen years before, on 27 July 2001, Belmullet publican Tony Lavelle lost his 14-year-old son Anthony during a boat trip from Frenchport to the Inishkea islands with fifty ewes on board. The animals shifted and the boat capsized. His son secured Lavelle to a piece of timber, which kept him afloat. Lavelle was rescued, but his son's body was never found.

It was also almost twenty years since Ballina diver Michael Heffernan of Gráinne Uaíle sub-aqua club had died during the Belderrig cave rescue. The garda superintendent on duty that night, Tony Heffernan, had continued his involvement with the RNLI Achill lifeboat after his retirement.[7]

Josie McGinty and Mary John Tom Breathnach were two of Annette Gallagher's army of women providing food in the Eachléim hall. Their parents' generation had been forced to evacuate from the Inishkea islands, north of Blackrock, after many of the active fishermen were drowned in 1927 in a violent storm.

***

Eight days after the helicopter's last flight, the black box and the main part of the helicopter wreckage were located just off

Blackrock Island. The three aircrew had now been missing for over a week. An outline of debris was captured by the camera of *Holland 1*, the remotely operated vehicle (ROV) deployed from the *Granuaile*. Driver of the ROV was Paddy O'Driscoll, on board the *Granuaile*, while a local vessel, MV *Ross Áine*, was also conducting seabed mapping. The ROV had been fitted with a 'homer' device provided by the National Oceanographic Centre at Southampton, England, to pick up signals from a black box.

A team of surveyors from Infomar, Ireland's national seabed mapping programme run jointly by the Marine Institute and Geological Survey of Ireland, had been brought in to examine the work of *Holland 1*. Imagery pored over by the surveyors in Belmullet Garda Station yielded the first clue – a helicopter door – which led to the wreck on the seabed.

On the morning of Wednesday 22 March, relatives were taken out to sea on the LÉ *Eithne*. They included members of the Fitzpatrick family, who had travelled to Blacksod after Dara Fitzpatrick's funeral to support the continued search effort. Weather conditions were challenging, with gathering north-easterly winds. The ship was close to Blackrock Island with its relentless swell when they were informed by Commander Brian Fitzgerald that the wreckage had been found. Ciarán Smith's mother, Teresa, knew instinctively there was only one way to mark this – she led the group in prayers and reflection for all four aircrew. It was a moment those on board the ship said afterwards they would never forget.

The weather was freshening, white horses galloping across the bay and a force 8 gale blowing as the *Eithne* dropped anchor on its return to port. Naval Service RIBs transported the families back to the pier. The next stage would involve divers, and Jurgen Whyte said this stage would be handled with 'great respect'. He told reporters on the pier, 'If we can access into the aircraft, then hopefully we will be successful in recovering the three missing crew members.' In one brief respite from torrential showers and driving wind, a rainbow lit up the sky, framing the Atlantic and Blacksod Bay.

By this stage, the course the search was taking was contributing to some tense moments. Senior Coast Guard personnel, who had been told early on that the gardaí were directing operations, were concerned that the primary focus was on retrieving the aircraft's recording system for the investigators. A week after the crash, one senior Coast Guard officer was told that his organisation was no longer required at co-ordination meetings, as this was a 'crime scene' and the Coast Guard was 'under investigation'.

Diving teams were on standby to descend, when it was confirmed that a body, believed to be that of Mark Duffy, was trapped amongst the main fuselage at a depth of 40 metres (130 feet). Although the flight data recorder was recovered by a Naval Service diving team on Friday 24 March, it would take another two days before the co-pilot's body could be released and brought to the surface.

The *Granuaile* remained on station close to the rock, deploying cutting equipment attached to the *Holland 1* to facilitate access to the fuselage and possible assistance with the delicate operation. However, the Naval Service was emphatic that its divers would make the recovery, and the harrowing operation was carried out by Naval Service Chief Petty Officer Courtney Gibbons and Leading Seaman Donal O'Sullivan.

On Sunday 26 March, the Rescue 115 helicopter escorted the Naval Service patrol ship LÉ *Samuel Beckett* into Blacksod on the first stage of Mark Duffy's journey home. The only small comfort for those waiting on the pier was the bright evening sunshine. A small canopy had been erected to allow for identification by close family friend and former colleague Loy McParland. A tricolour flag was placed over the coffin and a lone piper from Achill Coast Guard led the cortege along the shoreline from the pier, followed by members of the Coast Guard, Naval Service, Civil Defence and the Commissioners of Irish Lights.

***

'Words are not only inadequate, but well-nigh useless,' Fr Stephen Duffy, Mark Duffy's uncle, said at his nephew's funeral in his home village of Blackrock, County Louth, on 30 March 2017. He described the loss of four lives in the helicopter crash as a community catastrophe.[8]

'Length of days is not what makes age honourable ... God has taken him up,' his brother Gavan said. Close friend Garda Declan Whelan read the tribute written for her husband by Hermione Duffy: 'The sea pulled Mark to it – its ebb and flow, its colours, the wave and the stillness, the calm, the rage, the reflecting sun on the water, the low tide, the high tide – it was part of our lives.'

She described not only his love for his job, but his love for his family during the twenty-six years they were together. He was a 'Garda Cósta na hÉireann, but he was also our guardian,' she said. 'He put a safety net around us in our home. He was fearless. He lived consciously each day and for the moment.'

Coast Guard pilot and colleague Ed Shivnen read the words of *An Irish Airman Foresees His Death* – the First World War aviator's soliloquy written by W.B. Yeats in 1918. Such was the silence that it seemed as if there was barely a breath taken in and around the church as he read.

✳✳✳

Two days later, on 1 April 2017, Jurgen Whyte confirmed that mechanical fault had been ruled out as a cause of the crash. He explained that 'no mechanical anomalies' with the aircraft had been detected in an initial analysis of data retrieved from its health and usage monitoring system (HUMS) and multi-purpose flight recorder.

This ruled out any further speculation about the S-92 fleet, which had been leased by the Irish government with CHC Ireland from 2010. The S-92 produced by Sikorsky from 2004 replaced the Sikorsky S-61 at Ireland's four helicopter search and rescue bases, with a faster speed, longer range and advanced systems and hardware. The new contract had been part of a radical upgrade of the Coast Guard initiated by director Chris Reynolds, formerly of the Naval Service, when he took over from the first Coast Guard director, Captain Liam Kirwan, in 2007.

Investigators were required to issue a preliminary report within thirty days of the crash, and would now focus on operational elements, including navigational aids, procedures and human impact, Whyte said, predicting it would be a 'long ... arduous' process. 'There's a lot more evidence to gather and there's a lot of interviews to do,' he explained at a press briefing on Blacksod pier. 'We must talk to the different players involved. That takes time; takes time to gather facts, time to analyse and time to come to a conclusion.'

By then, frustration was building over several unsuccessful attempts to raise the helicopter's main fuselage from the seabed using airbags – attempts hampered by equinoctal weather and swell. Spring tides were making diving conditions very challenging at the crash location in the 40-metre-deep channel off the south-east tip of Blackrock. A series of dives was required to attach a number of airbags to the engine and gearbox section of the helicopter, using the local vessel *Gearoidín* as a platform, with the *Granuaile* on standby off the rock as support, and the LÉ *Samuel Beckett* providing on-scene co-ordination.

The plan was to inflate the airbags to tilt the wreckage to see if there was any trace of the two missing winch crew. Naval Service diving section lead officer Lieutenant Dan Humphries explained that as the tide rose the tide cycle became shorter – with eight-minute dives being cut back to six minutes in the increased depth. The dive team's cycle was planned to limit recompression, if required, on board the *Granuaile*, he said.

Advice offered by local fishermen on the conditions had been 'completely correct', Humphries acknowledged. The combination

of tides, currents and swell creating surges on the seabed meant
that divers were 'struggling to hold onto the wreck', and he said
it was the most difficult task he had personally been involved in.

The searchers decided to ask for help from Sean Harrington.
Harrington, in his early thirties and from Bere Island in west
Cork, was owner and managing director of salvage company
Atlantic Towage and Marine Ltd. In 2011, he had helped to
recover a Fastnet yacht race competitor, *Rambler 100*, when it
lost its keel and capsized off the Cork coast, and he had also
been involved in the salvage of the sail training ship *Astrid* after
it ran aground when its engines failed off Kinsale, County Cork,
in 2013.[9]

Harrington was contracted by the Coast Guard to send up
his salvage tug, *Ocean Challenger*. Waterspouts were sweeping
over the north of Achill as an inter-agency team worked with
Harrington to hoist the fuselage from the seabed on 2 April and
transfer it from the tug onto the deck of the *Granuaile*. Prayers
were said on deck before the ship left Blackrock for its anchorage.
The team on board had no 'good' news for the families of Paul
Ormsby and Ciarán Smith. There had been no trace of the bodies
of either man in or around the fuselage.

'It was a significant amount of wreckage, and it was very
important that we lifted it, not alone for the investigation, but
for the families ... we were hoping there would be something
underneath it, and we are desperately disappointed that there
isn't,' Whyte said.

The rotor head, main gear box, one engine and 'associated' pieces
would be taken by the *Granuaile* to shore and then transported by
road to Gormanston, County Meath, for further examination, he
explained. Along with Superintendant Healy and Gerard O'Flynn
of the Coast Guard, he paid tribute to all those who had endured
an 'extreme environment' over the previous days.

***

With relentless drizzle and low grey cloud obscuring Achill, there was a sense that the Atlantic horizon was almost closing in on the Mullet peninsula on the morning of Monday, 3 April 2017. The *Granuaile* was leaving Broadhaven Bay, bound for Galway Port with the helicopter wreckage, which was now the property of the investigators. The weather's mood reflected the sense of despair among those who felt the search priority had been overly focused on recovery of the aircraft while two men remained missing.

Caitlín Uí Aodha was sitting at a table in the Eachléim hall with Ciarán Smith's family, as kettles boiled and food was served. Uí Aodha was chair of the voluntary support organisation, Lost at Sea Tragedies (LAST), and had travelled from the south-east to offer support. She had a keen sense of the ordeal being experienced by the relatives, particularly the families of the two men still missing. She had been a fishing skipper, and the first woman to qualify for a state grant for her own boat, before marrying and rearing a family. Her husband, Michael, then 52, and four of his crew died on 15 January 2012 when their vessel, *Tit Bonhomme*, hit rocks at the mouth of Glandore harbour in west Cork. The sole survivor, Egyptian-born crewman Abdelbaky Mohamed, lost his brother in the incident.

'Sometimes local knowledge can be beneficial, and this is worth trying,' Uí Aodha said. Eamon Dixon of the Erris Inshore Fishermen's Association had suggested a concerted effort by the fishing fleet across the western seaboard to undertake a sea search, and the RNLI agreed to take on a co-ordination role. After some discussion in the hall about the logistics, Orla Smith, Ciarán Smith's sister, issued an appeal through those journalists still present in north Mayo, including RTÉ's western correspondent Pat McGrath and this writer, then with *The Irish Times*.

'We didn't get the result we were hoping for here yesterday,' Orla explained, paying tribute to the efforts of all those involved in the recovery who were, by now, exhausted, she said. The scope now had to be broadened, she said, but emphasised that safety was a prime consideration in any further search efforts:

It is absolutely essential that everyone remains safe and we want [the search] done in a co-ordinated and safe fashion. ... We need those boys home now ... we really do. To all fishing vessels, big and small, from Achill Island to Arranmore, we are appealing to them to please come to help us now. We need them, we need their knowledge and we need them in the ongoing efforts to find Ciarán and Paul.

Fleets in ports as far north as Donegal, as far south as Kerry and as far south-east as Waterford responded, and Malin Head Coast Guard drew up the search plan, extending some 35 nautical miles west. From daybreak on Saturday morning, 8 April 2017, over 3,300 square metres (8,500 sq. km) of sea was scanned by some 110 fishing vessels, along with RNLI lifeboats, Coast Guard, Garda Síochána and Irish Underwater Council vessels, and a group of volunteers with Carrick-on-Suir river rescue, who travelled from south Tipperary.

The Naval patrol ship LÉ *Ciara* provided support, and there were also air and shore scans by the Coast Guard, Air Corps and Civil Defence volunteers. Mountain rescue teams drawn from as far north as the Mournes in County Down combed the shoreline at low tide over the weekend, while the Garda Water Unit was at sea. The *Holland 1* ROV was once again deployed from the *Granuaile*, which had returned for this one-day search, to scan the seabed off Blackrock Island.

Orla and her brother Seán set out with fisherman Pearse O'Donnell on the *Éire Óg* and spent all day on the water with the Ballyglass inshore fishing fleet. Weather conditions could not have been better. 'To come here, to know so many fishermen are involved in this endeavour, to hear the boats on the VHF radio and see them all around us on the radar is very heartening,' she said afterwards at the RNLI Ballyglass lifeboat station, her face and that of her brother sunburned from the day on the water. 'They feel this as much as we do ... and they understand our need to find these two men. And there can be nobody at sea now who doesn't know that they are missing. We may not have found Ciarán and Paul yet, but to cover that amount of sea in such a short space of time ticks a massive box for us.'[10]

RNLI Ballyglass lifeboat coxswain John Walsh and his colleagues Paudge Kelleher, Agatha Hurst, John Gaughan and Pat Cosgrove shared a cup of tea with the Smiths. Visibility was excellent, Walsh said. The Ballyglass and Achill lifeboats had launched constantly for the past four weeks, and at this stage 'every buoy, every potential area' had been checked and rechecked, he said.

Farther up the coast, the RNLI Sligo and Bundoran vessels and Arranmore's all-weather lifeboat also launched that weekend, mindful that some debris from the helicopter had already been washed up as far north as Donegal. Superintendent Healy reported that small pieces of debris from the Sikorsky S-92 had been found in several areas, including Cross beach on the Mullet peninsula. He pledged there would be 'no scaling back' while debris was being washed ashore.

However, a joint statement from the Coast Guard, AAIU and gardaí on Monday 10 April confirmed that the *Granuaile* was leaving and the formal search was essentially being stood down. The statement expressed sympathies once again to the families, paid tribute to all the statutory and voluntary agencies involved, and highlighted the value of inter-agency effort. Superintendent Healy promised to continue targeted searches for the two winch crew when the *Granuaile* left Blacksod Bay to return to Galway. He said garda divers would remain and focus on shallower areas around the crash location off Blackrock Island and nearby Parrot Rock, while the Duvillaun and Inishkea islands to the east and north would be searched again by Coast Guard and Civil Defence volunteers.

***

One month to the day after the Rescue 116 helicopter crash, the topography of north Mayo's Mullet peninsula was firmly fixed in the public mind, as were images of all four aircrew. RTÉ's *Prime Time* current affairs programme had already broadcast the first of several reports by journalist Katie Hannon in the days immediately after the crash, suggesting that the twenty-first-century technology on board the Sikorsky S-92 was seriously deficient.

On 13 April, the precise nature of the deficiencies and the aircrew's last exchanges were released as part of the AAIU's preliminary report. The thirty-eight-page report found that the helicopter 'pitched up rapidly' and collided with the western end of the island in its final seconds. Visibility was down to 2-3 kilometres in mist and drizzle, with south-west winds of 20 knots, gusting 30-35 knots, and rough seas. The Met Éireann aviation weather report for Belmullet at 1 a.m. on 15 March gave visibility of 1,500 metres in mist, and the cloudbase was 91 metres (300 feet).

The pilots were relying on a programmed navigational route for Blacksod, which should have assisted their approach and warned them of Blackrock Island as an obstacle to the west. Instead, this obstacle was programmed into their systems as an actual waypoint – as in the first in a series of stepping stones to be crossed on the final southerly approach into Blacksod. In addition to this, the EGPWS, which is not a primary navigation tool but is equipped to provide a cockpit alert for approaching hazardous terrain keyed into its system, did not have co-ordinates for Blackrock as an obstacle programmed into it, so did not provide any warning.

The preliminary report also found that the satellite locator beacons worn by the pilots had been incorrectly installed, due to differences in instruction manuals, and would not function – hence no signals pinpointing the four on the night of the crash. What the report did not state (but something which would be identified in the final report) was that this was an ongoing issue, identified by employees prior to the crash and reported to CHC Ireland management.

The AAIU investigators had managed to extract information from the black box, comprising a flight data recorder, which records the technical performance of aircraft components, and the cockpit voice recorder. Captain Fitzpatrick was performing the 'pilot flying' role, while Captain Duffy was performing pilot monitoring, keeping an eye on the radar. A one-minute-forty-second extract from the cockpit voice recorder immediately before the accident was included in the preliminary report's appendices. The last thirty seconds of this transcript, which include the 'altitude, altitude' sounding and Ciarán Smith's warning of 'an island directly ahead', dominated new headlines generated by the preliminary report. It was revealed that in its last moments the helicopter pitched up sharply, then went out of control as it hit the rock, causing further automated calls, including 'smoke in baggage' and 'too low gear'. No further sound of the crew followed Duffy's heartbreaking, 'We're gone.'[11]

Several days later, the pilots' union, the Irish Airline Pilots' Association (IALPA), released a statement criticising the publication of the transcript. Both Dara Fitzpatrick and Mark Duffy had been members of the union. It said that the International Federation of Airline Pilots' Associations and the European Cockpit Association had also 'strongly' condemned the publication of the transcript extract. There was 'absolutely no justification for – or benefit from – publishing specifically the last two minutes of this flight, other than feeding a thirst for sensationalism', said IALPA president Captain Evan Cullen.[12]

In response, the AAIU said it was satisfied that it had 'followed best international practice and national legislation regarding the issuance of the preliminary report'. It continued, 'The section of transcript released in the preliminary report was deemed very relevant to the AAIU in giving the families, aviation regulators, operators and the many operational S-92 pilots around the world a better understanding of the sequence of events that occurred on the day of this tragic accident.'

The preliminary report had two recommendations – the first for helicopter operator CHC, calling on it to 'review/re-evaluate all route guides in use by its search and rescue helicopters in Ireland'. It also recommended that the manufacturer of satellite locator beacons on life jackets used by the search and rescue aircrew should review the viability of the installation provisions and instructions. The beacon had been installed in the same pouch as the GPS antenna, as per a service bulletin issued by the life jacket manufacturer. However, the beacon manufacturer had recommended a minimum separation distance of 30 centimetres between it and the antenna to ensure that the beacons functioned correctly and their signal was not blocked. This explained why no signals were picked up from the crew after the crash.

Less than a fortnight after the preliminary report's publication, the Irish state regulator, the Irish Aviation Authority (IAA), renewed approval of CHC Ireland's search and rescue operation for the Irish Coast Guard.

***

On the weekend of 22 April 2017, there was another concerted sea search, involving some 162 club divers trained in search and recovery, working in parallel with Naval Service and Garda Water Unit divers on the western perimeter of Blackrock Island. It was preceded on Thursday and Friday, 20 and 21 April, by a '360-degree' survey of the sheer terrain on the island by ten army mountaineers with garda support. Civil Defence volunteers searched sand dunes on the Duvillaun and Inishkea islands, while the Rescue 118 helicopter conducted another aerial search for the two missing men.

An air and sea exclusion zone around the island was lifted to facilitate the effort, which was one of the largest co-ordinated dive exercises of its type in the state's history. Up to thirty-five local boats offered to serve as diving platforms.

John Kearney of West Cork Underwater Search and Rescue, one of the co-ordinators, paid tribute to the 'phenomenal effort' of divers working in depths of up to 35 metres, focusing on rocks, crevices and gullies. 'The swells and currents around this island are well known, and to have weak tides and good weather is very rare – so these are once-a-year conditions,' Kearney said.[13] Still, there was no sign of either of the two winch crew.

That same weekend, at an Irish Medical Organisation conference, the silence about the decision to task the medical evacuation support was broken. Mayo GP Ken Egan questioned why two rescue helicopters worth more than 100 million euro, flown by eight expert professionals, were called out 'all for a tip of a finger'.[14] He pointed out that 'nobody seems to want to dwell' on the major resources deployed to treat the crewman's injury, a severed thumb, which occurred after the fishing vessel's skipper had been patched through to seek medical advice from a doctor in Cork University Hospital.

The previous month, when the details of the medical emergency were reported, medical sources had told *The Irish Times* that if the digit had been severed completely, time would have been of the essence in reconnection and would have justified a helicopter evacuation. However, in this case, the man had not lost his digit, and the fishing vessel could have been advised to proceed to shore, while dressing the wound to prevent infection and possible septicaemia. Criticising the 'indifference of the authorities' over investigating this issue, Dr Egan said, 'surely someone has to go back and look at why the helicopter was called out'.

***

Sun-tinted clouds tumbled down from Achill Head over Blacksod Bay as exhausted divers, aircrew, fishermen, RNLI, Coast Guard and Civil Defence volunteers stood around the lighthouse helipad, where a spray of white flowers encircling four roses had been laid shortly after they gathered on the evening of Sunday, 23 April 2017. Three of the roses were red, in memory of Mark Duffy, Paul Ormsby and Ciarán Smith, while a single pink was for their commander, Dara Fitzpatrick.

'Sometimes "thank you" sounds too small … but on this occasion, it isn't big enough,' Orla Smith began. There were lumps in throats, tears in eyes, as she paid tribute to the tireless efforts of all who had been searching, and supporting those efforts on shore, for almost six weeks since the helicopter crash.

Out on the helipad, members of the Roscommon Solstice Choir sang *Amazing Grace*, followed by a rendition by Eimear Reynolds of Sarah McLachlan's *In the Arms of An Angel*. Later that night, the choir performed a concert at St Brendan's church in nearby Tiraun for the families and for all those involved.

Local doctor and Fianna Fáil senator Keith Swanick was among those at the helipad, along with his baby daughter, Rosa Pearl, who had been born just a week before the crash. Lingering afterwards to talk to Vincent Sweeney, Dr Swanick recounted how he had received a card in the post from one of his patients, Sheila Doherty (92), in Castlerea, County Roscommon. She had sent a cash contribution to the Rescue 116 search effort.

'Doesn't that just say everything about how the country is feeling?' he said.

7

'THE PUREST FORM
OF HUMANITY'

Rescue 116 winchman Ciarán Smith was a 'drop-everything' kind of friend, remembered for his warm smile, sparkling eyes and 'sturdy, strong handshake', to whom time and distance meant nothing. Just over two months after the helicopter crash, his wife, Martina, painted vivid pictures of a man who had placed a 'blanket' around his family.

'My dream was always pretty simple – to have a happy home, and, boy, did I hit the jackpot', she told a packed congregation at Our Lady Queen of Peace church in Oldtown, north Dublin on Saturday, 20 May 2017.[1]

'Ciarán Smith, you are responsible for the majority of lines and wrinkles on my face', she said, adding that most of these were 'laughter lines' as 'you took me on a journey I had never explored alone, and I thank you for that'. She appealed to him now to 'help me steer this ship' and guide their daughters, Caitlin, Shannon and Finlay.

There was no coffin to touch, no grave to visit, for both winch crew were still missing. Members of the Fitzpatrick, Duffy and Ormsby families joined Smith's relatives and senior government representatives at the memorial service. Celebrant Fr Pat Reilly described the north Dublin airman as someone who lived his life to help others, and he paid tribute to the many members of the search and rescue community present.

The number of stories he had heard about his 'professional, competent, loyal, true, selfless' friend were 'overwhelming', colleague Sid Lawrence said, recalling how Smith had participated in 'hundreds' of rescue missions with the Air Corps and Irish Coast Guard, received marine meritorious awards and military service medals from the state, and raised €10,000 for charity during his Race Around Ireland cycle.

As a guard of honour was formed outside the church, the rumble of a helicopter could be heard and the Coast Guard Sikorsky S-92 from Dublin circled over the church grounds in the country village.

Less than a month later, on 10 June 2017, the S-92 flew over St Matthew's church, Ballyfermot, Dublin, for Paul Ormsby's memorial service. The government was once again represented by senior figures including Minister for Transport Shane Ross. Ormsby's sister, Angela, his brothers John and Patrick, and his niece and nephew, Jennifer and David Keating, heard celebrant Fr Joe McDonald describing the consummate professional who knew how to make people laugh and smile.

Captain Ed Shivnen recounted Ormsby's encounter with Prince William when on a joint RAF–Irish Coast Guard mission in the Irish Sea. Over a cup of tea afterwards at the RAF Valley base in Wales, Prince William joked that he had never seen so many Irish Coast Guard helicopters in one place.

'That's because we're invading,' was Ormsby's response.

'You can have the whole place as far as I'm concerned,' was the prince's rejoinder.

Shivnen went on to recount how his former colleague trained many of the crew he would later fly with, and he explained how a pilot hovering over a ship's deck is only as good as the winch operator directing position. Ormsby's voice was 'calming in the sometimes harsh environments we operate in', and Shivnen recalled a doctor's description of a winchman rescuing a casualty as the 'purest form of humanity' he had ever witnessed.

The voices of the Spirito Voci choir filled the church and surrounding grounds. One of the singers – Rebecca Murphy – had a close connection. Her father, Eoin, worked as an engineer with CHC Ireland at the Coast Guard's Dublin base.

***

That July, another RTÉ *Prime Time* report released more details about faulty navigational charts and issues with navigational software. Citing examples of flaws and 'phantom obstacles', the programme reported that the IAA had issued a revised map in June 2017, which increased Skellig Michael off the Kerry coast to its true height of 712 feet, from an original inaccurate height of 174 feet. The IAA told the programme that it had learned that Skellig Michael was inaccurately depicted on their official maps only nine days after the Rescue 116 crash.

Prime Time obtained details of a series of emails between Sligo-based Coast Guard pilots and a senior CHC manager referring to Blackrock Island and/or other omissions in the EGPWS – the secondary navigational tool – in 2013. However, the IAA said it had no record that it was advised that Blackrock Island was not in the EGPWS.

The pilots' union, IALPA, confirmed to *The Irish Times* that it had repeatedly expressed concerns to successive government transport ministers about issues relating to the state regulator's inadequate oversight.[2]

In the same month as these revelations appeared, another extensive search by the Garda Water Unit and Irish Underwater Council search and recovery divers took place in and around Blackrock Island, and a fishing vessel fitted with a specially designed net trawled the seabed around Blackrock. During that summer, and as the days shortened into autumn, Erris fishermen and local Coast Guard, RNLI volunteers and residents in north Mayo continued to walk and scan the coastline. In late September 2017, a life jacket with its PLB and a helmet were found on the Mullet peninsula shoreline east of the Inishkea islands. The equipment was handed in to Belmullet Garda Station and identified as belonging to Ciarán Smith.

A cross-border flotilla, fundraising cycles and a memorial concert in aid of the RNLI, hosted by RTÉ broadcaster Ray D'Arcy in Cootehill, County Cavan, as part of its arts festival, were among a number of events run over the following months. Dara Fitzpatrick's family had close connections with Cootehill. Messages of support included one from Britain's Prince William, who said, 'the crew of 116 lived their lives to the full, not just for themselves but for all of us' and 'will never be forgotten'.

In September 2017, the first annual five-kilometre run in memory of Dara Fitzpatrick was held at Waterford airport, where she had been based for so many years. It sold out, with 1,000 participants, and raised funds for the Waterford Hospice Home Care Team and the Search and Rescue Dog Association.

The following month, RTÉ *Prime Time* broadcast the findings of its latest investigation into the crash. One of the key issues in the AAIU preliminary report was the incorrect fitting of PLBs in pilots' life jackets, a key safety system ensuring that aircrew would be located quickly if they had to ditch in the sea. *Prime Time* reported that CHC Ireland had received repeated warnings dating back five years that PLBs on life jackets similar to those worn by pilots Dara Fitzpatrick and Mark Duffy were not installed according to beacon manufacturer guidelines and would not work. While the installation fault applied only to the pilots' life jackets, *Prime Time* said it had documents showing there had previously been ongoing issues with the beacons on the life jackets supplied to winch crews as well.

The programme reported that a number of life jackets were tested by CHC Ireland eight weeks after the crash. The type worn by the winch crews passed the test, but the type that pilots had been wearing failed to activate, and CHC Ireland immediately withdrew those life jackets from service. However, when approached about this by *Prime Time*, CHC Ireland said it would be inappropriate to respond to the programme, given that the crash was still being investigated. The life jacket manufacturer Beaufort Ltd said it was 'aware of the findings of the AAIU report, which are at this stage preliminary' and refused to make any further comment.[3]

The programme also reported that while new aviation maps published by the IAA since its first report on this issue in July corrected some errors, it now contained new ones. And it noted that a new electronic mapping system was being tested by the pilots of R116 on the night in question, though they would not have been relying on it. These electronic maps showed Blackrock Island at 46 feet, when it was 282 feet at its highest point.

Prime Time raised another issue relating to the safety oversight of helicopter search and rescue. It said that the Department of Transport had initially said that the IAA was responsible for search and rescue oversight, but the IAA's own safety plan said search and rescue was 'outside the remit of the IAA'.[4] This essentially meant that no one was overseeing CHC operations.

***

The crash's first anniversary was marked at Blacksod. A group entitled 'Miles in their Memory', led by the Coast Guard Ballyglass unit and involving Belmullet Cycling Club and members of the gardaí, cycled 347 kilometres from Dublin to north Mayo as a tribute to the crew of Rescue 116, to Coast Guard Doolin volunteer Caitríona Lucas, and to all those who had died at sea.

'There is no easy way to get through grief … grief is the price we pay for love,' Kilmore Erris co-pastor Fr Kevin Hegarty told a packed congregation in St Brendan's church, Tirrane on 14

March 2018.[5] He recalled the many losses off the Mayo coastline, including the First World War sinking of the SS *Tuskar* steamer, and the loss of ten fisherman from the Inishkeas in a storm ninety years earlier. The sea is a 'source of sustenance and sorrow,' Fr Hegarty said, and the four lighthouses in the area testified to its 'majesty and terror'.

While Blacksod and Blackrock lighthouses would be engraved on the hearts of the bereaved, 'we would like you to know you will always be engraved on our hearts,' he told the families. The night before, in a south-easterly gale, relatives of the four aircrew and over 100 people from the community and beyond marked four minutes of silence from 12.46 a.m. – the time that the helicopter lost contact a year before. Four LED lights placed between the hills of Cnoc an Tearmainn and Glosh shone like beacons over the Atlantic through the darkness and driving rain.

At Blacksod helipad, after the morning mass, community representative John Gallagher thanked people all over Ireland, and many children in particular, for their response. Peter O'Hagan of CHC Ireland paid tribute to all those involved in the search and support efforts. Wreaths were placed on the helipad by Dara Fitzpatrick's mother, Mary, and sister Orla; by Mark Duffy's two children, Esmé and Fionn; by Jennifer Keating for Paul Ormsby; and by Martina and Shannon Smith, wife and daughter of Ciarán Smith. A fifth wreath remembered Caitríona Lucas. Representatives of the five took the floral tributes out on the Naval Service ship LÉ *Niamh* to be laid off Blackrock Island. Just after daybreak that same Wednesday morning, a wreath had also been placed off Blackrock by the Killybegs fishing vessel *Father McKee*, in recognition of the role played by the rescue agencies in safety at sea.

Two days later, the AAIU published an interim statement into the crash as its investigation continued. It recommended that the transport minister, as the 'issuing authority' for the Irish national maritime search and rescue framework, should conduct a thorough review of such operations. It highlighted how an audit in 2010 by the International Civil Aviation Organisation (ICAO) observed an anomaly in relation to oversight of search and rescue.

The AAIU recommended that the helicopter operator, CHC Ireland, should review its safety management systems, with 'external input', and it recommended that Sikorsky Aircraft Corporation should update and modify software in the helicopters' flight data recorder. The interim statement also tracked progress made on its two previous recommendations, which called on CHC to review route guides and on life jacket manufacturer Beaufort to review installation information for locator beacons.

On 12 April 2018, AAIU chief inspector Jurgen Whyte told a preliminary inquest on the deaths of the four Rescue 116 aircrew in Belmullet Civic Centre, County Mayo: 'Everything that could be done was done under very challenging conditions.'[6] Convened by the coroner, Dr Eleanor Fitzgerald, it issued death certificates for all four of the crew, including the two missing members.

Whyte noted that he had been head of search and rescue with the Air Corps for twenty years, but this particular mission was 'the most challenging and most difficult' in his career, involving a number of agencies. The Sikorsky S-92 helicopter was lying 'literally between a rock and a hard place', between Blackrock Island and a smaller rock known as Parrot Island, he said. The helicopter's tail was found on Blackrock Island, but there were no personal items, and this led the search team to believe that three crew members had remained within the confines of the helicopter on impact, he said.

The inquest heard that the body of Dara Fitzpatrick was recovered from the water by the RNLI Achill lifeboat at a location south-east of Blackrock Island at 2.37 a.m., just under two hours after the last recorded contact with Rescue 116. RNLI Achill lifeboat coxswain David Curtis described how she appeared to be lifeless in the water, and that the lifeboat crew administered CPR. He recalled the rough sea conditions and how, after twenty-five minutes, the difficult decision was made to halt CPR. The Achill crew then continued their search for the other three aircrew, along with Rescue 115, which had arrived on scene from Shannon at 3 a.m.

'We were trying desperately to look for our colleagues in a search area south-east of Blackrock,' Eamonn Ó Broin of Rescue 115 recounted.

The RNLI Ballyglass lifeboat joined the search at 3.20 a.m., and two fishing vessels were also approaching from the north to assist. Rescue 115 finished its search over Blackrock lighthouse but could not detect any sign of the missing crew, and it then flew Dara Fitzpatrick's body to Mayo General Hospital, he confirmed.

The inquest heard how the helicopter commander was pronounced dead at 9.27 a.m. at the hospital, but coroner Dr Fitzgerald noted that it would be more correct to state that she was dead on being recovered by the lifeboat. She confirmed a deposition from Deputy State Pathologist Dr Linda Mulligan that the cause of death was due to drowning, and that there were no contributory factors.

Navy diver Courtney Gibbons told the inquest how he and colleague Donal O'Sullivan had recovered the body of Mark Duffy from the helicopter wreckage on 26 March 2017 in about 36 metres of water, some 100 metres from Blackrock Island. Dr Fitzgerald confirmed a deposition from Deputy State Pathologist Dr Michael Curtis that his death would have been almost instantaneous, due to multiple injuries.

Chief Superintendent Tony Healy gave an overview of the extensive search for the two winch crew over a forty-two-day period involving a number of agencies, along with fishermen, voluntary divers and members of the community. The coroner confirmed cause of death for Paul Ormsby and Ciarán Smith as being 'lost at sea' and paid tribute to the families and to the bravery of the search teams. Garda Inspector Gary Walsh of Belmullet station told the coroner that a joint garda/Health and Safety Authority investigation had been delayed by documentation sought from 'different parties'. 'We are trying to expedite the process as best we can,' he said, and noted that a file would be prepared for the Director of Public Prosecutions.

Tributes were paid to the crew by family members at the inquest hearing, with Niamh Fitzpatrick describing how her sister Dara 'lived her short life to the full', with an emphasis on 'values such as kindness and integrity'. Garda Sinéad Barrett, who had been a liaison for the families during the long ordeal in Blacksod, read tributes to the missing winch crew. The coroner adjourned the inquest.

A few days after the preliminary inquest, the four Rescue 116 crew, along with the late Coast Guard volunteer Caitríona Lucas, the Coast Guard organisation and the community of Erris were honoured at the annual People of the Year awards in Dublin.

In July 2018, Paul Ormsby's life jacket and helmet were found on the north Mayo coastline. It was sixteen months after the crash.

8

'AS NEEDLESS AS IT WAS PREVENTABLE'

Just over four months short of the fifth anniversary of the helicopter crash, the AAIU's final report was published, on 5 November 2021.[1] The families of the four Rescue 116 aircrew – two still missing – had lived for over two years with copies of the draft final report. The numbered copies had been furnished to all stakeholders in September 2019 in strict confidence, with a sixty-day period for comment and observations.

As the deadline for submissions closed in, it emerged that one of the parties – later confirmed as CHC Ireland – had applied for a review of the report under the Air Navigation (Notification and Investigation of Accidents, Serious Incidents and Incidents) Regulations 2009. This legislation permits an 'interested party' to serve a written 'notice of re-examination' relating to 'findings and conclusions that appear to reflect adversely on the person's reputation'. There was a lot at stake for the helicopter operator, CHC, given that the search and rescue contract for the Coast Guard, now running at 60 million euro a year, was due for renewal in 2023.

When Minister for Transport Shane Ross acceded to the request, IALPA was incensed, and it was a severe blow to the families: 'Ireland has an obligation to publish the final version of an accident investigation report as quickly as possible to ensure that safety recommendations, potentially applicable to search and rescue operations worldwide, are implemented at the earliest possible opportunity', its president, Evan Cullen, said.[2]

The review 'does not comply with the standards and recommended practices laid down by the International Civil Aviation Organisation', Cullen continued, stating that Annexe 13 of the ICAO sets out how states should investigate or delegate the investigation of accidents which have occurred in their territory. The Department of Transport said it wholly rejected the union's claim.

Senior counsel Patrick McCann was appointed to conduct the review, with technical expertise from Phillip Hanson, a senior British Coast Guard manager. However, in October 2020, Hanson resigned because of a conflict of interest, and the review board was reappointed with McCann as its sole member.

Three of the four families employed legal representatives for the review, which culminated in a series of online hearings conducted by McCann over forty-four days, from 23 November 2020 to 20 July 2021, to consider 'specific findings, contributory causes and the conclusion'. Latterly, Minister for Transport Eamon Ryan said he would meet all 'reasonable' legal costs that the families incurred.

The chairman submitted his review board report to Eamon Ryan on 1 October 2021, and a copy was sent to the AAIU chief inspector Jurgen Whyte. A 'revised text' was produced by Whyte and the original AAIU report's author, Paul Farrell, over the following month.

If CHC had sought, through the review, to somehow exonerate itself from responsibility for the crash and blame it on the pilots, it failed – although the AAIU did state in its foreword that the sole objective was the prevention of accidents and incidents, and it would be 'inappropriate' for its report to be 'used to assign fault or blame or determine liability, since neither the safety investigation nor the reporting process has been undertaken for that purpose'.[3]

The 350-page report found the 'probable cause' of the crash was a combination of poor weather, the helicopter's altitude and the crew being unaware of a 282-foot obstacle on a pre-programmed route guide, and it identified twelve contributory causes. These included 'serious and important weaknesses' in management of risk mitigation by helicopter operator, CHC Ireland. Aspects of the preliminary report were revisited and expanded upon, including the inaccurate navigational information provided to the crew, and equipment flaws, such as the malfunction of the PLBs due to a conflict in fitting instructions.

The twelve contributory causes were more directly critical of training and management factors in the final report than they had been in the draft, stating that the initial route waypoint, towards which the helicopter was navigating, was almost coincident with the terrain at Blackrock – as in, the island with the second highest lighthouse on the coast was marked as a waypoint or stepping stone – and that the activities of the operator for the adoption, design and review of its routes in the flight management system route guide were capable of improvement in the interests of air safety.

It said the training provided to flight crews on the use of the routes in the paper flight management system route guide, i.e. hard copy maps, and how these worked in conjunction with electronic flight management systems, was not formal or standardised, and was insufficient to address inherent problems, leading to an over-reliance on the electronic systems. The flight management system route guide also did not generally specify minimum altitudes for route legs, and the suggestion was that the flight crew probably believed their altitude would keep them safely above any features in the landscape below.

The report noted that neither pilot had flown recently into Blacksod, which was essentially another criticism of CHC management and training; that the EGPWS databases did not indicate the presence of Blackrock, and neither did other electronic navigation software to which they had access; and that it would not have been possible for the flight crew to accurately assess their position at night, under cloud, at 200 feet, 9 nautical miles from shore over the Atlantic Ocean.

The three final contributory causes were that the flight crew members' likely hours of wakefulness (between seventeen and eighteen hours) at the time of the accident would have correlated with increased error rates and judgement lapses; that there were serious and important weaknesses with aspects of the operator's safety management system; and that there was confusion at state level regarding responsibility for oversight of search and rescue operations in Ireland.

The highly detailed chronology and analysis began with question marks over the initial tasking, with 'a misunderstanding' at Malin Head Marine Rescue Sub Centre 'regarding the casualty', and a failure to follow in sequence procedures governing the tasking of a Coast Guard helicopter.

This was elaborated on in the report. Three minutes after Malin received a call that a man on a fishing boat 140 nautical miles off the coast of north-west Mayo had lost the top half of his thumb while working with nets, it tasked Rescue 118 in Sligo, stating that it 'sounds like he's lost his thumb and he's obviously bleeding quite badly'. The Rescue 118 commander agreed and he was told top cover would be organised; he asked Malin if the fishing vessel had turned towards land and was told by Malin they would instruct the skipper to do so and make best speed towards Eagle Island off the Mayo coast.

Subsequently, Malin organised a link call between the fishing vessel and Medico Cork, a twenty-four-hour telemedical support service for casualties at sea managed by Cork University Hospital emergency department. The fishing vessel's skipper explained to the doctor that he had a casualty on board who had lost his thumb and that he was just seeking some advice on pain relief, saying he had stopped the bleeding. The doctor advised him on how to administer first aid, give pain relief and keep the severed portion of the thumb in a saline bag with ice.

'So is he going to be medevaced then?' the doctor asked Malin, and it responded in the affirmative.

After the doctor hung up, the fishing vessel skipper confirmed to Malin that 'we've stopped the bleeding … I don't think he's in excruciating pain'. The report noted that 'at no time … was the doctor asked to assess the urgency of the medical condition of the injured seaman or to contribute to the decisions on whether and when to launch, as was required by procedure'. Instead, 'the scenario was framed for the doctor', who was told 'we are arranging a helicopter to go out and lift him [the injured party] off'. The commander of Rescue 118 took it in good faith that the airlift decision was taken on medical advice. This question as to whether there was any need at all for the call-out in the first place would become an issue in both the press and public imagination.

The report noted that 'At approximately 22.10 hrs, MRCC Dublin called the Dublin Duty Pilot of R116 for Top Cover for R118's MEDEVAC tasking'. It then drew on the cockpit voice recorder from Rescue 116 to chart the helicopter's route and progress after it left Dublin airport, noting how the initial plan was to refuel in Sligo. However, the report's authors did not publish the full transcript, even though the last section had been released in the preliminary report of April 2017.

After the decision was taken by Rescue 116 to opt instead for Blacksod, the report identified a number of factors that militated against the flight crew detecting Blackrock Island, west of Blacksod and on the approach route they had selected, in time to carry out an effective avoidance manoeuvre. The flight crew were using two primary navigation sources – the radar and the flight management system route guide, comprising 'three books' – the hard copy route guide, landing site directory and area navigation waypoint listing. They also had four secondary electronic navigation sources – Euronav aeronautical charts, an EGPWS,

Toughbook navigation software and the FLIR thermal imaging infrared camera monitored by the winch team. It noted that the radar was being operated on a 10 nautical mile range throughout the descent and the manoeuvre to start the approach route. Yet none of these sources effectively highlighted the danger.

Blackrock was not identified on radar because it was obscured by the magenta BLKMO waypoint marker and the magenta track line to the waypoint marker on the initial route for the approach to Blacksod. Flight databases also failed to indicate the presence of Blackrock. Lighthouses were not clearly marked, being indicated in the route guide simply with a small red dot and an elevation in numerical value, it said, and hazards and obstacles listed on the route guide title page were identified by white numerals, within red circles, outlined in black – in other words, they weren't clear enough, the report implied.

In addition, at least three of four secondary navigation tools had inaccurate or no information on Blackrock, the report concluded. 'Black Rock was not in the EGPWS databases', the '1:250,000 Aeronautical Chart, Euronav imagery did not extend as far as Black Rock', and the '1:50,000 OSI imagery available on the Toughbook did not show Black Rock Lighthouse or terrain and appeared to show open water in the vicinity of Black Rock', it said. Moreover, 'The AIS [automatic identification systems] transponder installed on the Helicopter was capable of receiving AIS Aids-to Navigation transmissions; however, the AIS add-on application for the Toughbook mapping software could not display AIS Aids-to-Navigation transmissions.' With so many inconsistencies in technology on state-of-the-art helicopters, it must have seemed to some readers of the report that a crew not regularly required to land at this particular refuelling point was as good as flying blind.

The report noted that, 'The Winchman announced that he had detected an island ahead on the EO/IR camera system when the helicopter was about 0.3 NM [nautical miles] from it, travelling

at a ground speed of 90 kts. The winchman called for a change
of heading and the flight crew were in the process of making
the change when the urgency of the situation became clear to
the Winchman.' Despite this, the report stated that there was
'no indication on the cockpit voice recorder that the flight crew
saw Black Rock, although in the final seconds of flight there was
a significant, manual input on the collective lever, an associated
"*droop*" in main rotor revolutions per minute and a roll to the
right'. Here, in the formal technical language of the report, was the
moment when disaster struck.

With regards to the helicopter operator, CHC Ireland,
the report noted its failure to have '"formalised, standardised,
controlled or periodic" systems of testing flight routes'. Other
failures included route guides not being fully proven and updated,
and an error in the length of one of the route legs for Blacksod
helipad which had gone undetected since 1999, while emails
provided by CHC Ireland to the investigation team showed
that one pilot had advised as early as June 2013 that Blackrock
lighthouse was not shown on the EGPWS.

The report noted that the reasons for selecting a 282-foot
obstacle – Blackrock Island – as the first waypoint or starting
point for what the operator described as a 'low level' route, could
not be determined, because the origins of the route design itself
were unknown to the operator. 'Furthermore, the operator did not
have formal processes or procedures to approve mapping data/
imagery for use in its helicopters,' it said.

One of the issues for Rescue 116, the report states, was that:

> The operating environment on the west coast would have
> been more challenging than east coast crews were familiar
> with, particularly regarding the availability of visual cues in
> the littoral environment. This meant that it would not have
> been possible for the flight crew to accurately assess their
> horizontal visibility. However, given that Black Rock was

only detected on the FLIR camera when the Helicopter was approximately 600 m from it, it seems that the horizontal visibility to the naked eye was probably less than 600 m.

The report did refer to 'automation and cognitive bias', where the flight crew may have been over-reliant on the electronic secondary navigation sources, but said that the CHC operation manuals provided guidance on primary and secondary sources of navigation which 'could be misinterpreted'. It suggested that it was 'possible that the Commander, who said that she was going to "stick on the map" … could have succumbed to what [Israeli psychologist Daniel] Kahneman described as a "*What you see is all there is*" effect where the flight crew may have felt confident that the white area of the chart margin where the BLKMO [Blackrock Island] waypoint appeared would not contain obstacles.'[4] The report also noted that the fact that the radar was not selected to a shorter range intermittently suggested the flight crew may have believed that hazards undetected at the 10-nautical-mile setting by radar would be 'detected and alerted by the EGPWS'.

In addition, both pilots had complained about poor cockpit lighting. The report noted that poor lighting had been an issue with the S-92 aircraft since their introduction, and the flight crew were bringing their own torches to read documentation and check lists in-flight at night. Between June and August 2015, components installed on the helicopters as part of a planned adoption of night-vision goggles had changed the lighting environment, but the report said anecdotal reports indicated 'a variety of views' on the impact of this on lighting during night-time operations, with some feeling it had improved it and others feeling it had made things worse. The report noted that some commentators also said that the standard of lighting varied from helicopter to helicopter.

Compounding the problems, the report suggested, was the fact that the commander had been awake for eighteen hours and her co-pilot for seventeen hours, and it noted that, if the flight crew were awake for the length of time suggested, research indicated they would have been 'more prone to errors in judgement and decision-making'. A sleep study of some of the operator's crew members working twenty-four-hour shifts – the only Irish emergency service to do so – found that they accrued less sleep than the US National Sleep Foundation recommended and that 'this may not be enough sleep for optimal operational duty'.

As well as this, 'The tempo of the mission was different to east coast missions, and furthermore, the SAR [search and rescue] support nature of the mission was known to be monotonous, increasing the risk of the Crew succumbing to fatigue.'

In a further focus on training shortcomings in CHC, the report analysed the transfer of roles between the pilots, and the plans for arriving into Blacksod, which were not fully verbalised. It noted that at 00.13 hours, the co-pilot was flying when he asked for an opportunity to look at the 'map' of the southern approach into Blacksod. The commander became 'pilot flying'. At 00.14 hours, when the co-pilot offered to 'come back on the sticks', the commander declined, saying she was 'happy enough there if you are actually … I'll stay on it'. It noted that the co-pilot had 'limited involvement in the development of the plan or how the Commander intended to fly the descent, route/approach and arrival into Blacksod', and the commander was 'subsequently briefing the Co-pilot on how she intended to fly a flight profile that she herself had planned'. In what was effectively yet another criticism of training and management, the report observed in its technical language that 'the level of independent review/ management of the flight/plan may have been adversely affected by the transfer of PF [pilot flying] and PM [pilot monitoring] roles'.

It also noted that:

> Routes were generally viewed as base-centric, and a level of local knowledge and familiarity may have been assumed, which was an invalid assumption when an east coast crew

was utilising a west coast route, a situation compounded by darkness and poor weather. The Operator [CHC] said that the routes were merely there as a framework on which to build a plan for entry/exit to a number of known sites. However, there was no formal training in the use of routes; there was no formal procedure for how a route was to be designed; there was no formal procedure for how a crew should use a route guide; routes did not include a vertical profile or minimum altitudes generally, for route legs; and routes were not available for use in the simulator.

The report outlined how:

the Route Guide was prefaced with the statement that it was 'a work in progress and should be used with the necessary caution until all routes/waypoints are proven'. Therefore, the routes were unproven, and the Operator [CHC] did not have a defined process for route proving. Consequently, in the absence of formal, standardised training, design procedure or procedure for how a crew should use a route guide, it is unclear what beliefs/expectations individual pilots may have had regarding routes and how they could be used operationally.

The investigation revealed that problems with a number of routes had been identified in the operator's SQID (safety and quality integrated database) system, but such reports were closed after personnel were emailed to resolve the matter, 'but without checking that the routes had actually been updated correctly'. In other words, management had allowed a box-ticking exercise to take place without checking to ensure problems identified had been addressed.

This was only one of a number of issues that the review found with CHC's safety management system: 'The investigation also found that safety meetings were not being held as often as called for; minutes were not being uploaded onto SQID; SQID closure was not following the protocols set out in the SMCMM [Safety Management and Compliance Monitoring Manual]; [and that] the quality of Risk Assessments could be improved.'

The report also noted that although the IAA had claimed responsibility for oversight of search and rescue before the accident, afterwards it questioned whether it had a mandate to do so. It said the Department of Transport lacked the technical expertise to oversee the IAA, and the Coast Guard did not have such expertise or a safety management system.

The report concluded that the crash was, 'in effect, what expert [Professor James] Reason termed "an organisational accident"'. In other words, it was the fault of the organisation, not the people involved.

It was recorded how, after the helicopter hit the water, Dara Fitzpatrick had managed to exit the cockpit at a depth greater than 10 metres and possibly up to 40 metres in a courageous bid to reach the surface. She had completed her dunker training, where crews were tested in procedures to escape from a helicopter if it ditched, just ten days before the crash.

'Notwithstanding the fact that the commander had experienced a very traumatic event and the subsequent effects of disorientation, cold-water shock and night-time darkness, it appears that she was able to unfasten her seat harness, egress by jettisoning her cockpit window (emergency exit) and inflate her life jacket,' the report said. As the post-mortem examination had stated, although she sustained some bruising, there were no significant injuries and the cause of death was drowning. The AAIU report noted, 'it appears that the combined adverse circumstances of water depth, cold-water shock, darkness and overall sense of shock militated against her survival'.

In all, the report made forty-two recommmendations, nineteen of which referred to CHC Ireland. These included reviewing navigational aids, improving crew training on route guides and improved monitoring of missions and decision-making. It also said the company should ensure adequate time is given for staff to attend safety-related meetings. It recommended specific guidance be given to crews about assessing visibility in conditions of darkness or poor weather, as well as an in-depth study of the cockpit environment of the S-92A helicopters, and suggested that CHC Ireland should have a 'fatigue risk management system' in place and should review training, so that crews are aware of the risk of 'automation bias' or over-reliance on secondary navigation systems when on missions.

A total of fifteen recommendations were directed to the minister for transport, including ensuring that those involved in decisions to launch search and rescue helicopter missions took account of the protocols and expertise of other agencies. Measures to ensure better administration and oversight of Coast Guard operations, with a particular focus on air rescue services, were also recommended, along with appropriate governance arrangements. Procedures on requesting and tasking of top cover for helicopter missions should also be reviewed by the minister, it said.

It recommended a review of the department's in-house expertise to ensure internal skills for oversight of search and rescue aviation and all activities of the IAA, as well as a detailed review of the IAA's regulatory and oversight mechanisms.

Five of the recommendations were directed at the IAA itself, including monitoring of exemptions granted by the authority, a review of its procedures for overseeing search and rescue services, and an examination of CHC Ireland's shift patterns. The report also called on the European Commission to review how search and rescue operations are managed across the EU to identify minimum safety standards.

***

On the eve of the final investigation's publication, RTÉ's *Prime Time* ran a report. Hermione Duffy, wife of the late Captain Mark Duffy, issued a statement that same evening, noting that her husband had been an excellent pilot and father and, together with his colleagues, shared a deep commitment to his search and rescue role, always taking pride and satisfaction from his work. She asked people to remember that 'four honourable souls lost their precious lives that night in the service of others, and in circumstances which are harrowing and traumatic to read of and which have left wives, children, parents and extended families bereft.'[5]

The family of pilot Dara Fitzpatrick said they believed that she and her fellow crew members were 'badly let down' by CHC Ireland, which had not provided them 'with the safe operating procedures and training that they were entitled to expect'. The family said there was an expectation that the operator of the search and rescue service would minimise the danger for crew by aiming to remove risk and providing them with safety procedures on which they could rely. 'Unfortunately, this was not done on this occasion,' they said.[6]

Their statement continued:

> We hope that the AAIU final report and the review board report will ensure that those responsible for this operation, both directly and at a supervisory level, urgently implement the necessary changes, and that in future they pay attention to the feedback that they get from flight crew as to any inadequacies and hazards in the operation, so that such an accident will never happen again, that no one else will needlessly lose their lives, and that no other families will have to endure the devastating loss that we endure with the untimely death of our beautiful Dara.

IALPA said the report showed that the loss of four aircrew lives was 'as needless as it was preventable' and made it clear that 'the crew of R116 were exemplary in the performance of their assigned task. Their planning, response, teamwork, and communication was exactly what would be expected from such a competent and seasoned crew, on a flight led by such professional pilots.' It concluded that 'They were let down by a regulatory system which left them ill-equipped to do the vital work that same system tasked them with.'[7]

IALPA president Evan Cullen described it as a fundamental betrayal, and called on the government and minister for transport to institute an immediate review of the failures identified in the report, and to 'bring forward concrete proposals to address each and every identified failure immediately'.

CHC Ireland welcomed the final report and said it would like to 'express its deepest sympathy towards the family and friends of our colleagues; Ciarán, Dara, Mark and Paul'. It credited the AAIU with producing a 'comprehensive' and 'extremely thorough' document, expressed gratitude to the chair of the review board, and said it 'continues to advance aviation safety by investing in ongoing employee training and development, working to global standards and engaging with aviation stakeholders'.

The company stated:

> We are committed to implementing the appropriate safety recommendations that are directed towards CHC Ireland in the final report. The report is clear that the organisation of search and rescue in Ireland involves many stakeholders including the Irish Aviation Authority, the Irish Coast Guard and the European Aviation Safety Agency. CHC Ireland will ensure that it collaborates with all the relevant stakeholders to address the recommendations. The most important thing is that we collectively ensure that all areas identified for further strengthening are actioned.

The IAA expressed its 'greatest sympathy' to the families and friends of the four crew, welcomed the report, and said it had reviewed and fully accepted the recommendations addressed to it, which had 'already been implemented or were being implemented'.

'At the time of the R116 accident, the IAA exercised safety oversight of the operator through their Air Operator Certificate and a national Search & Rescue approval,' the IAA said:

> As indicated in the AAIU report, Search & Rescue regulation is not covered by ICAO or EU safety rules. The AAIU has recommended that the EU Commission review search and rescue safety standards at European level with a view to developing guidance material, and the IAA supports this recommendation. The IAA continues to work on an on-going basis with the European Commission and EASA [European Union Aviation Safety Agency] in the development of safety rules.

It also noted that it was 'currently undergoing a programme of institutional restructuring, which will establish a new, single, independent aviation regulator for civil aviation in Ireland', conforming with 'best practice for institutional structure and governance for regulators in Europe and globally'.

The wording used by CHC in its statement was not lost on the four bereaved families; there was no apology. However, in an interview on RTÉ Radio 1's Saturday with Katie Hannon the following day, Dara Fitzpatrick's father, John, ruled out legal action on his family's part. He described the report as 'shocking', but told Hannon that 'anger really doesn't get you anywhere; I'm sad'. Legal action 'would prolong the whole thing', he explained to Hannon. 'It'd be another court case and it could go on for a couple of years.'[8]

He spoke of frustration over the previous warnings about issues which the company had ignored, and said, 'That's the thing that would really annoy you, there was an extraordinary series of unfortunate events, [and] that crew had been working for eighteen hours, then they were called out. And there's also the question of was it really necessary for the man to be taken into hospital at all?' he continued, referring to the decision to task two helicopters in the first place.

Inquests into the deaths of the individual crew members could be finalised, and 'that would mean an awful lot to all the families', he said. He recalled how, after Dara's death, people 'came from everywhere' to tell stories about the hundreds of lives she saved while with CHC.

In an interview with *The Mail on Sunday*, Ciarán Smith's wife, Martina, said there were many inconsistencies in the AAIU report which left her with 'little confidence in the process'.[9] 'I'm crushed and I'm heartbroken. This report leaves me very fearful that this could happen again and more families will be left without mothers and fathers,' she told the newspaper. 'I'm worried that Ciarán and the crew died in vain and I have grave concerns for the safety of other search and rescue crews,' she said, referring to the 'inconsistencies'. Smith said that her legal team was reviewing what options she had as 'Ciarán's voice'.

Several former search-and-rescue pilots who spoke off the record about the report felt the full cockpit voice recorder transcript should have been published. Given that there are only two coastal lighthouses in Ireland used for search and rescue refuelling – Blacksod in County Mayo and Castletownbere in County Cork – it was an organisational failure and a sign of weak management if all pilots were not obliged to fly regularly to and from all four Coast Guard bases as part of training, they noted.

As one former search and rescue pilot pointed out: 'Search and rescue is complex, dynamic and unpredictable. It is not possible, sensible or safe to write procedures for every possible scenario.' Every flight is an opportunity to train, he said, and 'basic airmanship' and rules of the air apply to all aviation, including search and rescue. 'If you cannot see terrain, you need to fly at least 1,000 feet above it,' he noted.[10]

It emerged that a confidential interview given by a pilot to the AAIU investigators had to be considered by the review board. In that interview, the pilot was asked about his previous experience of flying into Blacksod from Dublin and he spoke of how easy it could be to look at Blacksod on the flight management system and think there was 'nothing there' because it looks like a 'tiny dot'. And if one didn't know about Blackrock Island to the west of Blacksod, and 'if you missed that little red dot or if you had a waypoint painted on it, you wouldn't see,' he said.

The pilot recalled how he would approach from a height of 500 feet and would have been visual and not in instruments. He recalled how Blackrock was etched into his mind because on a training flight in daylight to Blacksod from Sligo several years previously the winch operator referred to the size of Blackrock Island and how 'some day, somebody is going to run into that island' as it was 'enormous'. He also recounted how there was no minimum altitude given in the route guide for APBSS or the southern route into Blacksod.

The pilot also recalled the shock he got one night when the crew was asked to try out new iPads for navigation for the first time. The pilot had reached down to get one of the 'three books' or route guides in his cockpit and it wasn't there. He then spent five minutes looking for the route guide he needed in the iPad and it wasn't there either. He asked the rear crew if there was a route guide and a few minutes later he was handed one.

***

On 17 November 2021, Minister for Transport Eamon Ryan told the Dáil that he accepted all the recommendations relating to his department. While it would take some time for his department to deal with each of the findings, he said he would formally respond to all the safety recommendations ahead of a ninety-day time frame for him to do so.[11]

Ryan outlined a number of measures already taken by his department to improve search and rescue operations, including publication of a national search and rescue plan. He said that a review of all training for Irish Coast Guard staff had taken place, and there had been a formal course on tasking of aviation assets. New legislation would formalise the role of the IAA on oversight of search and rescue.

Ryan explained that his department had asked that the IAA's role as civil regulator be reviewed by external experts in 2021, and it had found no gaps under the Irish Aviation Act 1993 in meeting obligations. He paid tribute to the work of the AAIU and to the four Rescue 116 crew, and expressed sympathies to their families.

Sinn Féin's transport spokesman, Darren O'Rourke, argued that accepting the findings of the report alone was not enough, and he called on the minister to provide a timeline for when each of the forty-two safety recommendations would be implemented. O'Rourke asked what mechanism would be used to ensure that the different parties to which recommendations were addressed would comply with the report on a co-ordinated basis.

Sinn Féin TD for Mayo Rose Conway Walsh and her Fianna Fáil constituency colleague Dara Calleary paid tribute to the communities in Erris and north Mayo who had rallied to provide support during the extended search effort. Alluding to the wider difficulties within the Coast Guard service, Calleary noted that Coast Guard volunteers who were on call 24/7 deserved respect, which they were not getting at present.

A number of TDs called for the state to resume direct control of search and rescue, while People Before Profit TD Bríd Smith questioned the 'light-touch regulation' and the role of the IAA. She said the minister must ensure the new search and rescue contract was not given to CHC Ireland. She noted that while Ryan had referred to it as 'a tragic, unforeseen accident', she didn't believe that, 'because when you prioritise costs in tendering out core services then you create very serious risk and cost of life'.

The TDs held a minute's silence for the four crew, as did senators during a debate on the report in the Seanad on 18 November.

In both chambers, Minister of State for Transport Hildegarde Naughton gave details of a series of measures already taken under six broad categories. She said:

> I am confident that measures taken to date since receipt of the final draft report in 2019 by my department will strengthen the safe conduct of search and rescue operations. Uppermost in our thoughts right now are the crew of R116 and their families and loved ones. We must all ensure the findings and recommendations set out in this report of the investigation are fully implemented to prevent similar accidents occurring in the future.[12]

Naughton stuck to her script, which, while comprehensive, failed to address some of the very valid issues raised by the Dáil deputies.

In early 2022, Ciarán Smith's mother, Teresa, spoke of her own family's continued sadness. Almost five years later, the bodies of her son and Paul Ormsby had still not been found. For her, Fitzpatrick's words enscapsulated how she felt about her son's employer.

'We gave them something precious, and they destroyed it, and in the process they destroyed so many lives,' she told this writer. 'It is like throwing a stone in the water, where the ripples spread far and wide.'

PART 2

Hours of Boredom, Moments of Terror: Irish SAR from the Early Years

9

A RARE AND CURIOUS SIGHT

There was a time when a helicopter was a rare and curious sight on the Irish coastline. When a small coaster named *Greenhaven* ran aground on Roaninish Island off Donegal in the early hours of 2 March 1956, the captain issued an SOS, which was picked up by a British navy frigate, HMS *Wizard*, and relayed to Donegal's RNLI Arranmore lifeboat.

Sean McKeon, one of two pilots on the sinking ship, remembered that all ten crew on board initially gathered in the wheelhouse, where they were 'like pigs in a lorry on a mountain road and all the glass from the wheelhouse windows was shattering in on top of us'.[1] When they eventually abandoned ship and took to the rocks with some biscuits, whiskey and gin, their flashlamp beam was picked up by the Arranmore lifeboat, which stood by all night in heavy seas, but a naval frigate close by signalled with Morse code that seas were too high for the lifeboat crew to make a safe approach.

Shortly before 3 a.m., a plane circled overhead and dropped flares to boost the men's morale. Most of them were soaked and singing songs like 'Sixteen Tons', Merle Travis's ode to a Kentucky coal miner. At around 4 a.m. HMS *Wizard* signalled, 'Food, clothing coming at daylight. Plane will try drop.' The ship's master, Captain Balmain, who had been torpedoed twice during the Second World War, knew that the only hope was a helicopter.

When someone thought of the British military base at Eglinton in County Derry, the men signalled with their lamp to 'send helicopter'. The frigate relayed the request through Malin Head coast radio station to Eglinton and was able to respond: 'Helicopters here at eight. Don't worry.'

The men had gone quiet by the time another British military plane dropped parcels with bread, biscuits and blankets at first light – about half of which the sailors managed to salvage. They were still opening them up when someone spotted a black speck in the sky – a British Royal Navy helicopter, the first of two aircraft sent to rescue them. When the helicopters landed for fuel at Narin, near Portnoo, after the rescue, Nora Shovlin and her husband, Peter, provided sustenance. After a tanker arrived by road with more fuel, the helicopter pilots were anxious to be airborne – they had no night navigation.

'With half of Downstrands looking on, the first helicopter took off and headed for Eglinton,' Frank Shovlin, Nora's son, recounted later. 'But when the second helicopter took off, it developed a fault and crashed into the field south of the strand. The crew sustained no major injury, but the helicopter was wrecked and had to be transported back to base on a 60-foot lorry which arrived next day and caused nearly as much excitement.'

The Donegal Democrat quoted several eyewitnesses, including Nora, who said: 'We thought it was going to fall on the house, but it crashed just ten yards away from the doorstep. We thought she was going to burst into flames, but there was nothing more than a loud crash as she broke.' The helicopter's wheels struck a hillock and it collided with a bank, severing the tail. However, the three crew on board stepped out, shaken but uninjured, and were assisted by the local gardaí, who also had to provide the helicopter with overnight security, sheltering in the Shovlin haystack.

Lodged fast on Roaninish, the hull of the *Greenhaven* attracted much interest and there was an unhappy sequel to what was the first recorded air-sea rescue by a helicopter off the Irish coast. During the summer of 1956, three visitors drowned between Roaninish and Portnoo. The two adults and a child who lost their lives were among a party of eighteen, mainly young people, which had set out on a sunny morning on an inshore boat to view the *Greenhaven*.

Burtonport brothers Michael and James Gallagher were out lobster fishing with their father, Michael, on his half-decker *Irine*, and remember a stiff breeze was washing seas over the bow of the visiting boat. As those on board retreated to the stern, the engine was swamped and the boat began to sink. The Gallaghers and their father, along with their uncle and cousins who had boarded *Irine* from their nearby fishing vessel, threw ropes to those in the water.

Michael remembered a young girl, no more than his own age of 17, seizing his hand. 'This must be what a death grip feels like,' he thought afterwards.[2]

Another young girl who was rescued had to be restrained from jumping back in when she couldn't see any sign of her father.

A yacht engaged in angling steamed over to help and two young brothers thrown from the punt swam over to its stern. The helmsman thought the engine was in neutral, but the propeller was still turning. One of the boys got caught in the blade, with fatal consequences. The Gallaghers heard the shouts, as the yacht, with the boy's body now trapped underneath, was blown towards the rocks. The young fishermen threw a line and towed it to safety. They secured the body of the young boy, while scanning the water around them. Thirteen of fifteen survivors were rescued by the fishing crews that day. The three who drowned were named later as George Warren, a solicitor from Enniskillen, County Fermanagh, Desmond McVitty, a Dublin businessman, and Christopher Chambers, seven years old and from Belfast.

By the time the Gallagher brothers arrived back home to Rutland Island, it was close to dawn and their mother was beside herself. She had heard the report on the radio of an incident out at Roaninish, and, as they remembered, 'she really thought it was us'. The Gallaghers heard no more about the survivors until they were invited to a state awards ceremony at Farmleigh House,

Dublin, in late 2019, where the brothers and their late father, Michael, were conferred with awards for saving thirteen people. They still have a photograph at home of the *Irine*, with a small boy standing on a rock close by: James's son, Jim, who took up fishing as a career and was instrumental in securing recognition for the three men.

The Royal Navy helicopter based in Derry that had taken part in the rescue of the *Greenhaven*'s crew would play a crucial role in another rescue later that same year. In October 1956, two technicians and a workman employed by the Commissioners of Irish Lights were working out at Blackrock lighthouse in Sligo Bay when they ran out of food. A relief boat with supplies was unable to make it out from Rosses Point due to bad weather. The three men – Dick Delaney (38), James Lambert (55) and Thomas McMorrow (50) – raised a distress flag. They were spotted standing out on the lighthouse balcony, pointing their hands towards their mouths, when Sligo businessman Kevin Murray and former Air Corps captain Padraig Ferguson flew over in a Miles Messenger aircraft.

The Royal Navy crew from Eglinton who rescued them and took them to Oyster Island near Rosses Point were named as Lieutenant Commander C.C. Thornton and Leading Telegraphist B. Brindley.[3] Afterwards, the three men recounted how they had to boil periwinkles gathered from the rocks when they ran out of meat and tea. For the two days before their rescue, their main meal was one tin of peas and an onion, divided between them, and pieces of turnip, cabbage and carrots. The helicopter's arrival was, they said, 'like an angel descending from the skies'.

***

Shortly before Christmas 1963, a French fishing vessel found itself in difficulties in heavy weather off the Connemara coastline. Its name was *Emerance* and there were sixteen crew on board. Details transmitted in a distress message were scant, but the vessel was believed to be drifting without engine power close to rocks, and the crew had been forced to abandon ship and take to inflatable life rafts.

Two trawlers, the *Melchior* and the *Balthazar*, relayed messages to say they were on their way to assist. Some 260 kilometres away on the east coast, an Alouette III helicopter prepared for take-off from Baldonnel aerodrome in west Dublin. The pilot was Commandant Barney McMahon, a tall, young and enthusiastic Air Corps pilot from Doonbeg, County Clare, and this was his first mission as detachment commander of Ireland's first air-sea rescue service.

Christmas trees were already up in thousands of houses below them as the helicopter flew west to Galway in deteriorating weather conditions. On board with McMahon were Lieutenant Fergus O'Connor and Sergeant Peter Sheeran. They had done some rough calculations and estimated they should be able to make it straight out to the Aran islands without refuelling.

This was the theory at least, but practice proved otherwise. It was less than a month since McMahon and Lieutenant John (J.P.) Kelly had delivered two new Alouette III helicopters, A195 and A196, from Marseilles in the south of France to Air Corps headquarters at Baldonnel. They hadn't established a regular training schedule in the Irish Sea, never mind flown over to the Atlantic seaboard.

'When I think of it now, we really were rookies, and I suppose I was a bit bloody mad to be taking that mission on,' said McMahon, who would rise to brigadier general rank in the Air Corps:

> We had very limited communications and an atrocious radio which took the heads off us because we had no helmets, and we had 1916 life jackets, no life raft in case of an emergency, and the most basic of gear. We knew the RNLI Aran Island lifeboat had also been called out and so

our plan was to try and make contact with it. But it took us ages to find it as it was heaving up and down in the swell – as were several fishing vessels nearby.[4]

Back at base, arrangements were made to have extra fuel delivered to Renmore Army Barracks in Galway. An Air Corps Dove aircraft was also dispatched to Galway to act as an airborne (top cover) radio relay station between the helicopter and Baldonnel. The Alouette battled its way west over Galway city and out over the bay towards the Aran islands. Scanning the turbulent seas, the crew could see nothing on the heaving grey and white surface below and could barely talk to one another with the noise of the engine and rotors. The pilot watched the fuel gauge constantly. There was still no sign of the *Emerance* or its crew in life rafts when they were forced to turn for land.

The aircraft wasn't going to make Galway city, and it was cruising in over north Connemara when McMahon spotted a likely landing place. Just outside the town of Clifden, he put the Alouette down in a handball alley. He needed aviation fuel (Jet Al), and fast, but he certainly wasn't going to get this in Clifden and there wasn't going to be enough time to wait for a delivery by truck, which could take almost six hours from Baldonnel.

A few minutes later the proprietor of the Stella garage was surprised to see a pilot in military dress in front of him asking for 120 gallons of petrol. The proprietor thought Christmas had come two days early – he hadn't sold that much petrol in a whole year. There was a problem, however; the pilot would need a certain amount of oil in the mix. The garage phoned the parish priest to see if he had any paraffin.

'Eventually we got sorted. We realised we had no filter, so I asked the garage owner if I could borrow a pair of ladies' nylons,' McMahon remembered. 'I think they were probably provided by his good wife, and they did the job.' Once the crew had enough fuel on board, they climbed into the aircraft, started up the engine and were airborne again in minutes, taking a south-westerly course towards Inis Mór.

'During that second search, we got a message to say the *Emerance* crew had been located,' McMahon said. One of the French vessels also searching the area that afternoon had found the crew and picked them up. The vessel sent out a radio message, relayed by a coast radio station in Brest in France, with a message of thanks to the Air Corps and the lifeboat for their efforts.

'We had been searching for 4 hours and 45 minutes in total when we turned back for Renmore again,' McMahon recalled. 'However, Clifden's handball alley became a frequent unofficial landing pad thereafter, and subsequently a fuel dump for contract company Irish Helicopters, servicing lighthouses. We got to know the nearest neighbours, Ciaran and Lavinia Joyce, quite well.'

Ciaran Joyce became an agent for Irish Helicopters and his son Pat became a helicopter engineer and held an autogyro pilot licence. Pat remembered McMahon's landing clearly as it was the first time he and most of his contemporaries had ever seen a helicopter. 'We thought Santa Claus had arrived a couple of days early!'

McMahon was glad he had Lieutenant (subsequently Commandant) O'Connor on board for that first mission. When he and J.P. Kelly had travelled to the Aerospatiale plant in southern France for their conversion training in early November 1963, they had been a little amazed and somewhat horrified at the French technique for sea rescue.

'They would drop their winch man into the sea and he would swim to the cable which was then lowered down by the pilot. It meant that no winch operator was necessary as the pilot could see everything,' McMahon said. 'You are talking flat calm Mediterranean seas, of course. We knew there was no way we'd survive with that in the much more turbulent Atlantic.'

McMahon immediately contacted Colonel Billy Keane back at base and suggested that he send two officers to train with the RAF

in Britain. By the time the two Alouettes had arrived in Baldonnel
on the dark and wet evening of 26 November 1963, after a historic
two-day delivery run from Marseilles via Lyon, Paris, London
and Cardiff, O'Connor and Corporal Jim Fahy had completed a
four-week helicopter search and rescue crewman's course at RAF
stations in Ternhill and Valley, and they had some idea of how
winching crews should work with pilots in hostile conditions in
these waters. However, they hadn't had a chance to pass these
skills on when the *Emerance* emergency arose. The first formal
course for Air Corps crewmen/technicians – for the ground crew
doubled up as winch volunteers in those early days – started on 31
December that year.

***

'Air-Sea Rescue Helicopters go to aid of French trawler' read
the *Irish Times* headline over a report from Christmas Eve 1963
recording the details of the 'newly formed' state air-sea rescue
service's first mission. 'The helicopter landed at Renmore barracks,
Galway, and will fly back to Baldonnel today,' the report concluded.
'It can fly on ordinary motor car petrol, but it has not the same
range with this type of fuel as it would have with the proper grade.'

In fact, the helicopter had to be given a special engine check on
its return to Baldonnel. And, as Captain Chris Carey – one of the
first four Air Corps search and rescue pilots – recalled, there had
to be 'a bit of a rethink' after the *Emerance* mission. 'The Alouette
was far better than the RAF's counterpart at the time, but it was
still a single-engine aircraft,' Carey explained. 'I suppose in a sense
we were all writing the operations manual. It probably helped that
we used to whirl miraculous medals up into that engine from time
to time!'[5]

Hardly a month had passed before the young search and rescue
crew were back out on the west coast again. Both McMahon and
Kelly were on duty when the call came through that a pregnant

woman was about to give birth on Inishturk Island in County Mayo. Would the helicopter be able to fly her to hospital in Castlebar?

McMahon, Kelly and Peter Sheeran weren't quite sure what was ahead of them as they flew north-west from Baldonnel to refuel at Castlebar before flying on out to the island. Effectively this was their first air-ambulance mission and they were still training. If the woman gave birth during the flight, would they be able to cope? They had a sense that they were invincible, O'Connor remembered. 'We would have gone anywhere, done anything, and that was simply because we didn't have the experience to say "no".'

The Alouette landed near the pier. There was no sign of anyone. They had been told that Mrs Flaherty would be there waiting for them. They climbed out of the aircraft. A very heavily pregnant woman was carrying two enormous suitcases towards the pier. McMahon couldn't believe his eyes. Her husband, smoking a pipe, was walking empty-handed several steps behind her!

The couple climbed on board and the suitcases were heaved in beside them; if Mrs Flaherty was in the advanced stages of labour, the pilot didn't remember her displaying much distress.

'We had to ask them to wear life jackets, but we couldn't get it on Mrs Flaherty due to her condition,' he recalled. The flight to Castlebar hospital took about forty-five minutes, and there was at least one press camera present and several medical staff when the Alouette landed. As Mrs Flaherty alighted, she turned to the pilot and handed him a £1 note.

'It took me a minute or two to realise that this was a tip and I couldn't accept it – certainly not when there were cameras there,' McMahon said. 'She wouldn't take it back. She was insistent, and so I had to put it back into her handbag myself. Unfortunately, that's what the camera caught – me with my hand in her purse!'

The RAF training which O'Connor and Fahy had undertaken involved a team of winch operator and winchman, who carried a rescue strop (or sling lift) first devised by the Royal Navy. Apart from looking after the winchman, the winch operator also had to guide the pilot in maintaining position while over a casualty or vessel by using a 'patter' or constant detailed dialogue. The two men were all set to adapt this expertise to the smaller Alouette III helicopter and pass it on to the first group of non-commissioned officers selected for the new helicopter – Flight Sergeant Peter Sheeran, Sergeant Peter Smith and Corporals Mick Fitzgerald, Seán Oakes, Bill O'Connell and Liam Sheridan. Funds were tight, however. So the strop design was adapted at Baldonnel, using old tyres which were tested out on various 'victims' suspended from a gantry in the Air Corps technical wing hangar.

The first overwater exercise took place on 14 January 1964 with the Rosslare lifeboat in County Wexford. O'Connor's logbook records that Chris Carey was the pilot and he was winch operator. 'It took place within Rosslare Harbour, and that should never have been agreed to,' he said. 'The lifeboat crew had to duck to avoid the helicopter descending to a dangerously low height while trying to maintain a hover overhead, and it clearly indicated our complete inexperience as a search and rescue crew.'

On 25 February 1964, a launch for training was hired by the Department of Defence from the Royal St George yacht club in Dún Laoghaire, County Dublin, and four days later the first deck winching course took place. By early March, the Air Corps was confident enough to demonstrate its new winching prowess at the Dublin Boat Show in the Royal Dublin Society (RDS) grounds at Ballsbridge.

Eventually immersion suits arrived and 'wet' winching training began; a Neil Robertson stretcher acquired from the RNLI in October 1964 added a new dimension to the exercise programme.

However, by November, a year after the Alouettes' arrival, the Department of Defence was already questioning the financing of the search and rescue service. It refused to agree a tender to supply a suitable training launch for the helicopter crews in the Dublin area, and so any deck training that took place from late

November to the summer of 1965 had to be done at the Naval base in Haulbowline, Cork harbour, where the commanding officer supplied his own launch, the *Colleen*, for use. The cost of one helicopter flight to and from Cork for training would have paid for several months' boat rental on the east coast. As for the aircrews themselves, their enthusiasm was certainly not reflected in their pay packets: winching, which was regarded as a hobby for the technicians who volunteered to do it, earned a bonus of around £3 a year.

The new helicopters were seven months old when the first actual rescue at sea was carried out. 'Helicopter to the Rescue. Night drama off Howth: Man and boy plucked from the sea' read the page one report in the *Evening Herald* of 8 August 1964. 'In a dramatic five-minute rescue operation, an Army helicopter plucked a Dublin car salesman and his 12-year-old nephew from the sea this morning after a sixteen-hour ordeal adrift in a rowing boat off Howth last night,' the *Herald* staff reporter wrote. 'The rescued man, Frank Kellett, a cousin of the noted show-jumper, Iris Kellett, gave a graphic description of the sea drama, today, at his residence, 163 Whitehall Road, Terenure.'

Barney McMahon was alerted at about 7 a.m. A small boat with two crew on board was in trouble around the Kish lightship in the Irish Sea, he was told. The Howth lifeboat, under coxswain Joseph McLoughlin, had been out searching since shortly after the alert was raised by Kellett's wife at 12.30 a.m.

Kellett and his nephew, Michael Maybin from Ballymena, had set off from Howth after tea to go sea angling in a rowing boat with an outboard engine. They got caught in strong currents and Kellett started the outboard engine, which worked for a while before packing up. When the boat began to drift out to sea, Kellett began to row desperately to try to keep sight of land. He rowed for over five hours while his exhausted nephew slept in the bottom of the boat. On several occasions he thought he saw lights – the spotlights of the lifeboat – and he tried lighting papers to act as flares. At one point he was within 150 yards of several fishing vessels, but they didn't see him in the darkness.

The helicopter had been out searching for about three-quarters of an hour when it located the drifting boat about a mile south-west of the Kish lightship. On board with McMahon were Airman Dermot Goldsberry and Corporal Bill O'Connell. Airman Donaí O'Leary was on Howth Head to communicate with the helicopter via a radio set. Winch operator O'Connell spotted the boat first and Goldsberry went down the cable, taking the young boy first in the rescue strop.

'Both of them were frozen and the sea was just a small bit choppy,' McMahon remembered. The actual rescue took about five minutes and the helicopter then flew to Baldonnel. Lightmen aboard the Kish lightship spotted the drifting, abandoned craft and notified the lifeboat by radio telephone. It was picked up by the lifeboat and towed into Howth Harbour; the voluntary lifeboat crew had been at sea for eleven hours by then.

'He was the bravest little lad I have ever seen,' Kellett said of his nephew afterwards. 'He never uttered a whimper, and when he became so exhausted he lay down in the bottom of the boat and fell asleep.' The following week Michael came fifth of fifty-six in his class in the children's horse-jumping event at the RDS.

A month later Captain Chris Carey recorded his first sea rescue. On 16 September 1964, a fishing vessel ran aground off Caher Island in County Mayo, and the crew of Carey, Sergeant Willie O'Neill and Corporal Alec Dunne rescued one man and two women.

However, it would be some time before there was any public awareness about the state's new service. 'No effort was made to advertise the fact that we were there and available,' Commandant Fergus O'Connor said. 'We would open the newspaper on a Monday morning and read about an accident that we might have been able to respond to – only no one thought to call on us.'

And yet it had been a calculated government decision to

purchase the new helicopters after the 'big snow' of late 1962 and early 1963. Weather conditions had been particularly harsh during that winter, with heavy snowfalls and severe frost cutting off upland areas for several weeks. The hardship and suffering, particularly among the farming community, caused a public outcry. In one instance, a pregnant woman had to be dragged on a sheet of corrugated iron to reach the hospital in south Wicklow.

In the absence of any state-supported air-sea rescue service, members of the Irish Parachute Club had been valiantly giving of their time to bring supplies to people cut off on high ground or on offshore islands in times of bad weather. Irish Parachute Club volunteers were often the first to the scene in emergencies where the assistance of British military helicopters had to be called upon.

'Is the machinery of the Department of Finance so creaking that it cannot produce the price of a helicopter tomorrow?' thundered an *Irish Times* editorial on 2 January 1963:

> And is the Department of Defence so entrenched that it cannot direct the Air Corps to crew and maintain such an essential piece of equipment within hours of its delivery? It seems nonsensical that anybody should have to campaign in such a safe cause. Perhaps the snowstorms of recent days, and the fact that there are votes to be obtained in County Wicklow, will suffice to prod the Government and its servants into immediate action. The winter, for all we know, may be only beginning.

***

In 1962, an interdepartmental committee had concluded that the state couldn't afford a helicopter service dedicated solely to search and rescue, although this was disputed by several minority reports. It was one of two such committees appointed to look at the feasibility of providing helicopters to complement the excellent work of the RNLI, which had first established itself on the Irish coastline in 1826.

As maritime historian Dr John de Courcy Ireland has shown, the history of search and rescue in Ireland started with the Dublin port authority's decision to set up rescue stations from 1801, the year after Captain William Bligh's major hydrographic survey of Dublin Bay.[6] These were designed to protect ships approaching one of the most dangerous stretches of coastline in Europe and as such represented the first co-ordinated lifeboat service – preceding by almost two decades the founding of the Royal National Institution for the Preservation of Life from Shipwreck (RNIPLS) in Britain (renamed the RNLI in 1854). Two years after its foundation in Britain, the RNLI set up its first station in Ireland, in Arklow. The organisation depended on largely voluntary crew drawn from coastal communities.

Ireland's first Coast Guard was formed primarily to combat smuggling in January 1822 by a British act of parliament. Stations were built on Dublin's southside in Kingstown (Dún Laoghaire), Dalkey, Bray and Greystones, and on the north side in Howth, Baldoyle, Malahide, Rush and Skerries. By 1870, there were also stations in Ringsend and on the North Bull. Lifesaving was a secondary role for former British navy ratings employed on Coast Guard gigs and galleys, and some also volunteered for the RNLI. Former Irish Coast Guard officer Joe Ryan has recorded how its first inspector general, James D'Ombrain, of Huguenot stock, clashed with authorities over his efforts to provide famine relief from 1831 – having witnessed terrible hardship on the west coast during his annual circumnavigation of Ireland.[7]

In February 1861, sixteen ships and many lives were lost in a terrible storm which swept up the Irish Sea. The following year, three lifeboat stations at Howth, Dún Laoghaire and the Pigeon House on the south side of the Liffey were transferred from the Dublin Ballast Board to the RNLI, and the board agreed to give the sum of £50 a year towards maintaining them. The volunteer crews at these stations often found themselves putting to sea in the most dreadful weather conditions, in 10-metre rowing boats fitted with a sail.

Throughout the latter half of the nineteenth century there were many acts of heroism, and there were also fatalities among lifeboat volunteers. One of the worst tragedies occurred in 1895, when the Dún Laoghaire number two lifeboat, *Civil Service No. 7*, was launched to assist a Finnish steamship, the *Palme*, which was dragging its anchors off Dún Laoghaire in a strong gale. The lifeboat capsized some 600 yards from the steamship, failing to right itself in the heavy seas. All fifteen crew died, while the crew of the *Palme* watched on helplessly.

A public funeral was held for thirteen of the fifteen bodies recovered, and the sum of £17,000 was raised locally for the families, which included a contribution from the RNLI.[8] Every Christmas the Dún Laoghaire station marks the fatality with a wreath-laying ceremony at sea. A granite stone in the harbour records the valiant contribution of those on the last mission by *Civil Service No. 7*.

On 20 February 1914, the RNLI Fethard-on-Sea lifeboat in County Wexford set out to rescue the crew of the Norwegian schooner *Mexico*, which had lost its bearings in terrible weather and been driven onto rocks at Keeragh Island. Nine of the fourteen lifeboat crew lost their lives when three large waves smashed their lifeboat to pieces.

The surviving five made it onto Keeragh and assisted the eight crew of the *Mexico* off their ship, which had struck the island. For three days, neighbouring lifeboats and a local tug made numerous rescue attempts in storm conditions to reach those now stranded on the island. Two of the survivors were rescued by the Dunmore East lifeboat, and ten by the Rosslare lifeboat and the tugboat *Wexford*. A crew member from the *Mexico*, who was badly injured, died on the island. When the centenary was marked in 2014, four of the volunteer lifeboat crew at Fethard RNLI were descendants of the 1914 crew – sisters Emily (22) and Nuala Carroll (20), whose great-great-grandfather was Patrick Cullen; Michael Roche (23), great-great-grandson of Patrick Roche; and lifeboat helm Eoin Bird (36), whose great-great-uncle was the coxswain, Christopher Bird, and whose grand-uncle was Richard Bird.

During the early years of the twentieth century, there was a revolution in lifeboat design when engines were fitted for the first time. The first motor lifeboat for the east coast was deployed at Wicklow in 1911. Then, in 1927, Rosslare Harbour station became the first to be fitted with a wireless set, which was housed in a watertight casing and promised a communication range of over 80 miles. Rosslare's selection was deliberate, given the exposed nature of the south-east coastline. Over the years its crews, along with fellow volunteers in the neighbouring Wexford fishing port of Kilmore Quay, were to distinguish themselves on many occasions.

One of the first such acts of heroism was at Kilmore Quay, nine years after the establishment of its first lifeboat station. An RNLI silver medal was awarded to Dennis Donovan, chief boatman on the 34-foot, ten-oared *John Robert* for the rescue of five of the crew of a brig, the *Isabella*, which had run up on rocks in a storm. Then there was the memorable morning of 27 November 1954, when the Liberian tanker *World Concord*, en route to Syria from Liverpool, broke in two during violent storms in the Irish Sea, and RNLI lifeboats from St David's in Wales and Rosslare rescued forty-two crew. When the Rosslare vessel reached Holyhead it had been at sea for twenty-six hours, earning decorations, and a letter from the Greek shipping magnate Aristotle Onassis with a sum of £5 for each crew member.

However, this was some way off the longest time spent at sea by a lifeboat. In 1936 the Ballycotton lifeboat set an endurance record off the east Cork coast, when it was launched to rescue the crew of the Daunt Rock lightship *The Comet*. The volunteers on Ballycotton's *Mary Stanford* were awarded a gold, a silver and four bronze medals for an extraordinary mission lasting for over sixty-three hours, with the vessel absent from the station for seventy-nine hours in total.

From the 1960s, distinguished Irish naval architect Jack Tyrrell, from Arklow, contributed to lifeboat design, but, in spite of improved safety, there were always risks. On 24 December 1977, volunteer crewman Fintan Sinnott of the Kilmore Quay Oakley class lifeboat, the *Lady Murphy*, was lost during a call-out which turned out to be a false alarm or hoax.

Despite the recommendation of the interdepartmental committee, several serious incidents within the previous five years prompted the government to move ahead with establishing an air-sea rescue service. Five people drowned in Clew Bay, County Mayo, on 22 October 1957, while en route from Clare Island to the mainland at Roonagh pier, near Louisburgh. In October and December 1961 there were two serious shipping incidents off Eagle Island, County Mayo, and the Wexford coast respectively. Though lives were lost, the RAF ensured there were survivors.[9]

That dependence on and relationship with British rescue services – developed initially during the Second World War to rescue British aircrews – was to extend well beyond the initiation of this state's new service at Baldonnel in late 1963. Irish pilots would learn much from their British counterparts, who had developed expertise during conflicts, including the Korean War, and emergencies, such as severe flooding in East Anglia and the Netherlands in 1953. They used equipment such as the airborne lifeboat designed by the famous yachtsman Uffa Fox, which was carried by plane and dropped by parachute, and was kitted out with engine, supplies and radio.

The rescue of 600 people from floods in the Netherlands influenced the design of the strop or rescue sling used by helicopter winch crews. Several ideas were also adapted from the German rescue services, including the use of yellow helmets in the water which could be easily seen. Other early developments included an agreement with Trinity House, provider of the lighthouse service and navigational aids, to fit all navigational buoys with ladders in case any ditched pilot was lucky enough to land near one.

British aircrews also learned that regular training over sea, at altitude and in darkness, was essential if crews were to maintain an edge. Royal Navy Squadron Leader Kearns, who held an individual record for rescuing 147 people during the Dutch floods, explained why:

> Low flying by day is one thing, with a clear horizon and objects to sight on all the time. But at high altitudes there is a feeling of being suspended in a rather flimsy glass cabin with nothing underneath you and vertigo is a very real danger.
>
> The engine sounds different, the rotor blades don't bite as they do near the ground and you have nothing to sight on. It is easy to feel unsure unless you do it regularly enough to have absolute confidence in your instruments and your machine.
>
> Flying over the sea can produce the same sort of problems. On a grey day in the North Sea, the sea and sky merge together, the horizon disappears completely and it is very easy to be much lower than you imagine.[10]

In the spring of 1964, the third (A197) of the fleet of Alouette helicopters purchased for the Air Corps touched down at Baldonnel. By 1972 there was a fourth, and four more were on order, due to arrive in 1974.

The RNLI Dún Laoghaire lifeboat station was the first to carry out official training exercises with the Air Corps, in the 1960s, and by a happy coincidence the then honorary secretary, Dr John de Courcy Ireland, was 'volunteered' for the first airlift from deck. 'I remember that the Inspector of Lifeboats told us to go way out off the coast, so that if anything happened the public wouldn't see,' de Courcy Ireland said. 'Just as I was dangling in mid-air the mailboat passed, and I think every passenger with a camera took a photograph!'[11] A 'body scoop' made by the Air Corps to lift a person or a body from the water was first used on a training sortie in September 1967.

If officialdom, in the guise of the Department of Defence, proved to be frustrating at times, many individuals around the coastline gave invaluable assistance to the aircrews, such as 'Skipper Pat' Griffin in Skerries, County Dublin. He never refused to launch his vessel when asked, even when in really rough weather in late 1966 he had to lash himself to the wheel for safety.

The helicopter crews found themselves responding to all sorts of missions in those early years, and they weren't all offshore. One such was on 16 November 1966, when constant heavy rain caused flooding and the River Suir burst its banks. Several Tipperary farmers who were out trying to rescue sheep got caught in high water, as did Army and Civil Defence personnel who had tried to rescue them. The Alouette III was called out, flown by Lieutenant Fergus O'Connor, with winch operator Corporal John Joyce and winchman Corporal Alec Dunne on board.

'When we located all four men, we tried to lower Alec down through the branches but the cable wasn't long enough,' O'Connor recalled. 'So we flew upstream, dropped Alec in the river and he used the current to bring him down to the stranded men. One of them panicked and wouldn't leave, and so Alec had to give him a bit of a clip to get him moving!'[12]

Corporal Dunne, who was nominated for a DSM by the military, lost his helmet during the rescue. 'It was almost fully dark when we later spotted the helmet in the swirling current while returning to an overnight base in Clonmel Army Barracks. Alec insisted on going back down on the wire to retrieve it from the river.'

The pioneers of the new air-sea rescue service – Barney McMahon, J.P. Kelly, Fergus O'Connor and Chris Carey – were on a constant learning curve, as were the ten non-commissioned officers who comprised the winching crew and provided the vital ground support. A high percentage of the early work involved air-ambulance missions and mountain rescue, which meant that winching crews also had to undertake medical training. Close links were forged with the Association for Adventure Sports and mountain rescue teams, and with specialist medical personnel, most notably the rehabilitation unit in Our Lady of Lourdes Hospital in Dún Laoghaire, where accident victims with suspected spinal injuries were treated.

Writing in a special edition of *An Cosantóir*, the Defence Forces' magazine, in March 1985, Dr Thomas Gregg of the National Rehabilitation Centre noted that co-operation between spinal unit medical staff and Air Corps crew had saved many accident victims from permanent paralysis over the years. The hospital medical staff designed a spinal stretcher with a traction facility for use on the helicopters.

The first air-ambulance mission on record was to Our Lady's Hospital in February 1964, when there had been a heavy snowfall along the east coast. The Alouette III A196 was fitted with snow skis to take a patient from Wexford up to Dún Laoghaire for specialist treatment. Another early medical flight, or 'casevac', required some diplomatic clearance, when a seriously ill Cork woman, Maureen Collins, was flown from hospital in Cork to the Royal Victoria Hospital in Belfast on 10 September 1965. The journey was done in two legs by the Alouettes – the first to Baldonnel by Commandant Barney McMahon, and the second up north by Lieutenant Carey.

Carey was told in his briefing that the Royal Victoria was on the right side at the end of the motorway into Belfast. In fact it was on the left. He landed the Alouette in a flowerbed in Musgrave Park Hospital and remembers he had to 'depart rapidly' when accosted by a formidable matron. After he landed successfully, he was asked by reporters if he had got lost.

There were also both ambulance and weather relief runs to the offshore islands, and it was here that crews experienced some of the warmest receptions on arrival. 'Of course many of these runs were emergencies, but when you had the time there was always the offer of tea and a little buidéal of poitín,' McMahon remembered.

On one air-ambulance mission to the Aran island of Inis Meáin, the pilot, Fergus O'Connor, was told that bed linen would signal his destination. Fortunately, the 'flag' was kept well free of down draught and rotors as the helicopter approached to land on a piece of level ground running up from the island's eastern shore.

However, as he descended, O'Connor realised that the field was too small, as were all the fields around it – designed over centuries by island farmers who used drystone walls as a form of shelter. The pilot signalled to several men close to the house. Without any hesitation five of them walked over and pushed down a dividing wall which may well have been standing there for over 100 years. The quick demolition was enough to give the Alouette room to land.

10

A DEVELOPING SERVICE

John Oglesby was a skipper who commanded enormous respect among his peers. Born on Donegal's Owey Island, he had fished for most of his life and was in his early forties when he acquired the 36-metre vessel *Neptune*. At the time it was one of the largest and most modern vessels in the west coast fishing fleet.

In the early hours of 12 February 1988, Oglesby was on deck off the Mayo coast when a sheave pin lifted, loosening a trawl warp which severed his leg. Crew member Tom Rawdon was also injured. Malin Head Coast Guard radio was alerted, but the nearest lifeboat station was Arranmore Island off Donegal, and the Air Corps rescue squadron was on the east coast at Baldonnel, so a call was put through to Britain, which had long-range search and rescue capability. The *Neptune* was steaming as fast as it could to Broadhaven Bay in north Mayo. It was estimated that it would be near land before a helicopter from Prestwick in Scotland would have time to reach it.

Among the crew trying desperately to help John was his son Martin. Three and a half hours later the skipper lost his battle for life. He was within sight of land when he died.

Joan O'Doherty, a Donegal-based mother of four young boys and trained community worker, was angry and upset. Her husband, Mick McGinley, also a fisherman, had family connections to Owey and had grown up with Oglesby. Only three weeks before, the Killybegs fishermen's leader, Joey Murrin, had spoken on RTÉ Radio about the need for a rescue helicopter on the west coast, an issue that both he and Dr Marion Broderick, GP for the Aran islands, had raised before. Murrin said that Air Corps helicopters were being used to transport politicians, while those who toiled off the Atlantic seaboard were dependent on Britain for air-sea rescue.

RTÉ Radio broadcaster Gay Byrne had initially been sympathetic but returned to the subject when a female listener phoned to say that there was a fine helicopter already based up in the north-west coast at Finner Army camp in Donegal. Byrne reacted as if he felt he had been taken in by Murrin.

O'Doherty contacted the radio programme to defend the fishermen's leader. The helicopter at Finner was a single-engine Alouette III which had limited range, she pointed out. She also had a tea towel hanging over her washing machine which clearly showed the concentration of lifeboats on the east and south coasts. There were only three stations along the entire western seaboard, and fourteen on the east coast, all within range of a plethora of British search and rescue facilities.

Now, several weeks after that exchange, an experienced fisherman had died unnecessarily. O'Doherty – then known by her married name of McGinley – organised a public meeting for 31 March 1988 in Killybegs. Some people took several days to travel from various compass points and islands off the coast. Fishing industry representatives from Dingle in Kerry to Greencastle in north Donegal pledged support. Posters showing fourteen lifeboat stations on the east coast and three on the west, with five Dauphin helicopters based at the Air Corps base in Baldonnel, were distributed. Politicians were invited to attend but not to speak from the platform. 'It's so rarely that the fishing industry – whitefish, pelagic and fish farming – unites on anything, but it will on this,' O'Doherty predicted.[1]

The consensus from the packed meeting was that she should form an action committee of her choosing to campaign for a better service. 'I knew I needed helicopter expertise, a master mariner, someone from the Naval Service, someone representing fishing interests, medical expertise and legal input. It had to be small and geographically spread,' she said.

O'Doherty enlisted Commandant Fergus O'Connor, formerly of the Air Corps and now working with private company Irish Helicopters; two former Navy officers, Eamonn Doyle and Paddy Kavanagh; Joey Murrin of the Killybegs Fishermen's Organisation; Bryan Casburn, manager of the Galway and Aran Fishermen's Co-op; Dr Marion Broderick, Aran islands GP; and Peter Murphy, a solicitor from Letterkenny. Their budget for the campaign was just over 12,000 punts or Irish pounds (15,200 euro), comprising individual and corporate donations. One of the first contributions came from Donegal playwright Brian Friel. Aran islanders held door-to-door collections. Within a few short months the voluntary committee had published a comprehensive report on the current state of search and rescue off the Irish coastline, largely written by Eamonn Doyle.

As a coastal state, Ireland was obliged under international law to establish, operate and maintain an effective coast watch and search and rescue service, the report stated. The frequency with which British helicopters responded to taskings in the designated Irish search and rescue zone - equivalent to the air-traffic control zone - showed that this international obligation was not being met. By then, there had been countless British responses to assist fishing vessels in Irish waters. Major operations included the response to the Whiddy Island emergency of 8 January 1979, when fifty-one people died after the 120,000-ton French oil tanker *Betelgeuse* was ripped apart in an explosion at the oil terminal on Whiddy Island off Bantry in west Cork.

Eight months later, there was another major co-operative air-sea rescue effort when the August 1979 Fastnet yacht race was hit by a serious storm. Seven British military helicopters, three RAF Nimrod aircraft, six Royal Navy ships, a Dutch frigate, four lifeboats, the Irish Continental Line ferry *Saint Killian* and the Naval Service patrol ship LÉ *Deirdre* were involved in the response.

Three Irish lifeboat stations played a leading role. Lifeboat crews from Baltimore, Ballycotton and Courtmacsherry in County Cork and Dunmore East, County Waterford, spent seventy-five hours at sea in 60-knot winds. Kieran Cotter was a young volunteer with Baltimore lifeboat at the time and was working in his shop that evening when the wind began to freshen around 6 p.m.:

> I was not long in the shop when I got a call about a press boat overdue in Schull. We launched and searched for an hour or a little longer. We went into Cape Clear and about 10.30 p.m. or 11 p.m., the boat turned up in Schull – it had been sheltering in Schull harbour.
>
> Then we got the call about a yacht named *Regardless*. The wind was southerly or south-east gusting 8 or 9 or even stronger, and there were boats everywhere. The LÉ *Deirdre* located *Regardless*, and we put a tow line on and it took us from 3 a.m. that morning to around 7.30 p.m. to 8 p.m. that night till we arrived in Baltimore, with the wind now west nor-west and storm force.
>
> We were still on the pier when we got called to assist a yacht named *Marionette*. So we went back out and located *Marionette* about ten to fifteen miles south-west of Galley Head with the help of an RAF Nimrod, and we took her in tow early afternoon.
>
> By the time we got to Baltimore again about twenty-three hours later, the weather was abating, the sea moderating and it was a beautiful evening.[2]

Two years after Fastnet, in 1981, an Aerospatiale SA 330 Puma medium-range helicopter was leased by the Defence Forces at a time of increased security commitments related to the Northern conflict. It was the first twin-engine helicopter to be based at

Baldonnel and was to prove its worth in search and rescue when severe snow hit the eastern half of the island and cut off many hill and mountain communities in early 1982.

Over a ten-day period, the Puma and the Alouettes carried out 148 snow relief missions, saved or assisted ninety-eight people and airlifted livestock stranded on hillsides in the blizzards. Flying and technical crews worked around the clock, and for this the squadron was later presented with the Fitzmaurice Award for Services to Aviation by IALPA.

Early in 1983, however, the Puma lease was terminated, and the helicopter was flown back to its French owners. The decision, which was later criticised in several government reports, was a severe blow to morale and one that was to mark a turning point in Air Corps search and rescue. It seemed to put paid to all hopes of developing medium-range rescue capabilities, which would reduce reliance on British air-sea rescue units.

However, a fleet of Pumas would have made little difference to the survival chances of 329 passengers travelling on board an Air India aeroplane on 23 June 1985. The aircraft was in transit through Irish airspace, en route from Toronto in Canada to Bombay in India, and its progress was being monitored by Shannon air-traffic control.

Michael Quinn, procedural air-traffic controller on duty, had just returned from his breakfast break and had sat down to a busy 'board' or screen. Four aircraft had entered Irish airspace about the same time and had called up the Shannon tower. Quinn assigned them codes and gave airway clearance. Three of the aircraft appeared on the radar. However, when the fourth disappeared from the screen, he alerted his supervisor, Michael O'Hehir. It was just eight minutes after the plane, Air India Flight 182, had reported it was on course. It did not respond to Quinn's repeated calls. By that stage, it had broken into thousands of pieces in the Atlantic below, after a bomb placed on board exploded above the south Irish coastline.

Sergeant John McDermott was on an Air Corps Beechcraft surveillance plane, which had just taken off on a fishery patrol when its captain received a message that 'something was in the water off Cork' and an EPIRB was transmitting a navigational fix. 'We were 15 minutes in the air en route to the south-west fishery zone, and within half an hour we saw the wreckage in the water,' he said.[3] The Beechcraft flew for nine hours that day, providing top cover for all the other agencies, and it also served as communications control until the RAF and the United States Air Force took over.

Up to twenty aircraft in all were involved in the search for bodies, with the RAF sending Chinooks, Sea King helicopters and Nimrod reconnaissance planes. A US Air Force Hercules C-130 transport plane supported American HH-53 or 'Jolly Green Giant' helicopters, and the Royal Navy sent several Sea Kings from Culdrose in Cornwall. The Air Corps alternated its Beechcraft reconnaissance planes.

Alan 'Rocky' Boulden, then a flight lieutenant with the RAF at Odiham in Hampshire, was on duty that Sunday when the alert was raised. He had been assigned to a Chinook, which has far greater range and endurance than the Sea King and is used for military support or for major incidents. 'We recovered about a dozen bodies and took them to Cork Airport in one run,' Boulden said. 'There was really nothing much more we could do than that, because there was nobody to be saved.'

Working with Boulden on the Chinook ZA714 were co-pilot Flight Lieutenant Steve Ingham, winch operator Denis Gaunt and winchman Gerry Maher, and Boulden remembered that 'Maher had not been trained for search and rescue, and yet there he was down among the debris and the carnage.'

The harrowing recovery proved also to be challenging for Petty Officer Muiris 'Mossy' Mahon, Leading Seaman John McGrath and Able Seaman Terry Brown, on board a Naval Service Gemini inflatable launched from the patrol ship LÉ *Aisling*, under the command of Lieutenant Commander Jim Robinson. They would subsequently receive DSMs for their actions that day.

Among the many smaller craft working in tandem was the RNLI Valentia lifeboat, under the command of coxswain Seanie Murphy. The lifeboat was assigned to work with one RAF helicopter, which would drop smoke signals every so often to guide it to bodies. Crewman Nealie Lyne told reporters he had seen a solitary photograph floating in the water, and a pair of socks with the manufacturer's label still attached. A Sea King helicopter pilot, Lieutenant Gordon Jones, described the distress of seeing children's bodies in the water. 'It was consistent with a catastrophic failure at height.'[4]

Helicopter winchmen were constantly in and out of the water, while winch operators also dispersed green and yellow dye to mark specific locations. Many of the bodies were transferred to the LÉ *Aisling*. Medical orderly Jim Sperin remembered that, as he approached the crash site, he felt angry, frightened and powerless. He worried that if someone was brought aboard alive, he wouldn't have the medical training to save them.

'First the engineer's office on board was filled with bodies, then the carpenters' store, end to end,' throughout the day and into the night, Sperin recalled in an *Irish Times* article fifteen years later. 'We had no body bags, so we wrapped them in sheets. Nor did we have gloves ... By 10.30 p.m. there was no light left in the sky and, full of bodies, 38 in all, we turned for home.'[5]

The ship spent the rest of that week as part of an extensive search operation gathering the remaining pieces of wreckage, while concentrated efforts were also being made to recover the aircraft's cockpit recorder and flight data recorder. Naval Service ship LÉ *Aoife*, under the command of Lieutenant Commander Rory Costello, was tasked to search for the two recorders, collectively known as the 'black box'.

Among Costello's crew was Dave McMyler, who subsequently moved to the Coast Guard. He recalled that the ship's technology wasn't suitable for the depth involved, so specialised equipment had to be flown in from Boston. 'We had virtually built our own charts of the search area, and we were just about to pack up when we got the first signal,' McMyler recalled. 'We had to do a couple of runs to get a reasonable fix, which we did, as we were coming to the end of our patrol. We gave the position to the LÉ *Eithne*, and it was involved in the recorder recovery.'[6]

There were eighty-four women, thirty-three children and fifteen men on board the Air India flight. A memorial was dedicated to their memory at Ahakista, a tranquil west Cork location overlooking the Atlantic where they lost their lives.

***

The West Coast Search and Rescue Action Committee's report, published in September 1988, just a few months after the death of John Oglesby off north Mayo, focused on the inadequate resourcing of air-sea search and rescue within the twenty-six counties. It highlighted how most rescue resources were based on the east coast and that the Air Corps Dauphin helicopter fleet had limited range. It described the lack of modern radio communications equipment at the MRCC, which was without even a VHF or medium-frequency radio. Contact between the coast radio stations at Malin in Donegal and Valentia in Kerry was limited to telex.

The report also highlighted the lack of a coast watch service, in spite of repeated calls for the setting up of such a service by maritime historian and Dún Laoghaire lifeboat honorary secretary Dr John de Courcy Ireland. It noted that most effective search and rescue cover in Ireland's sea area – ten times the size of the island – could be provided only by the Sea King, an aircraft which could also carry up to twenty survivors, depending on range. It advised that, as there appeared to be no plans to purchase long-range aircraft for the Air Corps, the British model of inter-mixing public and private services to provide search and rescue should be 'looked at'.[7]

Another of its recommendations was that an Air Corps search and rescue squadron should be based at Shannon, with one helicopter detached on a rotational basis to Finner in south Donegal, and it called for a long-range helicopter, with a capability for carrying up to twenty survivors, to be stationed on the west coast to allow unrestricted operation out to fifteen degrees west longitude. It suggested that a coast watch service should be established, that EPIRBs should be fitted on all commercial seagoing vessels and pleasure craft above a certain size to give a satellite fix, and that a new rescue co-ordination structure be established. And it said that emergency air-ambulance missions from the twenty-one inhabited islands off the west coast of Ireland should be considered as 'search and rescue' and given the same priority.

The government set up its own review group in February 1989, chaired by retired Garda Commissioner Eamonn Doherty. In the intervening weeks another spate of incidents had highlighted the pressure on existing services.

On 13 January 1989, three fishermen were drowned when a Spanish fishing vessel, the *Big Cat*, ran aground in heavy seas on Beginish Island off Valentia. Winds were gusting to gale force 9 when the distress signal was picked up by Valentia coast radio at 7.34 a.m. The Valentia lifeboat could not make a safe approach and an RAF Sea King from Brawdy in west Wales was en route when the local Coast Life Saving Service managed to use nineteenth-century breeches buoy equipment to winch the eleven survivors ashore. The five volunteers with Valentia Coast and Cliff Rescue Service – Michael O'Connor, Patrick Curtin, Owen Walsh, Aidan Walsh and Peadar Houlihan – were recognised subsequently by Comhairle na Míre Gaile, the awards for bravery council, at a ceremony in Cahirciveen district court on 16 July 1992.

The breeches buoy equipment had been dropped by Britain, and Ireland had purchased some of it at a bargain price. After the *Big Cat* incident, Captain Peter Brown, superintendent of a state body then known as the Coast Life Saving Service, said the equipment would continue to be used in Ireland until such time as there was adequate helicopter rescue cover.

Even as the *Big Cat* rescue was underway, a British cargo vessel, *Gladonia*, had gone aground in Tramore Bay on the south-east coast, and *Yarrawonga*, a bulk carrier with thirty-two crew on board, was reported to be in danger of sinking some 360 nautical miles north-west of Shannon, while a light aircraft had crashed on the Aran islands several nights before. The United States dispatched several MH-53 Pave Low rescue helicopters to the *Yarrawonga* to winch off the crew. The abandoned tanker was around 170 nautical miles west of the Aran islands when the Naval Service flagship LÉ *Eithne*, under Commander John Kavanagh, was sent to locate it, but was unable to put a boarding party on the vessel. Kavanagh sought the assistance of the Air Corps – after all, the LÉ *Eithne* had been built with a helicopter deck.

The Air Corps Dauphin was working at extreme range, in fresh weather, and conditions made a landing on the patrol ship impossible. Instead, it refuelled while hovering over the ship in a procedure known by its acronym, HIFR (helicopter in-flight refuelling). A salvage party from the *Eithne*, including Lieutenant Commander Gerry O'Donoghue and Leading Seaman Kieran Monks, was then winched on board and transferred onto the tanker. Two Filipino crew from a Dutch salvage tug, the *Typhoon*, were also taken on board to assess the scene. The *Typhoon* had last been in Irish waters when the *Kowloon Bridge* hit rocks off the Irish south coast in 1986 – an incident which caused extensive pollution along the south coast and highlighted the Irish state's lack of preparedness for a major shipping incident.

In 1989, the government's Doherty Committee produced an interim report which recommended that an Air Corps Dauphin be relocated to Shannon and that Finner camp in County Donegal should be 'increasingly used' for search and rescue operations.

It also called for the re-equipping of the MRCC and the streamlining of the alert procedure. The committee's final report, signed off in February 1990, recommended that a new division of the Department of the Marine should be established for rescue, shipwreck and sea and coastal pollution, called the Irish Marine Emergency Service (IMES).[8] It said the MRCC should be moved from Shannon to Dublin, that three marine rescue sub-centres should be established at Dublin, Valentia and Malin Head, and that two medium-range helicopters – Sea Kings or similar – should be purchased for the Air Corps and based at Shannon. An interim private contract to provide medium-range helicopter cover should be negotiated 'as a matter of urgency'. Once this contract led to these helicopters arriving at Shannon, the Dauphin service based there should be moved to Finner camp on a twenty-four-hour response basis.

The report highlighted the contribution made by the British military helicopters in the Irish search and rescue region over the years, principally by RAF Sea Kings from the military base at Brawdy. It praised the professionalism of the RAF and noted that the military wing was eager to continue this service. However, it also noted the disadvantages of the arrangement, including a time delay of one to two hours' transit from Brawdy to Shannon, and the fact that the RAF could not provide the service where safety of life was not directly at stake. And there was also the fact that the RAF's first priority was military search and rescue.

There was much more in the fifty-four recommendations, all of which vindicated the campaign fought by Joan O'Doherty and her committee. A government contract for a medium-range service at Shannon was drawn up, even as the Air Corps continued its duty there with the Dauphin. However, the recommended purchase of new craft for the defence wing was put on the long finger.

The government's decision to concede Shannon as a west coast air-sea rescue helicopter base was to prove its worth just a month after the report was issued, when the Air Corps search and rescue crew, relocated to the west, were involved in a most dramatic mission.

'I have never seen such a sea state in my [fifteen-year] flying career,' Commandant Jim Corby noted afterwards.[9]

The distress call came shortly after midnight on the night of 8/9 March 1990. A 20-metre fishing vessel, *Locative*, with four crew on board, had lost engine power and was taking in water somewhere off Arranmore Island in Donegal. Commandant Jurgen Whyte, Dauphin commander on duty, alerted the crew – co-pilot Commandant Corby, winch operator Sergeant Ben Heron and winchman Corporal (subsequently Flight Sergeant) Daithí Ó Cearbhalláin. Whyte was one of the search and rescue unit's most experienced pilots, having flown initially in fighter squadron jets. He had held several key posts, including officer commanding the Naval Service support squadron, and officer commanding search and rescue.

Earlier that evening the crew had abandoned a winching exercise due to bad weather. A north-westerly gale was gusting to severe gale force 9, with seas of 3 metres and a very heavy swell of up to 10 metres in height. Whyte was concerned about the wind conditions and the lack of information on the vessel's position. He requested support from an RAF Nimrod and a Sea King helicopter from Britain; the Arranmore lifeboat was also en route.

Corby got a detailed weather briefing. The worst conditions would be in and around Arranmore Island, with winds of over 70 knots and a heavy rolling sea. The captain decided to fly to Finner, refuel and reassess the situation there.

The Dauphin took off from Shannon for Finner at 1.55 a.m., and by Castlebar it had made contact with the RAF Nimrod. Flares had been sighted by another fishing vessel south of the island of Arranmore and close to Rathlin O'Birne. However, the helicopter crew was under pressure as the MRCC had informed them that the RAF Sea King had had to turn back due to icing weather conditions.

The Dauphin made visual contact with the Nimrod when it reached Sligo Bay at about 3.10 a.m. Nothing had been heard from the fishing vessel for thirty minutes. By chance the Dauphin heard the *Locative* on VHF channel 24. Using direction-finding equipment, the Air Corps crew estimated its position to the west. Several minutes later both the helicopter and the Nimrod spotted a red flare. There was no time to refuel; in any case they had enough fuel for ninety minutes. The helicopter flew out to the vessel, which was drifting broadside in an enormous Atlantic swell. The four crewmen were huddled at the stern of the heaving vessel, fortunately visible under a full moon. All were wearing life jackets, a rare enough occurrence in such emergencies at the time.

It had taken an hour and fifteen minutes to get there, but the work was only beginning. The aircrew spent another thirty minutes trying to hold the aircraft over the vessel to allow winchman Ó Cearbhalláin down safely. As he recorded afterwards, the pitch and roll of the vessel was the worst he had seen to date during his career. He had to take account of the gear on deck, including a large ship's aerial, a derrick at the bow and several lines and aerials running between it and the wheelhouse.

'The vessel was rising and falling 80 feet [24 metres] in the swell,' Whyte said. 'This successive rate of change exceeded the capability of the Dauphin's automatic hover system.' The hover system allows the pilot to set the minimum height between the belly of the aircraft and the sea; the aircraft will rise and fall with the swell – and automatically fly away if that sequence is broken. Whyte opted to fly the helicopter with manual height control, which involved the continuous calling of heights by the co-pilot, while the winch operator monitored how close they were to the sea's surface. As Ben Heron explained, 'You can see the clearances. It is the pilot's job to do what he or she is told, and it is all based on trust.'[10]

There was an additional danger: the aircraft was at constant risk of being skewered by the mast of the vessel below. 'Due to the wind position of the *Locative*, I couldn't see it below me and under these conditions the chance of collision is very high,' Whyte said. He decided to stand off and wait for the arrival of the Arranmore lifeboat.

Within fifteen minutes the lifeboat arrived – to the relief of the Dauphin crew. It was now 3.35 a.m. Over the radio the aircrew explained that they couldn't attempt a lift with the vessel lying parallel to the swell and at 'cross decks' to the helicopter in hover. The lifeboat made several unsuccessful attempts to approach the *Locative*. At one stage Whyte recorded, 'We witnessed the trawler bearing down on top of the incoming lifeboat' and only 'prompt, evasive action' by the coxswain averted a collision:

> We thought the lifeboat would be able to come alongside and drag the guys off the deck. Instead, we witnessed this incredible sight where the lifeboat was trying to dart into the vessel and the *Locative* would rise up over the swell and fall down towards it. The coxswain was incredible, but we knew then that the lifeboat wasn't going to do it.[11]

There was just forty minutes of hovering time left. The fishermen were totally dependent on the helicopter; if it flew away to refuel, the four men might not survive. The pilot and winch operator remembered reading an account of a rescue where a lifeboat had pulled a powerless vessel around. 'Picture the situation where the helicopter was hovering north–south, and the vessel was lying east–west. If the vessel could be pulled into a north-east position, we could at least see part of it,' Whyte explained.

The aircrew suggested that the lifeboat try to secure a line aboard and pull the vessel to a thirty-degree heading off wind, which might be enough to provide visual clues for the helicopter in hover. Coxswain John O'Donnell managed to get two tow lines on board and manoeuvred the *Locative* successfully into position.

'Once the vessel was lying at this 30-degrees offset, I could see a pattern,' Whyte said. 'The two vessels – lifeboat and *Locative* – were engaged in a surreal dance across the swell, to the extent that the captain could anticipate the movement of one by the other. That sequence developed a distinct pattern, and this allowed us to go in safely.'

At this point the winch crew lowered the hi-line, a light line with a weight on its lower end, attached by a weak link to the helicopter's winch cable. This allows the crew of a vessel to guide the main winch wire while the winchman, a stretcher, or a lifting strop is lowered and lifted away again, but it must never be attached to anything fixed. The winch crew hoped that the fishermen would know what to do with it and wouldn't secure it to anything on the deck.

Ó Cearbhalláin descended and within a few minutes he had sent one of the crewmen up. 'Due to the big swell the finer points of winching … were discarded and the survivor was "snatched" off,' Ben Heron said afterwards in his report on the mission.[12]

Once Heron had hauled the first survivor into the helicopter, he winched the strop back down to Ó Cearbhalláin. The hook got caught in a fishing net, but the winchman freed it and placed the second crewman in the strop. However, 'at this point things started to go wrong', Heron said. A large wave hit the boat, throwing it up towards the helicopter and snapping one of the two tow lines from the lifeboat. The pilot had to climb rapidly and move back to avoid being hit by the ship's aerial. Heron winched out as much slack as he could to prevent the second crewman from being dragged off the deck when the boat went over the top of the wave.

With one tow line gone, the coxswain on the lifeboat had to reduce his towing speed to maintain the second line. If it snapped, the vessel was gone. However, in reducing the tow the lifeboat and helicopter had to cope with the more erratic and haphazard motion of the vessel, which made winching all the more difficult.

As if there wasn't enough going on, Ó Cearbhalláin noticed a problem with the hi-line, which was no longer attached to the helicopter's hoist hook as it should be – a very rare occurrence. With great presence of mind, he stuffed a bundle of the hi-line into the strop with the second crewman, just as the boat slid down the back of a wave and the crewman was dragged off and scooped up in a violent swing with the hi-line tangled around him. Heron recalled that he only knew he had the man when he felt the shock coming back up through the cable. 'He spun around and got all caught up.'

The winch operator untangled the hi-line furiously as he had no knife to cut it. He then had to replace the 'weak link' with one from a spare hi-line and winch the strop back down to Ó Cearbhalláin. It took a good ten minutes to make the repair. Fuel was running low and the winchman was getting anxious. The delay seemed like an eternity, according to Corby. His colleague, Whyte, had to maintain a hover which was 'too close for comfort' over the vessel, without the vital assistance of 'patter' from the winch operator.

'The strain on all concerned was particularly severe, as we had been in the manual hover for over an hour in the worst conditions any of us had ever seen. The crew didn't know for how much longer the hoist would hold out in the violent snatch lifts,' Corby said.

With just twenty-five minutes of fuel left, winching resumed, with the third 'snatch lift' as hazardous as the previous two. Shortly after the last fisherman was taken off, and as the lifeboat was towing the *Locative*, the second tow line snapped and the vessel was left to the mercy of the sea. The helicopter routed directly to Finner with the four fishermen and landed with just five minutes of fuel remaining. Coxswain O'Donnell later told the Air Corps board of inquiry that it was a 'hellish night', a fitting statement, the Air Corps noted, from a man who had received a citation for his courage from the RNLI.

The aircrew agreed that the lifeboat was crucial in helping to position the fishing vessel and in acting as a visual reference. Both crews had demonstrated great courage, stamina and seamanship. The pilots knew that the winching crew were the very best they could have hoped for – 'top guns', Whyte remarked afterwards.

The vital need for constant radio communication between winchman and aircraft was raised by members of the aircrew in their reports to the Air Corps. For their efforts they were awarded a DSM with distinction, the first time a Dauphin crew had been recommended for one. It was also the first such medal for a sea rescue, and the first night rescue by a Dauphin attached to the Air Corps fleet.

11

A SHANNON SIKORSKY'S NEAR-DITCHING

Two years after the *Locative*, a search and rescue helicopter was involved in a very close call off the west coast. Less than three weeks before Christmas 1993, weather conditions were so bad at Shannon airport that cargo palettes were airborne, and a Fiat Uno was lifting up and down in the wind. That was how John McDermott, formerly a sergeant with the Air Corps, remembered it. He was now working for Irish Helicopters, which held the search and rescue contract at Shannon for what was then the IMES.[1]

McDermott and his partner, co-pilot Carmel Kirby, finished duty about 9 p.m. and headed home to Quin, County Clare. Kirby, from Renmore, Galway city, was the first female pilot on the Shannon search and rescue unit. The storm was so severe that they had to make several detours. When they eventually arrived, a front wall had collapsed, a tree was down and there was no electricity. As they lit candles in the house, they remarked that nothing would happen that night. Conditions were too bad for anyone to be out.

However, several Spanish fishing vessels had put to sea in the teeth of the gale warning. Among them were two Irish-registered Spanish vessels, the 35-metre *Dursey* and the 42-metre *Dunboy*, owned by Eiranova Fisheries of Castletownbere, County Cork, a subsidiary of a Spanish company. Like most of the Spanish vessels working in Irish waters, they were under pressure to earn their keep and make the most of the fresh market before Christmas. They were about 40 kilometres apart off the west coast when they began experiencing communication difficulties in storm-force winds.

In the early hours of 9 December, the *Dunboy* reported an engine failure and gave its position on VHF radio as 40 nautical miles west of Slyne Head, County Galway. To the south-west of it, a third Spanish vessel, the *Mara Sul*, also reported engine difficulties about 75 nautical miles west of Loop Head, County Clare.

McDermott was woken by his bleeper at 1.55 a.m. At that time the simple call-out system gave no further information. The winds had only abated slightly and were still blowing at up to 70 nautical miles per hour as he and Kirby headed for the car and drove back through floods to Shannon. 'We were told there were thirteen crew on a Spanish boat in trouble. I remember thinking that was a great number – thirteen.'[2]

The Naval Service patrol ship LÉ *Aisling* had picked up the alert and was heading for the *Dunboy* but was hours away. Shannon had been tasked by the MRCC, along with an RAF Nimrod aircraft from Kinloss, Scotland, to provide top cover. Captain Liam Kirwan, first director of IMES and on duty that night at the MRCC, had decided to put in a request for Air Corps and RAF helicopters. There didn't seem to be any great need, he recalled afterwards, but his instincts told him he should.

As the Sikorsky prepared to take off at Shannon, the lanky duty engineer, Pat Joyce, almost lost his life. The helicopter engines had started and the rotor brake was released. 'There is no great centrifugal force when the blades start initially,' he explained. 'In high winds the blades can hit the cockpit or the tail during that start-up phase. I could see that starting to happen and had to get out of the way.'

The pilot, Nick Gribble, who had left a British helicopter charter company to join Irish Helicopters in September 1991, was normally pretty jovial. There was usually a bit of banter as the crew set off on a call-out to keep spirits up. 'I was trying to crack a few jokes, but got no response this time from the cockpit,' McDermott, on the winch team, said.

The crew of the *Dunboy* were wearing life jackets when the Sikorsky arrived overhead. Co-pilot Carmel Kirby could only spot an intermittent single light. 'We thought at first that the light was going on and off,' McDermott remembered. 'In fact, the seas were so bad that the vessel was just disappearing behind the swell.' As the Sikorsky tried to hover overhead, the radio altimeter showed that the waves were between 18 and 24 metres high.

'The waves were just heaped up behind each other, like the film set for *The Perfect Storm*,' McDermott recalled: 'I'd never seen anything like it before … We tried to put the hi-line on the boat and it broke … I don't know how I got down … At one point I remember landing on the wheelhouse and the radar reflector and aerial crashing up around me, and then I was whipped back up again.'

He had to organise three crew at a time to winch off, as the cable burned through his gloves:

> We were all falling all over the deck, it was so bad. I got three off, and then I remember another three came towards me and one walked away before I had a chance to put on the strop. It was so wet that the radio had stopped working, and I couldn't hear myself talk. I had just got one guy into the strop when the boat listed 70 degrees.
>
> A lot of slack cable got caught up on the deck and the guy was dragged away from me. I remember I grabbed him by the ankles, and he was pulled right across deck … It was a miracle he didn't go over the side. At this stage,

about 120 feet [36 metres] of cable had wrapped around the helicopter blades, but I only found that out afterwards. All I had seen was a flash as the cable broke, and I didn't know how.

The winch operator and winchman were trained to make a splice or a hook assembly if a cable snapped. 'So I thought they'd fly around and come back and we'd fit this. Instead, I saw the helicopter descend to within 20 feet (6 metres) of the crest of the waves. If it had gone in, there is no way they would have survived. The sea would have just swallowed them up.'

On board, co-pilot Kirby heard a bang, looked round and couldn't see winch operator Peter Leonard. She thought at first he had fallen out. In fact he had been hit by the rebounding cable, knocking him back into the cabin, before the cable sliced into four of the five rotor blades.

'I heard the captain roaring to Peter to winch in. I put out a "Mayday" call because I believed we were going to ditch,' Kirby said.

'It all happened in a flash,' Peter Leonard remembered:

It had taken two to three attempts to get John on the deck. Because of the conditions, we were trying to winch up as many as we could as quickly as possible ... When I winched down a third time, one of the crew was waiting for the other two to come forward, and then all of a sudden the ship lurched away from us. The winch got caught and ripped off just above the hook at the deck end.

All I heard was a whooshing noise, and I didn't know much about it until I came to my senses a few seconds later. My headphones had become unplugged, and I ended up in front of the winch operator's seat on the other side of the cabin. I realised I had cut my nose. I looked at the winch and all the wire had come off. That 80 feet [24 metres] of cable had snapped from the ship's end, and with the tension it sprang back towards the aircraft and wrapped itself around the rotors and ripped itself off from the hoist.

I heard Carmel putting out a 'Mayday', and Nick Gribble began flying away. We knew there had been damage, but there was no visual warning in the cockpit about damage to the blades. It was only when we had shut down that we saw the extent of the damage. It was quite horrendous.

The MRCC picked up the alert and relayed it. Out on the Aran island of Inis Mór, Dr Marion Broderick, medical officer with the lifeboat, and Coley Hernon, Aer Arann airport manager, were asked to prepare for a possible crash landing on the airstrip at Cill Éine, but there was no electricity on the islands due to the storm. Fortunately, the Air Corps and the RAF were en route, and the lifeboat from the Aran islands had been alerted.

'All I can remember is a slight descent, seeing a bit of Atlantic, and then flying away', Gribble told *The Irish Times* the following day. 'My primary consideration was getting the aircraft into a safe flight regime, whether in the air or on the water. It's really not a major thing unless the vibration gets too bad, and it wasn't. We were only doing our job, but we were very lucky not to have ditched.'

The professional 'speak' about safe flight regimes belied the drama of the situation. McDermott saw the helicopter fly off and then vanish. 'I thought it was gone, I had no radio and I was on this vessel with absolutely no power on board.'

He made his way into the wheelhouse and saw that all the windows had smashed, and the metalwork was bent and twisted by the force of the waves. 'The skipper was pretty calm and told me the vessel wasn't going to sink. A number of guys below deck were just holding on to a bar. The boat was broached to the sea, it was pitch dark, and I was violently ill.'

Lying on the wheelhouse floor, McDermott took off his helmet for some relief. However, he got cold and put it back on again. Seconds later he heard the crash of metal behind him. A fire extinguisher had broken loose in the pounding and struck the back of his head, leaving a crack across his helmet.

Shortly afterwards another Spanish vessel came close. 'There was a lot of shouting in Spanish, and I then witnessed one of the finest acts of seamanship I have ever seen,' McDermott recalled. 'The skipper of the other vessel had a hand-held radio, which he bound up in bubble wrap. As the vessels passed in the swell, he threw it over.'

Grabbing the radio, McDermott heard it crackle with the words 'Rescue 51' – it was the RAF Nimrod overhead. The first question he asked the pilot was about his fellow helicopter crew. He was told the S-61 was ten minutes from Galway.

Like the Aran islands, the city was also in darkness, the storm having felled electricity cables throughout the county. However, power was restored as the crippled helicopter flew east and it landed safely at Galway Airport with the crewmen it had taken from the *Dunboy.* The pale face of co-pilot Carmel Kirby, photographed by Joe O'Shaughnessy of the *Connacht Tribune*, spoke volumes in the newspapers the next morning.

Back out at sea, an Air Corps Dauphin, flown by Captain Donaí Scanlon from Finner camp, had refuelled at Blacksod and was approaching the *Dunboy*. McDermott knew the winch operator on board, Sergeant Dick O'Sullivan, having been trained by him. The Dauphin did not have the hover capabilities of the Sikorsky and there was difficulty getting the hi-line on board. Three times it broke. At one point the deck was swamped with the lights of the helicopter.

'It seemed as if it was going to crash down on top of us,' McDermott remembered. 'As soon as they came round again, I just waved them away. It was too risky after what had happened before.'

Hours passed. McDermott fixed his gaze on a lone gull, which hovered constantly at the back of the boat. He was sick several more times but felt no fear. He thought of family at home who were asleep and 'completely unaware of what was going on'. At one point a fisherman approached him and showed him photographs of his own family.

'It was a bit sobering. I didn't have pictures of my kids with me. I got the feeling he thought this was the end.'

The second fishing vessel continued to stand close by, which was comforting. At about 6.30 a.m., over an hour before daybreak, the wind died.

'It was like the flick of a switch,' McDermott said. The MRCC had informed him that the RAF was en route, and he consulted with the skipper and crew. The fishermen decided that they wanted to stay with the vessel and take a tow. 'I had to reassure the MRCC that there was adequate survival equipment on-board.'

And so, after all that effort, McDermott was taken up by the RAF Sea King on his own and flown to Galway. That night the helicopter crew had their Christmas dinner. 'I didn't have any aftershock,' McDermott recalled. 'It hit Carmel several days later.'

The *Dunboy* was taken under tow to Killybegs, County Donegal. Farther south, the *Mara Sul*, also in difficulties, was offered a tow by another vessel and both headed for Spain. The RAF Sea King remained at Shannon on standby until a relief Sikorsky could be flown to the base.

There were tributes from all quarters. The Minister for Defence and the Marine, David Andrews, and his junior minister, Gerry O'Sullivan, sent congratulations to the rescue units, as did various fishing industry representatives. It was the Sikorsky helicopter's 302nd mission since the service had been established under contract to Irish Helicopters by the Department of the Marine in July 1991.

Joan O'Doherty, founder of the West Coast Search and Rescue Action Committee, also paid tribute to the rescue crews but was very critical of the decision by the Spanish fishing vessels to put to sea in spite of storm warnings. Just three years before, the Naval Service had lost its first crewman on duty, Leading Seaman Michael Quinn, who died while trying to assist a Spanish vessel that had also chosen to disregard an unfavourable weather forecast. Quinn was serving on the patrol ship LÉ *Deirdre* on 30 January 1990 and volunteered with Able Seaman Paul Kellett to launch a RIB and investigate a distress call from the *Nuestra Señora de Gardotza*, a British-registered Spanish fishing vessel with seventeen crew on board. The vessel had gone aground in force 8 winds on rocks close to Roan Carrigbeg, off Bere Island in west Cork's Bantry Bay. Quinn, who was coxswain of the RIB, realised that sea conditions would make evacuation from the fishing vessel very difficult and was bringing the RIB around to return to the navy ship when a large wave caught the inflatable and threw both men into the sea. Kellett made it ashore, but Quinn didn't and his body was recovered by the Air Corps the following day.

The crew on board the Spanish fishing vessel were airlifted off by an RAF Sea King helicopter from Brawdy in Wales during an intense twenty-four hours for the British air-sea rescue services. Over on the east coast, the air wing had been involved in an alert when the Sealink ferry *St Columba* reported a fire in its engine room while on passage across the Irish Sea. The ship had 199 passengers on board, all of whom were called to muster stations and told to put on life jackets as helicopters flew firemen to the vessel. After about two hours the fire was extinguished and a potential evacuation was called off.

O'Doherty said that the series of events added focus to the debate on the need for a medium- or long-range helicopter service. The government was still 'foot-dragging' on the issue, she said, while it had spent £1.3 million (€1.65 million) leasing an additional jet for the duration of Ireland's presidency of the European Union.

As local fishermen in west Cork pointed out, the *Nuestra Señora de Gardotza* was the fourth fishing vessel to have run aground in Bantry Bay in that fortnight. That particular vessel was well known to the Naval Service: it had been detained on six separate occasions for alleged illegal fishing offences in Irish waters, the last offence being in 1985.

Leading Seaman Quinn had been engaged to Sarah Buckley. She attended a ceremony hosted by the Spanish government some months later, along with Michael's two sisters, Angela and Kathleen, where the King of Spain's award of the Spanish Cross of Naval Merit was presented posthumously to Michael by the Spanish Ambassador to Ireland, Dr José Antonio de Yturriaga. The Irish government gave DSM medals to Able Seaman Kellett and, posthumously, to Quinn. A plaque from the Spanish Navy marking the event was mounted on the bridge of the LÉ *Deirdre* and was later transferred to a new dining complex built at the naval base when that ship was decommissioned.

The Sikorsky and Air Corps crews were decorated for their actions in the *Dunboy* rescue. Captain Nick Gribble and winchman John McDermott received silver medals at the first award ceremony hosted by the IMES. Appreciation awards for meritorious service were given to co-pilot Carmel Kirby and winch operator Peter Leonard, as well as to Captain Donaí Scanlon and his crew from the Air Corps Dauphin.

12

THE TREACHEROUS SOUTH-EAST

Long-term observers of search and rescue accidents in Ireland are well aware of tragedies where official bodies have been accused of serious negligence. The most notable of these, prior to Rescue 116, occurred in 1999, with the loss of four Air Corps crew in a Dauphin helicopter crash in County Waterford. The four crew were killed instantly when their helicopter collided with a sand dune near Tramore, County Waterford, in thick fog.

It was the first night mission from a base which had switched just the day before from daytime to twenty-four-hour search and rescue availability. The Air Corps had run a daytime service there for the Irish Coast Guard from 1998, using an Alouette III aircraft, and the government had opted to upgrade it after the series of fishing industry fatalities off the south-east. The Coast Guard's north-west base was also run at that time by the Air Corps from the army barracks in Finner.

Captain Dave O'Flaherty (30) from Tullamore, County Offaly, had been with the Defence Forces for over eleven years and had started flying the Dauphin in 1997. O'Flaherty loved sport, particularly basketball, and was keenly interested in the hurling fortunes of his native Offaly, where his mother, Lily, still lived. One of his more unusual taskings during some 2,910 hours of flying had been to rescue a man 'in a sheet' stuck up on a tower in the old Dublin lead mines. The man had been out on a stag night and could not remember how he got up there.

The following year, he was part of a rescue mission which had tested the aircraft's limits. The Coast Guard's Shannon-based Sikorsky S-61 had answered a call-out on 25 February 1998 to lift an injured fisherman from a Norwegian vessel, the *Leinebjørn*, off the Mayo coast in 50-knot winds with a 6-metre swell. The Sikorsky was forced to leave its winchman behind on the vessel when the controls registered a gearbox failure.

The Air Corps Dauphin at Finner was called out as support, as were an RAF Nimrod, two RAF Sea King helicopters and a relief S-61. Commandant Seán Murphy, Captain O'Flaherty, Corporal John O'Rourke and Airman Jim O'Neill escorted the Sikorsky with the gearbox issue back to Blacksod on the Mayo coast and refuelled. They then flew out to the fishing vessel to airlift both the injured man and the Shannon winchman from the heaving deck. The Dauphin had barely touched down when the crew were tasked to take a sick man on Inishbiggle Island, County Mayo, to hospital in Castlebar.

O'Flaherty's colleague, Captain Mick Baker (28) from Enniscorthy, County Wexford, had joined the Air Corps in 1988 and had accumulated 2,327 flying hours. One of a family of five, he loved literature, played several musical instruments including the trumpet, was a keen artist at school and loved hurling. He was accepted for a place at the Royal Military Academy in Sandhurst, but opted for the Irish Air Corps. His long-term aim was to return to study law at Trinity and fly part-time for an airline, as he had a civilian aviation licence. He played Gaelic sports with several clubs, including the local Rapparees and the Air Corps, and took part in the Round Ireland yacht race – twice – with his defence wing colleagues. At the time of his transfer to Waterford he was living in Castleknock, Dublin, with his long-time girlfriend, Siobhán Dunne.

Sergeant Paddy Mooney (34) from Stamullen, County Meath,

was married to Monica, and they had known each other since primary school. The couple had three children, aged between two and ten. Paddy had joined the Air Corps in 1981 and had also served in the Curragh with the Army Rangers. He had saved many lives during his time as a winch operator, clocking up 3,500 flying hours as rear crew, and he was also a search and rescue aircrew rating examiner. He had served overseas with the Defence Forces as part of the 55th Infantry Battalion in Lebanon.

Among his many missions had been a rescue in very heavy seas on 4 November 1996 off the Mayo coast. 'One of those white-knuckle jobs' was how Commandant Seán Murphy, the pilot on duty at Finner camp that night, described it afterwards.[1] A fisherman with head injuries on board the *Benchourn*, some 75 miles west of Blacksod, required airlifting to hospital in a westerly storm blowing to 75 knots. The helicopter's only communications link, other than the fishing vessel, was the semi-submersible exploration rig Sedco 711, which was drilling on the Corrib gas field off Achill.

Two hi-lines snapped during the rescue effort. The crew only had one left when Airman Jim O'Neill reached the deck and found himself sliding around in the horrible conditions. 'Once hooked up, I remember yanking both [the winchman and the casualty] off with the finesse of a catapult,' Murphy recalled afterwards.

Murphy and co-pilot Captain Kevin Daunt had just enough fuel left to get to Sligo Airport, but not to the hospital. On approaching Sligo, Mooney noticed that the hi-line was trailing. It had become snagged in the undercarriage; fortunately, it hadn't done any damage. That same night, after the Dauphin returned to Finner, the hangar roof blew off.

The youngest of the four on that first night mission from Waterford on 1 July 1999 was Corporal Niall Byrne (25), who had transferred to the search and rescue service the previous December. He had 175 flying hours as rear crew when posted to the south-east base. He had originally joined the army and had served overseas in Lebanon with the 78th and 82nd Infantry Battalions. On returning from his second Lebanon trip, he forfeited some leave to start training with the Air Corps. He was engaged to Teresa Bolton and the couple had put down a deposit on a house. A keen canoeist, he had competed in several Liffey Descent kayaking races.

The four Air Corps crew had flown the aircraft three times on 1 July – the official date for Waterford's upgrade to twenty-four-hour search and rescue availability – before the call-out later that night to search for a small boat missing off Dungarvan with four men and a young boy on board. The 4.5-metre fibreglass vessel had only two life jackets for the five, and no one knew how to work the VHF radio on board when thick fog came down and they became disoriented. They had called what was then the IMES (subsequently the Irish Coast Guard) by mobile phone seeking help.

'We have a job for your shiny new Dauphin,' Dublin's MRCC told O'Flaherty when he got the call.

'Very good. I had a feeling you'd call us out on our first night,' O'Flaherty replied. The Rescue 111 crew were on their way from accommodation in Dunmore East by minibus to Waterford airport when O'Flaherty received a second call from the MRCC to say that VHF radio communications had been established with the small vessel and they weren't required. After some further discussion at the MRCC, OFlaherty was asked if they were at the airport and said they were 'on the road out'.

'You might as well go then if you're en route,' the MRCC said.

The child on the boat was very seasick and the skipper was heading into the weather to try to keep the craft stable as the Dauphin became airborne. After the boat had been located by the Helvick inshore lifeboat, the helicopter informed the airport tower that the lifeboat had the casualties under tow. The helicopter remained on scene to ensure a safe passage home in poor visibility. Ballycotton lifeboat was also making its way to Dungarvan harbour. By this stage, Waterford airport's manager, a qualified aerodrome officer, was in the tower with the technician.

The Helvick lifeboat's navigation system wasn't working properly, so it needed help from the aircraft to guide it back safely in the fog to Helvick pier, some four kilometres away. The Dauphin commander agreed to stay overhead and descend if the lifeboat got into any trouble. O'Flaherty said he was in 'a lot of cloud, a lot of fog'.

At 11.11 p.m. the helicopter said it was approaching Waterford Airport, but it did not land. The tower couldn't see it, and it couldn't see the runway's landing lights. The pilot made several attempts, before opting for a coastal landing at Tramore instead. The helicopter didn't have the fuel at this stage to fly to Baldonnel aerodrome, where weather conditions were reported to be better. Tragically, the aircraft never made it to Tramore, colliding with a sand dune and killing all four crew instantly.

Tributes flowed in from President Mary McAleese, Taoiseach Bertie Ahern and individual members of the government and opposition parties. Minister for Defence Michael Smith and his colleague Dr Michael Woods travelled to Tramore. 'The aircraft itself had flown in about 450 missions, saving hundreds of people,' Smith said. 'On this occasion, we're faced with the loss of four great men who went out in high-risk conditions to save people … They were within minutes of getting down safely when they hit the dune.'

An RAF Sea King flew to Baldonnel the day after the crash and stayed for five days, its crew attending several of the funerals. 'It was a very moving time for everybody, and it could so easily have been us,' said RAF Squadron Leader Al Potter. A unit of the Royal Navy's Fleet Air Arm joined members of the Air Corps at a multi-denominational service in Kinsale, County Cork.

One of the most heartfelt tributes came from the Aran islands GP Dr Marion Broderick, long-serving voluntary medical officer to the Galway Bay lifeboat, who outlined how all islanders 'depend for our safety and security on the selfless dedication of the men and women who provide our rescue services'.

✳✳✳

Lieutenant Colonel Thomas Moloney of the Air Corps was appointed to head the AAIU team looking into the crash, which included an inspector from the British air accident investigation branch and a military psychologist from the Swedish armed forces. A separate military investigation was also initiated.

The final AAIU report, released in late September 2000, identified two active causes, six contributory causes and nine systemic causes for the crash. 'Serious deficiencies' in support by Air Corps senior management, the Department of Defence and the Department of Marine and Natural Resources were identified. Weather in Tramore Bay was so bad that a successful landing would have been 'virtually impossible', it said.

Weather information emerged as a key factor. The MRCC stated that a flight forecast from the meteorological service at Shannon must be obtained for 'all missions', but the first weather-related communication between the Dauphin crew and the control tower at Waterford was one hour into the mission on the night of 1 July.[2] The staff relaying information to the Dauphin from the airport tower were technicians supporting helicopter maintenance, who 'unwittingly found themselves, through no fault of their own, placed in a situation outside their training and experience', the AAIU report noted. It was possible that had an experienced air-traffic officer with a meteorological observation rating been on duty, he or she could have communicated details of poor visibility and low cloud base earlier, and even recommended diverting from Waterford, but the Department of Defence had failed to conclude an agreement with the airport on this issue.

There was much more in the AAIU report, which found that pressure on the detachment commander to accept the rescue mission had been 'very high' and crew fatigue was a contributory factor. The call-out had come at the end of a day of official and press duties to mark the initiation of the twenty-four-hour south-east base, and the crew had been on duty for sixteen and a half hours at the time of the accident. It also highlighted the lack of an agreement on the provision of after-hours air-traffic control staff, and the failure to organise a dedicated accommodation block and catering for the search and rescue crews.

These issues were flagged as crucial by Maria O'Flaherty, widow of Captain O'Flaherty, when she made her first public comment in an interview published in *The Irish Times* in November 2000. The four men had been badly let down by their employers, she said, and one of the most shocking aspects of the official report was the revelation that her husband and crew were not informed until 1 July that no after-hours air-traffic control was being provided, when the Air Corps had specifically requested it.[3]

The Representative Association of Commission Officers' general secretary, Commandant Brian O'Keeffe, said that those responsible must be held accountable. He said the report clearly illustrated the potentially disastrous effects of 'substituting, cherry-picking, cost-cutting, split authority and micro management'.[4]

In the separate military inquiry into the crash, it emerged that attempts had been made to obtain weather information before take-off by the airport fire officer, but the technology wasn't working.[5] The military court of inquiry, which finished its deliberations on 30 August 2001, concurred with most of the AAIU report findings. Its report stated that the pilots' actions must be considered within 'the context of the pressure they were under' and 'serious organisational deficiencies'. It found the absence of a qualified air-traffic controller on the night in question to be a 'very significant contributory cause of the crash' but concluded that there was no single cause. It said it was struck by the genuinely high regard in which the four men had been held and said that, in view of the level of activity at Waterford Airport on 1 July 1999 and the pressures on the new Dauphin service, 'that same crew should not have been available for call-out on that night'.[6]

A memorial was erected in Tramore on the first anniversary of the crash – a stainless steel sculpture by Waterford-based artist John O'Connor. The Air Corps helicopter wing paid its own personal tribute at Finner camp, with a bench cut from limestone by Creevy stonemason Joe Roper commanding a clear view of Slieve League, St John's Point and Donegal Bay, dedicated to the four men on 12 November 2000.

In December 2004, over five years after the crash, the four men were given state recognition. The posthumous 'Marine Gold Medal for Meritorious Service' presented by junior marine minister Pat 'The Cope' Gallagher came two months after the Air Corps' involvement in search and rescue was axed by the government with the disbanding of a unit based in Sligo. The citation for the award noted that the Air Corps had carried out 1,140 missions and saved 878 lives, besides providing air ambulance and island relief missions, over forty-one years.

***

The names of the four men killed off Tramore are among those that appear on a memorial wall in Dunmore East, County Waterford, which stands as a testament to the sometimes treacherous nature of Ireland's south-east coast. The fertile valleys and plains, which once attracted Vikings, Anglo-Saxons and Normans, and the wetlands and rampart-like dunes overlook beautiful sandy beaches. However, fast-running currents and uneven seabed contours off this coastline have earned it a reputation for being a 'graveyard of a thousand ships'.

One of the Irish state's most serious air accidents, off Tuskar Rock lighthouse, County Wexford, in 1968, claimed sixty-one lives. There were four crew and fifty-seven passengers – thirty-three Irish, nine Swiss, six Belgian, five British, two Swedes and two US citizens – on board the Aer Lingus Viscount 803 when it took off from Cork, bound for London.

The flight never reached its destination. 'Twelve thousand feet descending spinning rapidly' were the last words, later assumed to be those of First Officer Paul Heffernan, heard by London air traffic control from the plane.[7]

Gardaí, the Air Corps, local fishing vessels and lifeboats from Rosslare, Kilmore Quay and Arklow were all involved in the extensive search, which recovered the bodies of fourteen of those on board. A total of forty-seven were lost at sea around the lighthouse, a familiar seamark for the busy ferry routes linking Wexford to Wales and France.[8]

The memorial wall was conceived after three local fishermen died off the Wexford coast early in 1996. Skipper and owner Peter Nolan (39) from Dunmore East, Niall Power (25), also from Dunmore East, and Conor O'Grady (22) from Annestown had set out to fish for cod off Brownstown Head in their 40-foot vessel *Jenalisa* on the morning of 4 February. Last radio contact from the vessel was around 4 p.m. that afternoon. There had been no distress call but, around 6 p.m., another vessel, *Atlantic Warrior*, reported fishing boxes and other debris on the surface. Conor O'Grady's body was recovered about 4 miles south of Brownstown Head. The *Jenalisa* was eventually located by Naval Service divers and brought to the surface a month later, on 6 March, but the bodies of the missing skipper and crewman were never recovered.

The sinking marked one of the darkest periods for the fishing industry right around the coast. During a fourteen-month period, twenty-five crew died, including six Donegal fishermen on the vessel *Carrickatine*, which was last heard of some 50 nautical miles north of Malin Head on 15 November 1995. The search for the *Carrickatine* crew – skipper Jeremy McKinney of Moville and his brother, Conal; John Kelly of Ballymagroarty and his son, Stephen;

and Terry Doherty and Bernard Gormley of Greencastle – lasted well into the new year of 1996.

Just a day after the *Carrickatine*'s disappearance, Wexford crewman Timmy Currid died off Howth harbour in north Dublin Bay when his vessel, *Scarlet Buccaneer*, hit rocks. The official investigation into his death recommended a twenty-four-hour air-sea rescue helicopter for the east coast – there was no Air Corps night-time helicopter available at the time at Baldonnel.

Niall Power's mother, Kathleen, was one of the members of a committee formed to raise funds for the memorial wall, and it was chaired by former RNLI lifeboat coxswain John Walsh. Unveiled by President Mary McAleese in March 2000, the wall incorporates a boat held high by four oarsmen created by sculptor Pat Cunningham. In her speech, McAleese referred to the loss of so many fishermen from the area, the four Air Corps crew, and the death of two young canoeists – Keith Crowley (21) of Tramore, County Waterford, and Ros Davies (14) of Mount Pleasant, Waterford – after a party of eight paddlers got into difficulty close to Dunmore East harbour in February 1995.[9]

The wall was originally designed by architect Ken Wigham to commemorate 128 people who had lost their lives at sea. Two decades later, that number had almost doubled.[10] There were times when it seemed as if the south coast was synonymous with tragedies at sea.

***

In 2002, the south-east was back in headlines again after a pleasure trip went badly wrong. The *Pisces*, a half decker used for sea angling, sank a mile from Fethard-on-Sea in fog. There had been nine anglers on board with the skipper, and three of the five who drowned were from one family.

In November 2005, the Kilmore Quay fishing vessel *Rising Sun*, which had set out to haul crab pots, capsized off the Saltee islands. Crewmen Jimmy Myler (46) and Ian Tierney (29) were both rescued, but Myler died in hospital, while skipper Pat Colfer (37) was reported missing. Dave McMyler, who had moved from the Naval Service to the Coast Guard, was en route to a training session in Drogheda, County Louth, when Coast Guard assistant director Norman Fullam phoned and asked him to head south. He called in to Tierney, the sole survivor, in hospital in the early hours of the morning and then drove out to Dunmore East. He recalled that the Coast Guard's decision to impose an exclusion zone, once the vessel was identified, caused a lot of upset as Colfer had not been located. It was for good reason, however, given that the *Rising Sun* was estimated to be in about 50 metres of water and could be searched only by experienced trained divers.

The exclusion zone had been lifted when two experienced club divers, Billy O'Connor (51), an engineer and father of two from New Ross, County Wexford, and Harry Hannon, planned a descent to search for Pat Colfer's body. Former Coast Guard director Chris Reynolds, then with the Naval Service, recalled speaking to O'Connor beforehand and advising him not to go, but he explained he was under pressure to do so. Both O'Connor and Hannon were ascending when, inexplicably, the sinking claimed a third life – O'Connor died during the ascent.

Comhairle Fo-Thuinn (CFT), the Irish Underwater Council representing recreational divers, defended O'Connor's decision to dive and pointed to his many years of experience on one of the most treacherous parts of the coastline. He was a former vice president of CFT and had trained many colleagues.[11] Chris Reynolds noted afterwards that, like Mayo diver Michael Heffernan, O'Connor had sacrificed his life during search and recovery in highly challenging circumstances.[12]

Tensions were high when Naval Service divers began their recovery attempt, and at one point the Coast Guard requested a garda escort. Support was provided to the Navy divers by the Irish Lights ship *Granuaile*, equipped with a recompression chamber.

Doolin coxswains Caitríona and Bernard Lucas on a training exercise off County Clare. Caitríona lost her life off Kilkee in September 2016, the first Irish Coast Guard volunteer to die on duty. (Courtesy of Bernard Lucas)

A Sikorsky S-61 coming in to land at Blacksod lighthouse in December 2001. (Courtesy of Fergus Sweeney)

Dawn at Blacksod lighthouse on 14 March 2017, hours after the Rescue 116 crash. An ambulance stands by in readiness as the search for the air crew continues. (Courtesy of Fergus Sweeney)

Captain Dara Fitzpatrick and winchman Ciarán Smith of Rescue 116, who lost their lives off north Mayo in March 2017.
(Courtesy of the Fitzpatrick and Smith families)

Rescue 116 air crew winchman Paul Ormsby (above) and (left) Captain Mark Duffy with his children Esmé and Fionn in 2014. (Courtesy of Ed Shivnen and Hermione Duffy)

Irish Coast Guard winchman Neville Murphy (extreme right), who is also an RNLI lifeboat volunteer, with his Dunmore East lifeboat station colleagues marking the arrival of a new Shannon-class vessel. On the boat are Roy Abrahamsson, Joe Molloy, Brendan Dunne, Jonathan Walsh and Peter Curran. On the pontoon with Neville are Alex Coleman, Bill Deevy, Maryia Balbachan, Raina Frieberg, Hugh O'Sullivan, Nicole Whelan, Paul Sheehan, Oisin Fitzgerald, David O'Halloran, Gus MacNamara and David Murray. (Courtesy of Patrick Browne)

Dr Marion Broderick, Inis Mór GP, who was part of the West Coast Search and Rescue Action campaign and a long-serving voluntary medical officer to the RNLI Aran Island lifeboat. (Courtesy of Joe O'Shaughnessy)

Rotor-blade damage to the Shannon Sikorsky S-61 after the near-ditching off the west coast in December 1993. (Courtesy of Joe O'Shaughnessy)

Sikorsky S-61 co-pilot Carmel Kirby at Galway airport after the near-ditching. (Courtesy of Joe O'Shaughnessy)

Captain Seán Redahan (left) and winchman Gary Robertson. Robertson was awarded the Billy Deacon Award for his part in the rescue of a fisherman off Arranmore Island in April 2016. (Courtesy of CHC Helicopters)

RNLI Kilmore Quay lifeboat crew members Jack Devereux, Philip Walsh and Ryan Thomas on board the Tamar class lifeboat *16-18 Killarney* at sea for a training exercise, with Irish Coast Guard helicopter Rescue 117 from Waterford. (Courtesy of RNLI/Nigel Millard)

The RNLI Baltimore lifeboat assisting sixteen of the twenty-one crew on the hull of the upturned supermaxi yacht *Rambler 100*, which capsized after it lost its keel off the Cork coast during the Fastnet yacht race in August 2011. All of the crew were rescued. (Courtesy of RNLI/Nigel Millard)

Italian-born Lorenzo Cubbedu windsurfing. The lifeguard, windsurf and dinghy instructor survived many hours at sea in November 2018 after he was carried from north Kerry across the Shannon estuary to the Clare coast. (Courtesy of Lorenzo Cubbedu)

Italian brothers Giovanni and Riccardo Zanon on the Aran island of Inis Mór. Both were swept towards the Atlantic by seas at Poll na bPéist (the Wormhole) in February 2019, and were rescued by the Rescue 115 helicopter from Shannon. Winchman Phil Wrenn received the Billy Deacon Award for his bravery. (Courtesy of Riccardo Zanon)

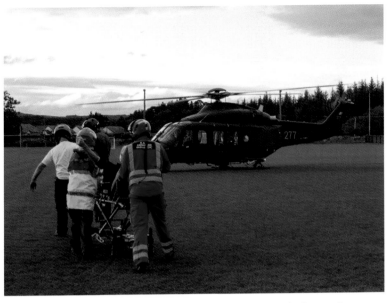

The crew of AC112 prepare to board a patient in need of critical care, assisted by members of the National Ambulance Service.
(Courtesy of 105 Squadron, Photographic and Airborne Imaging, Irish Air Corps)

The O'Connor family with three of the crew of the Air Corps Emergency Aeromedical Service who helped save Glyn O'Connor's life. *Left to right*: Captain Eugene Mohan, Advanced Paramedic Pat Moran, Alan, Celyn, Glyn and Cilian O'Connor, and Commandant Stephen Byrne.
(Courtesy of Cpl David O'Dowd, Irish Air Corps Press Office)

Ellen Glynn and Sara Feeney, the Galway cousins who survived fifteen hours at sea on their paddleboards in Galway Bay in August 2020.
(Courtesy of Joe O'Shaughnessy)

Father and son Patrick and Morgan Oliver, who rescued Ellen Glynn and Sara Feeney after they were found off Inis Oírr in August 2020. With the Olivers are RNLI Galway lifeboat crew members Olivia Byrne, Sean King, Ian O'Gorman, Cathal Byrne, Stefanie Carr, Declan Killilea and Lisa McDonagh, who were out all night on the search. (Courtesy of Joe O'Shaughnessy)

McMyler recalled that the subsequent recovery operations were extremely challenging in an area of strong currents and tides: 'The tides were so strong at one point that one of the strongest Navy divers was parallel with the sea surface when he ascended, and we just managed to get him out.' O'Connor's body was recovered, but Colfer's was not on board his vessel when it was salvaged from the seabed.

In March 2006, a steel-hulled fishing vessel, *Maggie B*, with three people on board, set out from Kilmore Quay to fish south of Hook Head. A 'Mayday' call was made by skipper Glen Cott at 11.05 p.m. The vessel appeared to be sinking by the stern and had rolled to starboard.

The RNLI Dunmore East lifeboat launched with coxswain Joefy Murphy and eight crew, and battled 6-metre (20-foot) waves and gale-force winds, locating crewman Krzysztof Pawtowski, a Polish national, clinging to a capsized life raft some seven miles from Dunmore East at around midnight. Pawtowski later described how there had not been enough time to put on life jackets, and the life raft had inflated upside down and did not right itself. He had been in the water for over half an hour and was already suffering from severe hypothermia. In spite of an extensive search, the bodies of Glen Cott, from Ballycotton, County Cork and Polish crewman Jan Sankowski were never recovered.

Polish ambassador to Ireland Witold Sobków paid tribute to the RNLI Dunmore East crew, which had included two of its most experienced members, Brendan Dunne and Neville Murphy, the latter of whom was also a paramedic and part of the winch team with the Coast Guard helicopter run by CHC Ireland in Waterford.[13] Formerly with the Air Corps, and from Skibbereen, west Cork, Murphy had already been nominated for several state awards when he was transferred to Waterford in 2005. The first was for the rescue of a woman who sustained serious injuries when she fell down a gully on Hungry Hill, close to Castletownbere in County Cork, on 19 September 2002. Kerry Mountain Rescue

Team members were on the scene when the Coast Guard Shannon helicopter flew in and Murphy remembered the woman was at the bottom of a crevice. It was a 'pure team event', he stressed, paying tribute to winch operator Steve Dodd:

> I had to winch down and move laterally, and as I was going down the cliff I went over on my ankle on a bit of rough terrain. I gave the signal to stop winching and we moved into the casualty and I unhooked. They sent down a stretcher and I managed to move her onto it but she was very sick with severe head trauma and spinal injuries.[14]

The helicopter flew the woman to Cork University Hospital for emergency treatment. After the handover, Murphy asked one of the medical team if they could take a look at his ankle when they were free. 'They X-rayed me, as I thought I had sprained my leg. Actually, I had broken it! I could only feel the pain in A&E when the adrenaline wore off. Thankfully, the woman did survive.'

In late January 2003, Murphy and his Rescue 115 crew of Captain Rob Goodbody, Tony O'Mahony and Eamonn Ó Broin undertook a very difficult medical evacuation of an injured crewman from a large coaster, *Princess Eva*, off the Donegal coast. The challenging mission was some 150 nautical miles off the coast in force 11 north-westerly winds and was recognised the following year with a state marine award.

'We knew it was rough, but we refuelled at Blacksod and thought it would be straightforward – a classic error in this job,' Murphy recalled:

> I remember the ship was being tossed around like a corkscrew. We wanted the ship to turn head to wind but he couldn't in the weather conditions, so we had to fly 30 degrees off the wind and then cross it amidships which is not the most comfortable position to be in.

One of their life rafts had come loose on the deck in the bad weather, killing one of the crew, and injuring a second man who lost a leg. I had to treat him on deck in the dark with the ship moving around in a big way. The skill of the two pilots and Eamonn, as winch operator, were crucial, and thankfully we had also fuelled up.

Murphy had never lived in close range of a lifeboat station until he was transferred to the Waterford base. On the call-out to the *Maggie B*, he remembered that Pawtowski was in a very bad way when the lifeboat spotted him that night. 'Conditions were brutal, but we saw the flashing light of the upturned life raft, which was semi-submerged, and the fisherman in the water had one of the handles wrapped around his arm. We had one go at catching him, really, and Joefy Murphy was such a brilliant coxswain.'

***

Christmas decorations were barely down in January 2007 when fishing vessels in the south-east put to sea to take advantage of a short weather window. The winter so far had been gale after gale, with much lost fishing time. Heading out from Dunmore East was the French-built steel vessel *Père Charles*, which was over 19 metres in length, while the 22-metre wooden-built *Honeydew II* was leaving Baltimore in west Cork.[15]

Within the space of less than a week, these two vessels were among three which sank – the third being the 27-metre steel vessel *Renegade*, which had been part of the search for the other two boats. Seven men lost their lives – on the *Père Charles*, skipper Tom Hennessy of the Maharees, County Kerry, his uncle Pat Hennessy, Billy 'the Squid' O'Connor from Dunmore East, Pat Coady from Duncormick, County Wexford and Andriy Dyrin from Sevastopol, Ukraine; and on *Honeydew II*, skipper

Ger Bohan from Kinsale and crew member Tomasz Jagla from Poland.

Neville Murphy had been out on the RNLI Dunmore East lifeboat searching for the *Père Charles* crew and was in the air hours later with his Waterford crewmates looking for survivors from the *Honeydew II*. He was standing at the cockpit door, talking to his two pilots on the intercom when, for some reason, he turned around to glance out one of the rear windows of the helicopter into the black night. It was a momentary sighting – a red flare 'dropping like an arc'.

'Lads, flare, eight o'clock,' he told the pilots, and Captain Mark McDermott banked the helicopter to the left in time to see the flash of light before it hit the water. Calculating it must be at least five miles away, the pilots flew straight ahead. Minutes later, on the infrared camera, winchman Paul Truss spotted a life raft with two people on board.

Lithuanian crewmen Victor Losev and Vladimir Kostvr had been surviving on crackers and water for at least seventeen hours in the life raft and had drifted 15 nautical miles from where the *Honeydew II* sank. The operation to winch them up was more than challenging, at night in 3–5 metre seas and with 30 knot winds. In spite of their ordeal, they had not developed hypothermia, and their pulse and respiratory rates were normal.

On 16 January, skipper and owner Kevin Downes of the *Renegade* and his crewman Ken Doyle were on the way to Howth for repairs after their participation in the searches, when their vessel sank east of Tuskar Rock lighthouse. The two men managed to take to their life raft and were located by Rescue 117 from Waterford, flown by Dara Fitzpatrick and Mark McDermott. Winchman Keith Devanney and his operator Neil McAdam rescued the pair, and both were being checked on board the helicopter when Captain McDermott flicked on the landing light. The *Renegade* was slipping beneath the waves, and the helicopter's FLIR camera captured its last 20 seconds before it vanished.

'A bit freaky,' Fitzpatrick said afterwards, noting it 'went so quickly and left very little debris'.

As Damien Tiernan recounted in *Souls of the Sea*, the sinkings stunned the entire island and stretched the rescue services to their limit in appalling weather conditions. In spite of an intensive air, sea and coastal search, the bodies of the seven men missing from the *Père Charles* and *Honeydew II* were never found. Coast Guard officer in charge Jim Griffin, who co-ordinated the search, was one of the many recipients of state marine awards for the intensive effort, as was skipper Johnny Walsh of the *Rachel Jay* and his crew.[16]

***

Sometimes even a training run off the south coast could be hazardous. In November 2009, three crew members of the Wexford inshore lifeboat were on a routine exercise when their boat capsized. Two managed to stay in contact with the upturned lifeboat and were winched to safety by the Coast Guard helicopter from Waterford, while a third crew member was recovered a mile and a half north-east of the scene by Rosslare lifeboat.

The Wexford crew were wearing life jackets. Life jackets, which became mandatory by law from 2002 on decks of fishing vessels and on craft under 7 metres in length, were crucial in saving lives in another incident in late August 2015. Ten people, all members of the extended Horan family from Moneydurtlow, Ferns, were rescued from the hull of their overturned boat by the crew of a small ferry boat, *An Crosán*. The alarm had been raised after the angling vessel failed to return to Kilmore Quay from a sea-angling trip to the Saltee islands.

The group had gone out for a day of fishing and concern grew when they did not return at sunset. A member of the family called 21-year-old Sam Nunn, a member of the Kilmore Quay lifeboat crew and a summer crewman on *An Crosán*, owned by his uncle,

Declan Bates. Sam was in Wexford when the call came in and by the time he reached Kilmore Quay the lifeboat was just launching. He took *An Crosán* with his brother and two other members of the local lifeboat crew and split the search area.

Nine of those rescued survived. The tenth person, 73-year-old Englishman Francis Smith, from Salisbury, in Wiltshire, died. The Rescue 117 helicopter lifted Mr Smith and flew him to Waterford Regional Hospital where he was pronounced dead. The survivors, including two teenagers, Jill and Eddie Horan, were brought back to Kilmore Quay by the small ferryboat.

***

RNLI Dunmore East crewman Brendan Dunne had been driving to Dublin on the night of the *Père Charles* sinking, and he remembered that the wind was so strong passing Carlow it was shaking his jeep. The losses from that tragedy brought back memories of the sinking of the *Jenalisa*, in which his cousin, Niall Power, was lost. 'Like that, Niall was never found. His family had been very involved in the lifeboat. You don't ever forget it,' Dunne said.[17]

Dunne volunteered with Dunmore East from the mid-1980s, when the station's Waveney-class vessel, *St Patrick*, was built to a US Coast Guard design. His grandfather, Johnny Dunne, and other relatives had been with the lifeboats over many years, and it was only natural that he would also sign up. Back then, the crews were mustered with the firing of a maroon – a type of rocket emitting a bang that would alert a lifeboat crew and its surrounding community.

'Our house was half a mile up from the harbour and the maroons would rattle the windows. It worked, as not only you were aware, but so was the entire community, whereas the modern bleepers tend to be very personal.'

Along with many RNLI volunteers, Dunne has been involved with highly challenging rescues that have not made the headlines.

One such was that of an injured man on board the 35-metre trawler *Saltees Quest* in April 2018. The vessel was 70–75 nautical miles south-south-east of Dunmore East when the shout, as call-outs are known, came for the lifeboat to be launched.

'It would be unusual now for a lifeboat to be tasked that far out, but we could only presume the Irish Coast Guard helicopter was on another shout,' Dunne recalled. 'The weather couldn't have been better, though – and on so many shouts close to shore, you don't get time to prepare. We had plenty of time on this one.'

The lifeboat was tasked at 11.30 a.m., and coxswain Michael Griffin headed to the position given by the Dublin MRCC. Dunne had been assigned to first aid and prepared his medical kit for an arm injury with possible sepsis. He recalled:

> We were apprehensive about getting there on time, because the distance was the equivalent of Dunmore East to The Seven Heads near Courtmasherry in west Cork by sea, and we were in contact with the fishing vessel and MRCC to check on the crewman's condition. We knew that if fluid was coming from his arm and he did collapse, we would have to be ready for all eventualities including cardio-pulmonary resuscitation.
>
> The *Saltees Quest* was heading for us and we met up with her about 55 nautical miles off, took the man on board and began treating him. We had oxygen ready, tried to keep him alert and reassure him. I'm not a paramedic, but as RNLI casualty care crew we are trained to a very high level so our training automatically kicks in on a shout. I was also referring back to our on-board medical check cards and making notes to be ready for the handover when we met the ambulance crew ashore.
>
> It was about 5.30 p.m. when we were back in Dunmore East, met the ambulance, where we did a full handover debrief and he was brought to Ardkeen hospital. He didn't

lose his arm and he was out the next day, but it had been a serious call-out for us.

I think the crew saw a porbeagle shark and gannets and shearwaters on the way out, but to be honest I was so busy preparing inside that it all passed me by... you become a different person when you step on the lifeboat.

His colleague Neville Murphy said Dunne's calm and methodical approach was crucial in a medical situation that could have been critical.

The year before that tasking, Dunne's fellow volunteers across the county border in Wexford's Courtown were faced with a different medical challenge off Ardamine, a popular beach close by. The volunteers who responded to the call-out on the afternoon of 11 August 2017 were told that a teenage girl was in difficulty in the sea with suspected back injuries. The teenager had been thrown from a 'donut' being towed by a jet ski, after the ski was disabled when a rope became caught in the water intake.

Coxswain Peter Browne on the Courtown D-class, or inshore, lifeboat launched and could see the girl in the water. A kayaker and the girl's father were both trying to support her in the water. Courtown crew Fergus Slevin and Fr Tom Dalton got into the water to assess the teenager and they transferred her father to the lifeboat. The teenager was in pain and it was clear that a helicopter would be required. The Waterford-based Rescue 117 helicopter was out on an exercise and needed to refuel.

Slevin and Dalton immobilised the teenager and put a neck brace on her. Treading water, they worked to ensure she remained afloat but flat and straight in the water. For forty minutes they chatted to her, reassuring her at all times. When Rescue 117 arrived, the winch crew advised Browne to drop the drogue anchor, keep the vessel head on to the waves and cut the engine. The teenager was then transferred from the water to the lifeboat using a rigid stretcher. The boat transported her to nearby Glendoyne beach, where the local shore-based Coast Guard unit assisted with the next delicate stage. This involved beaching the lifeboat to allow the helicopter to perform a high lift, lowering a basket, carefully transferring the stretcher, winching it back up and flying the teenager to University Hospital Waterford for further treatment.

The RNLI's Arklow lifeboat had also launched and took the two people on the jet ski and the kayaker back to Courtown harbour, where they were treated for shock and cold by a waiting ambulance crew. RNLI Courtown lifeboat operations manager Sam Kennedy commented afterwards that it was a great example of the RNLI and Coast Guard 'working well together', and paid tribute to the Rescue 117 crew and a member of the public who had raised the alarm.

Several months later, the neighbouring RNLI Rosslare crew faced a very different challenge when they were called out during Storm Ophelia in October 2017. As Rosslare coxswain Eamonn O'Rourke recalled, the storm had been well forecast and the 'whole country was bracing itself'. Public transport and ferry sailings had been cancelled, businesses had closed, staff were told not to travel to work, and O'Rourke and other leisure-craft owners had called down to the harbour early that day to put some extra rope on vessels in the lagoon. He was on his way to see his aunt in hospital before the storm hit, when he got a call to say there was a 'ten-metre yacht in a bit of bother up the coast'.[18]

Three yachtsmen had been attempting to move the 1968 Dehler 101 from Rosslare harbour to a more protected mooring farther up the coast. They had left Southampton three days earlier to deliver the yacht to Malahide in north Dublin and had reached Rosslare twelve hours ahead of the bad weather.

'A lot of people might not realise that we didn't go sailing in a storm,' yacht skipper Mark Adrian Corbett explained afterwards:

> We were manoeuvring the boat a few miles north of Rosslare harbour for safer anchorage. We left Rosslare

harbour in 10 knots of wind and flat seas. By the time we reached our destination, the wind had increased to around 60 knots and the surf conditions were so big that I couldn't get into the harbour. We would've broached had we gone in there.

Essentially we were in a sailor's worst nightmare - a lee shore. That's when the wind is blowing towards the shore. The surf is heading that way and all the pressure is heading that way. You're being pushed that way and you can't sail or motor out of it. It's an environment I've never been in before. We were so overpowered by the wind. The engine was never going to survive. That's when I called in the 'Mayday'.

We were relieved when we saw the lifeboat. But when I saw the size of the lifeboat in comparison to the size of the waves the lifeboat was in, I realised that I'd got these guys into trouble as well.

We spent some time trying to establish a tow and were then towed back into the weather. When you sail into a hurricane, it's like sailing into a 100mph sandstorm. It's like an industrial pressure washer. Everything on the yacht was just getting destroyed and the boat was getting smaller and smaller.[19]

RNLI Rosslare mechanic Michael Nicholas remembered that there were 50–55mph winds whipping around the end of the pier when the lifeboat launched, after the 'Mayday' call from the yacht. 'I kept watching the gauges. From the time we left to the time we got back, the wind speed kept on climbing. I have never, ever seen that before,' he said.

'The yacht was out of control,' coxswain O'Rourke said. 'It was moving very erratically. At one stage, the skipper reported sailing 17 knots down a wave, and a moment later falling back to 2 knots. We decided to try to stabilise it using a drogue – a device trailed behind a vessel to slow down its speed. But first we had to get the drogue onboard.'

He continued, 'The wind made it extremely difficult. The fear was that if we tried to go alongside we'd fall down on top of them or they'd fall down on us.'

The lifeboat was slightly upwind of the yacht when the crew managed to swing the drogue's heaving line across, on the second attempt. This allowed O'Rourke to manoeuvre the lifeboat close enough for a tow. There was another challenge, however, as the lifeboat was facing south.

'We could go on up to Arklow or we could turn the yacht around, which would make the tow that much shorter. The fear was that if we carried on, and the tow came apart on the sandbanks, we'd never recover,' O'Rourke said. 'The yacht would capsize and the lads would be in the water. We decided to turn, but there was no let-up in the waves so we couldn't choose our moment. We just had to go for it.'

The yacht had no choice but to follow, knowing if it went broadside on the waves it would have rolled over. Both vessels were heading straight into hurricane-force winds, with a tow rope attached to two small cleats on the yacht. O'Rourke was 'absolutely amazed' that the cleats held.

Three years later, in October 2020, the lives of nine more people were saved and a major environmental incident averted by three of the south-east's lifeboats, when a cargo vessel of more than 4,000 tonnes named *Lily B* sent out a 'Mayday' call. The vessel was en route from Germany to New Ross, County Wexford, with a cargo of coal when it lost all power some 2 nautical miles south-south-west of Hook Head.

A force 8–9 southerly gale was churning up 6-metre-high waves and there was a rising spring tide when coxswain Roy Abrahamsson of the Dunmore East lifeboat assessed the situation. Rescue 117 from Waterford was tasked to provide top cover to the lifeboat fleet, including Kilmore Quay and Rosslare all-weather vessels.

'I was collecting the kids from school when the bleeper went,' Neville Murphy said. 'I remember looking out at the sea earlier and thinking this was not the day to get a shout, so I jinxed it!'

'I think we faced into some of the worst conditions ever when we hit a wall of sea after the breakwater,' he recalled. 'It was so bad you couldn't go downstairs to get the helmet with the camera. The ship was broadside when we picked it up, and we calculated it had about twenty to twenty-five minutes before running aground.'

RNLI Dunmore East was designated as on-scene command, and the coxswains of all three lifeboats showed 'fantastic skills', Murphy recalled, going on to recount:

> The only thing we had in our favour in those extreme conditions was the fact that it was daylight initially.
>
> We made three attempts to get a line on board and three times it failed. It was nearly impossible to hear each other, and then there was the language barrier with the crew of the *Lily B.* We fired two rocket-propelled ropes – the first snapped, but the second from the Kilmore Quay lifeboat got a tow on.
>
> We knew at this stage that a tug was on the way and our main aim was to try and hold the ship from being driven up on the lee shore. A vessel of this size couldn't be towed by a small lifeboat.
>
> The only reason the two towlines we had on board did not part was because of the skill of the coxswains, throttling the engines back and forth to try and keep some tension on. Every time a wave smashed us, we had to pull back ...
>
> It was a local tug that arrived at about 8 p.m. and we were never so glad to see it, but it didn't end there.

It was the *Tramontine,* owned by the Port of Waterford, that arrived on scene. Murphy's account continued:

The ship had no electrical power to deploy an anchor and the tug couldn't get the normal lines on, so the ship had to drop other lines and there was a co-ordinated effort involving the three lifeboats, the tug and this big ship to hand over the tow … in pitch dark.

We used spotlights, and Rescue 117 also illuminated the sea area with its lights. Eventually we escorted the ship and tug back to Waterford harbour, and there was a second failure of the towing bridle on the way in.

It was within a safe anchorage at that stage, and the ship could drop anchor.

There was such a contrast in seas when we rounded Hook Head and it was flat calm, and we arrived in at 02.18 hours, having been almost twelve hours at sea. The captain and crew were very grateful, and the first mate sent us all a lovely letter.

The RNLI recommended the three coxswains – Dunmore East's Abrahamsson, Kilmore Quay's Eugene Kehoe and Rosslare Harbour's Eamon O'Rourke – for bronze medals for gallantry for 'their fine display of seamanship and boat-handling skills in atrocious weather conditions, in securing a tow and determination to succeed, resulting in the saving of nine lives'. RNLI Medal Service certificates were also recommended for the three crews: Dunmore East coxswain Abrahamsson, David Murray (mechanic), Neville Murphy (navigator), Peter Curran, Jon Walsh, Luka Sweeney and Kevin Dingley; Kilmore Quay coxswain Kehoe, Philip Walsh (mechanic), Aidan Bates (navigator), Trevor Devereux and Sam Nunn; and Rosslare Harbour coxswain O'Rourke, Mick Nicholas (mechanic), Keith Miller (navigator), Padraig Quirke, Michael Sinnott, Eoghan Quirke and Paul McCormack.

The RNLI also recommended a Medal Service certificate for the crew of Rescue 117 for 'their top cover and reassurance to all the crews below for the duration of the service', when a potential 'tragedy and environmental disaster was averted'. It said signed letters of appreciation would also be presented to the staff of the National Maritime Operations Centre in Dublin, and to the master and crew of the tug *Tramontine*.

Murphy's colleagues in Rescue 117, including the Irish Coast Guard's first female winch team member Sarah Courtney, were further lauded when they received national bravery awards in November 2021 for their collective efforts to save the lives of seven fishermen from a sinking vessel off the south-west coast earlier that year.

Courtney, winch operator Adrian O'Hara, and pilots Ronan Flanagan and Aaron Hyland were on duty when the vessel was taken under tow by the Naval Service patrol ship LÉ *George Bernard Shaw* in high winds and a very heavy swell some 70 nautical miles west of Bantry Bay on 27 March 2021. The fishing vessel was at serious risk of sinking. As the citation stated:

> In fading light and worsening conditions Rescue 117 successfully evacuated the crew of seven from the vessel in force nine gales and 10–12 metre seas. Without doubt the lives of the 7 crew on board the fishing vessel were saved due to the collective bravery and physical efforts of the crew of Waterford-based Irish Coast Guard helicopter Rescue 117 … In particular winchman, Ms Courtney, deserves special credit. On this occasion her individual bravery and physical effort in such arduous conditions showed her to be an individual of immense capability and significant courage.[20]

All four were awarded certificates of bravery, and Courtney was also awarded a silver medal for her actions.

13

THE MIGHT OF THE ATLANTIC

The sailor and writer Wallace Clark once wrote about how some of the oldest rock found anywhere on Ireland forms Inishtrahull, a once inhabited island off the north Donegal coast. Clark described it as the 'Ultima Thule' of Irish islands due to its size and inaccessibility – this part of the coast being prone to sudden weather changes.[1]

Rescue crews off the north-west coast are very familiar with the might of the Atlantic in all its moods. So when Donegal's RNLI Arranmore lifeboat coxswain John O'Donnell spoke of a 'hellish night' during the rescue of the fishing vessel *Locative* in 1990, it would have been particularly challenging. The lifeboat station on the north-east of Arranmore Island in County Donegal had been saving lives since 1883, and its crews have secured ten medals from the RNLI – one gold, three silver and six bronze – to date.

Eight Dutch medals for gallantry were also conferred for saving lives during the Second World War. Coxswain John Boyle, motor mechanic Teague Ward and crew Philip Boyle, Philip Byrne, Neil Byrne, Bryan Gallagher, Patrick O'Donnell and Joseph Rogers were recognised by the Dutch government for the rescue of eighteen people from the Dutch steamer *Stolwijk*, which was forced onto rocks at Inishbeg on 7 December 1940. The steamer was one of a convoy of ships from north America that had come through three days of a rising north-westerly gale and was making for the sea passage between Scotland and Northern Ireland – then the only remaining safe entrance to British ports – in a 'hurricane of wind and snow'.[2]

Queen Wilhelmina of the Netherlands paid tribute to 'exceptionally outstanding courage, unselfishness and devotion to duty'. The owners of the *Stolwijk*, the Netherlands Shipping and Trading Company, gave £20 (€23.51) to be divided among the crew.

Arranmore coxswain Francis Bonner was recognised by the RNLI for a thirteen-hour service on 19 December 1994 to save five people and the fishing vessel *Claudia Marie*, which had lost its rudder 24 nautical miles north-east of Arranmore in winds gusting to force 9, with very rough seas and a large metre swell.

Eleven years later, the station's crew were lauded for yet another long call-out. The Coast Guard Rescue 118 helicopter from Sligo and the RAF from Kinloss were also involved in the mission to rescue solo sailor Keith White on his yacht *Nephele* on 2 July 2005. White, who had lost the use of his left arm in a motorbike accident, had been sailing since the age of 16. From London, he was sailing around Britain and Ireland to mark the 200th anniversary of the Battle of Trafalgar when he was caught in south-westerly force 10–11 winds and 10-metre seas. Malin Head radio initiated the search when it lost contact with *Nephele*.

White had managed to right the yacht after it capsized and was unwilling to leave his vessel. Conditions were too bad in any case when he was located some 40 miles off Tory Island. The Arranmore lifeboat stayed with the yacht throughout the night, until it was safe to establish a tow as conditions eased the following morning. Coxswain Anthony Kavanagh and crew were exhausted when they berthed after twenty hours at sea.[3]

***

Donegal-based fisherman Ross Classon (45) had no family background in fishing when he opted to pursue it as a career. He was barely a few wet years in the job when he was earning more than his father, Michael, who was then principal of Newpark Comprehensive School in Blackrock, County Dublin.

It wasn't the money that attracted him, but the pull he had felt since he began catching salmon at the age of 12 on holidays in Rosbeg, County Donegal. He was still in school when he got his first half decker, *Naomh Seosaimh*. He would embark on gillnetting and seining trips off the south Donegal coast with friends Pat Johnson and Cathal Boyle on the *Dun Laoghaire* and the *Lorella*.

His career took a leap when Mick Doyle enlisted him for a beam trawler in the Irish Sea. Mick, originally from Wicklow, was one of the successful Irish fishermen who had pioneered the lucrative mackerel fishery. 'I learned a lot, and during my time in Newlyn I took an interest in the fishery for crab with vivier boats, which had been developed there,' Classon said.[4]

This led him to apply for his own crab vessel, the *Ainmire*, which was built in Holland in 1993. It arrived in Donegal to great celebrations within the Classon family, which included Ross's wife, Anna, and four sons, shortly before St Patrick's Day. The vessel then spent a number of seasons working the rough, tough grounds between Mayo and Scotland.

Seventeen years later, on 29 April 2010, Classon, his son Christopher and three Latvian crew were on board the *Ainmire* when it began taking in water 30 miles off the Scottish Butt of Lewis. 'The BBC reported that the *Ainmire* was sinking – I'll never forget it,' he says. 'The engine room flooded and there was no way of stopping it.'

Classon called all hands, instructed them to don survival suits and issued a 'Mayday' on VHF channel 16. Lachlan Murray, skipper of a neighbouring vessel, *Our Hazel*, was 6 nautical miles away and set a course for the location, while a British Coastguard helicopter and the RNLI Stornoway lifeboat were tasked.

Murray took the *Ainmire* crew on board and deployed a petrol-driven pump to the vessel, but to no avail. *Our Hazel* took it under tow, but it began listing after about five miles and the tow had to be released. The crabber sank in about 100 metres of water; its life raft and satellite beacon floated to the surface and were recovered. *Our Hazel* took the shocked crew of the *Ainmire* to Ullapool. 'It happened so quickly … and then she was gone!' Classon said.

Five years later, an Aran island crew had a shockingly close shave off the Scottish coast. On 20 January 2015, the 23-metre *Iúda Naofa* began taking in water about 80 kilometres north of the Butt of Lewis and called the British Coastguard on VHF radio for assistance.

'It wasn't a "Mayday" at that stage, as we thought if we got a pump on board we'd sort it,' recalled Micheál Conneely, who was on board with his father Mairtín '20' Ó Conghaíle of Inis Mór and three fellow crew.[5] However, the crew still put on their immersion suits and life jackets. A British Coastguard helicopter was on scene in forty-five minutes and by then the vessel had started to list.

'We gathered at the stern, and my father was thrown back by a wave and I just managed to catch him,' said Conneely. 'When we were in the water, we had a rope tangled around us, which I had to free – if it was attached to the boat, we'd be gone, but once I had untangled it I knew we would be okay.'

It took just thirty-five seconds for the seas to engulf the hull – an image captured by the helicopter and one that broke his father's heart. 'The boat was like his sixth child, so it's a big loss for him, even though we were all saved,' said Conneely.

Standing by was the *Star of Hope*, skippered by Mike 'Twin' Ó Fatharta, which had been pair trawling with the *Iúda Naofa* and which took two of the crew. Three were airlifted to the Western Isles Hospital in Stornoway. Weather conditions were difficult at the time, according to British Maritime and Coastguard Agency (MCA) duty-watch manager Paul Tunstall, with 'very rough seas' and southerly force 6 winds.[6]

Coincidentally, TG4 television had commissioned Conneely to make a documentary on an Aran island fleet's winter pursuit of mackerel. He had completed a postgraduate degree in communication, with film studies being part of his thesis. Fortunately, he had already recorded a lot of footage of fishing before the sinking, and the British MCA supplied him with the rescue material.

'One of the helicopter winchman told me it was the first time in fourteen years he had actually seen a boat go under, as usually the rescue crew arrive after that has occurred,' he said. The footage became one of the highlights of *Snámh in Aghaidh Easa* [Swimming Against the Current], broadcast later that year.

***

Rescue 118 winch team member Gary Robertson was on duty at the Sligo search and rescue base on 9 April 2016 when a call came in to assist a fisherman off Arranmore Island, County Donegal. The fisherman's 6-metre vessel had capsized in Innisinny Bay, and he was clinging to a lifebuoy when the Sligo-based helicopter was scrambled by Malin Head Coast Guard.

The location was 60 nautical miles north-west of Sligo, and the weather en route was 'post frontal, with a cold air temperature of two degrees Celsius, scattered clouds, clear skies, a light tail wind'.[7] Sea state was classified as six, meaning very rough, with wave heights of up to 6 metres, a large swell and a sea temperature of 10 degrees. The RNLI Arranmore all-weather lifeboat had been tasked and was on scene in ten minutes from the island, but the extreme sea state and building surf made an approach too difficult.

The fishing vessel had already begun to sink, and the casualty, a 67-year-old man, was 'seen to be clinging to a life buoy [with] his left arm and had managed to inflate his life jacket but had no survival suit. With waves repeatedly crashing onto the casualty, frequently submerging him and pushing him toward the shore, it was clear that a swift rescue was required to save this fisherman's life.'

However, it was also going to be a complex rescue for Robertson, as he was lowered on the winch through heavy seas. As he approached the fisherman and tried to apply two strops or slings to carry out a hydrostatic lift, he noticed that the man was entangled in many metres of thick rope. The rope was 'wrapped three to four times around the casualty, attached also to the lifebuoy which in turn was still tethered to the submerged boat'.

The heavy swell and the downwash from the helicopter were consistently submerging the two men in the water at this stage. Robertson's winch operator, Alan Gallagher, took action to minimise this, directing the aircraft to a position some 18 yards offset and around 250 feet above to monitor his colleague as he struggled to attach both strops.

The helicopter was now very vulnerable, with all three – helicopter, winchman and the fisherman – effectively attached by the coiled and tangled rope to the sunken vessel. As a citation for an award conferred on Robertson noted, 'the winch operator deftly raised the winch, whilst the co-pilot maintained a steady hover, to a position where the winchman could access his knife and cut the ropes which were now under tension'. This allowed Robertson to swing free, lifting the fisherman clear of water and swell – some forty minutes after the boat had capsized.

'If they arrived moments later, he would have gone down with the vessel,' a Coast Guard spokesman said. 'The winchman could not cut the rope until there was tension on it, so it was very tricky. When he cut the rope, the bow of the vessel bobbed under the water. By the time they were back in the aircraft, the boat was gone.'

Robertson realised the fisherman's left arm had been caught in a spasm, meaning he was unable to release the lifebuoy he was clinging to and had to be prised away. He also knew from his advanced paramedic training that the fisherman was in a bad way, being semi-conscious and showing signs of a lack of oxygen. He worked with Gallagher to apply immediate lifesaving medical care, as pilots Seán Redahan and Ciaran Ferguson flew to Letterkenny General Hospital.

'The swift and extraordinary physical … efforts … of Gary Robertson, both in the water and in the aircraft, resulted in this casualty's life being saved,' the citation said. He was given the Billy Deacon award, which was established by Bristow Helicopters in memory of a winchman of the same name who died during a British Maritime and Coastguard Agency search and rescue helicopter mission in 1997.

The helicopter's work wasn't quite finished as it took off from Letterkenny Hospital. En route back to Sligo, it was tasked with rescuing two surfers off the tiny bit of County Leitrim that borders the Atlantic. One man was pulled from the water by the winchman, while the RNLI Bundoran lifeboat rescued the other.[8]

**

Rathlin, the 'L-shaped island' renowned for its strong tides off the Irish north-east coast, was the nearest location to an extraordinary helicopter rescue in May 2017. On a Sunday morning that month, Matthew Bryce (23) from Airdrie in north Lanarkshire set out to catch some surf off Westport Beach, on Scotland's Argyll coast. When the surfer was rescued, he had been thirty-two hours at sea with no life jacket or buoyancy aid.

Speaking to the media from his Belfast hospital bed, Bryce described how wind and strong currents swept him out, how his paddling was 'ineffective' but kept him warm, and how he headed for a shipping lane after seeing fishing vessels in the distance. He had tried calling and waving, to no avail. After two days and one full night at sea, he was watching his second sunset and had 'pretty much made peace with it all', thinking he was going to die.[9] He calculated he had only three hours left when he heard the helicopter overhead.

'So I jumped off the board ... I started waving the board in the water, and they flew right over. I thought they'd missed me. But then they turned round ...'

Some 500 feet above him, Captain Andrew Pilliner and his crew with the British MCA had been out for five hours from their base at Prestwick, Glasgow, and had refuelled once already. 'Whenever we are searching for anyone over water or over land, any movement, any contrasting colour ... that's what the human eye is drawn to, and that's what allowed us to find him,' Pilliner recalled.

It was 7.30 p.m. on Monday evening, with fading light, when the co-pilot spotted something in the water some 13 miles off the Scottish coast. Winchman Duncan Tripp said that it resembled a marker buoy with a flag on it.

'We came round again only because that buoy shouldn't have been in that area,' Tripp said. 'And there was a bloke sitting on a surfboard.'

Tripp was winched down, placed two strops over Bryce and gave him a 'man hug'. He could ascertain his casualty was in an advanced state of hypothermia.

'To put the surfer's situation into perspective, the body temperature is 37 degrees Celsius, and the Irish Sea at this time of year is around 10 degrees Celsius – so the sea will do its damndest to pull that body temperature down to its level,' Ray Johnston, National Maritime College of Ireland services operations manager, said afterwards.

Water Safety Ireland chief executive John Leech noted that Bryce's experience was 'pretty remarkable' and may have set a new record for the north Atlantic, although two Scotsmen wearing some survival gear had come close. Fife anglers Bill Hepburn and John Gowan were twenty-five hours in the water and had had the sense to stay with their upturned angling boat when they were rescued by the Dublin-based Rescue 116 helicopter crew 13 miles north-west of the Isle of Man on 1 September 2003. Only part of the hull was visible above the waterline by that point and the pair had been surviving on some crisps and a banana when lifted aboard by winch team Derek Everitt and Alan Gallagher.

The fact that the Scottish surfer was wearing a heavy neoprene wetsuit and kept his head covered were key factors in staving off hypothermia, Leech said. Bryce did the right things – staying with the surfboard being crucial, he noted. 'Wearing a black suit, he would never have been seen on his own, but the white surfboard saved him.'

Although the surfer had broken a golden rule in adventure sports – that is: never kayak, sail, paddle or surf alone – Leech said it was 'fantastic that he held his nerve'.

***

In May 2018, the wreckage of a Mayo vessel was washed up on South Uist in the Outer Hebrides. The *Aisling Patrick* had drifted 300 kilometres in a month after it capsized 16 nautical miles north-west of Eagle Island in north Mayo. Two of the three crewmen survived the accident, having managed to make a broken 'Mayday' call before taking to the life raft. An Air Corps Casa maritime patrol aircraft located the vessel, and the Rescue 118 helicopter from Sligo winched them aboard. Sadly, 57-year-old John Healy from Erris in north Mayo did not survive.

Eighteen months later, another Mayo crabber, *Seán Óg 2*, was the focus of a combined response from three RNLI lifeboats on the north coast – Arranmore, Lough Swilly and Portrush.

The Lough Swilly lifeboat, established in Buncrana in 1988, often found itself being beaten to a tasking by a helicopter – what the RNLI termed an 'ineffectual shout' – because it has a 16-mile steam out of the lough to reach the sea. However, in November 2006, Lough Swilly's second coxswain, Mark Barrett, and deputy second coxswain, George O'Hagan, were recognised by the RNLI for a particularly challenging task, towing in a fishing vessel, the *Mary Ellen*, with six crew on board. In gusting gale-force winds and a 10-metre swell, the tow line parted twice before the vessel was brought into Greencastle.

Conditions were similarly poor on 14 December 2019 when the Mayo crabber *Seán Óg 2* got into difficulty 20 miles north of Fanad head. As Joe Joyce of Lough Swilly lifeboat recalled, it had been a 'terrible, terrible day'. The weather had deteriorated, with force 9–10 gales and sea swells of 15 metres (50 feet). The boat lost power and couldn't steer, even as violent waves smashed in the wheelhouse windows.

Belfast Coast Guard tasked Lough Swilly RNLI, which launched its all-weather lifeboat for a 34-nautical mile steam to the location. RNLI Portrush was also tasked and had 50 nautical miles to travel. The Arranmore lifeboat was asked to launch shortly after, at 4 p.m. At the time, its crew were at the station putting a star up in memory of Lee Early, one of their volunteers and son of coxswain Jimmy Early, who had died just a month before. Lee, who worked on the island's ferry service, had been trying to turn his car at Poolawaddy pier when it slipped into the sea.

'The sea conditions [during the rescue] were so severe that one of the Portrush crew was thrown off the seat and tore leg muscles,' Joe Joyce said. 'We managed to secure a tow, but it parted a number of times. The Portrush lifeboat was climbing up and falling off the tops of waves, and we were doing the same, so Arranmore took up the tow from us.'[10]

'We weren't back in the lough till 2 or 3 a.m. after fifteen hours out,' Joyce continued. 'Two big container ships out that day were also getting it hard with weather, and Jimmy Early asked one of his crew for the name of the ship that passed them on the way out. It was the MV *Lee*.'

***

Charlie Cavanagh's home overlooks the harbour in Greencastle in north Donegal, and so he often found himself counting the boats berthed at the pier on a bad night. 'You'd be very conscious of who is still at sea, and it was like that the night of the *Carrickatine*,' he said, recalling the events of 15 November 1995 and thereafter.[11]

Cavanagh knew the six crew well, including skipper Jeremy McKinney (27) and his brother Conal (29). He had once fished with John Kelly (38), and knew his son Stephen (16), the youngest of the crew. Terry Doherty (23) lived a few doors away, and he knew Bernard Gormley from the post office – he marked his eighteenth birthday on the day the *Carrickatine* disappeared.

Cavanagh, who had then been ten years with the Coast Guard Greencastle unit, rang around all the harbours to see if the vessel had made it to shelter before the alarm was raised. It had been a 'horrendous, stormy night', Cavanagh recalled. The weeks to follow were harrowing for the families, waiting for news. The search was one of the most extensive in Irish waters, but no trace of the six men was ever found.

'It never leaves you ... and the families have carried it with them all the time.'

Cavanagh, one of the longest-serving and most experienced members of the Coast Guard, was a key member of an advisory group that devised a new system for coast and cliff rescue, known as 'Tag 07' (Technical Advisory Group 07).[12]

'When I joined in 1985, we had inherited the old horse carts, ropes and rocket gear used by Her Majesty's Coastguard, and it also used a system of stake boards to anchor ropes at the top of a cliff. It was very basic, and we felt we needed a better mechanism for situations where the helicopter could not gain safe access,' he said.

The Tag 07 system, used since about 2009, has proved very reliable in situations such as that which occurred on the night of 28 May 2019, when a group of three Derry climbers encountered difficulties at a chasm on Malin Head through which the Atlantic surges, known locally as Hell's Hole. One of the group became trapped about 45 metres (147 feet) down, and could neither move up or down on an unpredictable rock face. It was well into the night when the Coast Guard Greencastle unit deployed its team to locate him.

As Cavanagh explained, sitting in a climbing harness for a long period of time can induce suspension trauma where one loses the power of one's legs. 'We managed to get him out by around 1 a.m, and take him to Letterkenny Hospital, so it was a long but successful night.'

Not every call-out has such a good outcome, and the dates of those rescue shouts that became search and recovery remain etched in Cavanagh's memory. One such was the evening of Sunday 20 March 2016, when an Audi Q7 SUV drove down the slipway at Buncrana pier.

The slipway commands a fine view of Lough Swilly and the ferry crossing to Rathmullan. Within seconds, however, the car was in trouble as its wheels lost friction on the ramp. A local man, Francis Crawford, noticed the car at the bottom of the slip with about 10 centimetres of water up around its wheels, and called to the driver to ask if he was okay. Sean McGrotty (49), who was at the wheel, shouted back to him to phone the Coast Guard, which Crawford did. Minutes later, the car had drifted 20–25 metres into the lough.

Former League of Ireland footballer Davitt Walsh from Kerrykeel, County Donegal, had driven to Buncrana with his girlfriend, Stephanie Knox. He stripped down to his underwear and swam out to the sinking vehicle. McGrotty managed to break the front driver's window with his elbow, and partially hauled himself out to hand Walsh a baby.

With water rushing through the car, Walsh also tried to grab a young boy's arm to pull him out – but the force of the surge was too strong. 'The father had the window half ajar and started hitting it with his elbow,' Walsh recalled afterwards. 'When the window was broke, the father … handed me the baby and said: "Take the baby." I took the baby, I held it above my head and I swam back to shore,' he said. 'The father could have saved himself because he was out of the car, but he went back in to save his family. I think deep down the father knew I was only going to be able to save one person.'[13]

McGrotty, his sons Mark (12) and Evan (8), his mother-in-law Ruth Daniels (59) and Ruth's daughter Jodie Lee Daniels (14) from Derry city were all inside, unable to open the doors to escape.

Fighting off exhaustion as he swam back, Walsh managed to hand four-month-old Rioghnach-Ann to Knox on the slipway and she took the baby up to her car to keep her warm. Walsh, whose feet were now cut and bleeding, could barely breathe and had to be taken to Letterkenny Hospital.

'I was exhausted on the pier, I just lay there on the algae … I just feel really, really terrible that I couldn't do any more for the family,' he said.

The Coast Guard Greencastle unit worked with the RNLI Lough Swilly lifeboat on the recovery at Buncrana. Walsh was later awarded a state gold medal for gallantry, while the Lough Swilly lifeboat crew received a ministerial letter of appreciation.

Over four years later, the Greencastle unit was once again called out to another unforgettable emergency involving a family.

John and Geraldine Mullan and their two children, Tomás (14) and Amelia (6), were well known in Moville, just a few miles from Greencastle on the Inishowen peninsula. John owned the local garden centre and Geraldine is a nurse in Letterkenny Hospital. The family were driving home from the cinema in Derry on the night of 20 August 2020 when their Mitsubishi ASX SUV left the road near Quigley's Point. It careered down an embankment into Lough Foyle and overturned.

The night was wet and windy, Cavanagh recalled. Geraldine and the two children managed to escape from the vehicle, but John was trapped inside.

'One of our unit volunteers, Kevin Barr, who lives close by, was first on the scene. Geraldine was hanging onto the car, but the two children had drifted away. Kevin managed to get Geraldine up out of the water and pull her up the embankment,' he said.

Garda sergeant Charlene Anderson took Geraldine's arm, stayed by her side as she was wrapped in a blanket to prevent hypothermia, and was with her when she was taken by paramedics to identify the bodies of her husband and children. Fr John Farren, parish priest of Iskaheen in Muff, anointed them and gave them the last rites.

'When you land on a scene in the dark, you don't know what you are dealing with and who ... but then when you recognise the vehicle, and you know the children when they are taken from the water, it's very, very difficult,' Cavanagh explained. 'You wish the ground could open up and swallow you, but you have to keep working. I remember there were times when there was no sound. There was just a stillness over the whole scene ...'

Over the years, Cavanagh has trained with many helicopter search and rescue crew, including the four members of the Air Corps who lost their lives in the crash in Tramore in July 1999. He also knew the crew on the Rescue 116 helicopter mission that crashed in north Mayo in March 2017.

His brother-in-law Patrick McClenaghan was fishing off the west coast on the *Foyle Warrior* when he heard the traffic on the VHF about a helicopter missing, and phoned Cavanagh at home.

'I went up to Malin Coast Radio Station in the early hours of the morning because I knew there was probably only a couple of radio officers on watch, and even to have someone there to make a cup of tea would help,' Cavanagh recalled. 'I was there until late afternoon, when they were recovering the wreckage and Dara Fitzpatrick had been found ... We all knew her – as a female pilot she had broken the mould.'

After the outbreak of the Covid-19 pandemic in early 2020, training proved to be a challenge for search and rescue units. 'There is a sacrifice for volunteers, but there is also a social aspect, and that was something we all missed when we had to restructure training for Covid-19,' Cavanagh explained. 'For instance, as officer-in-charge, I couldn't train with my deputy Cathal McGuinness, as we can't both afford to be sick. Living close to the border also meant we were aware of different restrictions – mask-wearing has not been a big thing in the North.'

Cavanagh has been conferred with a thirty-year long-service Irish Coast Guard medal, and he has two daughters in the Greencastle unit, Maeve and Caitríona. During a thirtieth birthday celebration for one of his daughters on 15 August 2021, the pagers went off for an incident where a woman had broken her leg at Malin Head. 'We were about to cut the cake, but it cost no one a thought to get up and go. In the event, we weren't all needed, but you have to have a very understanding family,' he explained.

14
SOUTH-WEST SEA SENSE

Tea, coffee, dried milk, cans of corned beef, maybe a loaf of bread. Retired coxswain of Baltimore lifeboat Kieran Cotter had a consistent supply list for shouts, much of which he might source in his own shop in the village.

'A pound of butter, a couple of packs of ham were always handy,' Cotter recalled. 'And plenty of biscuits and bars of chocolate, so we never starved.'[1]

Cotter grew up close to the RNLI lifeboat station in west Cork, as he lived on Cape Clear Island. He joined the merchant marine but didn't complete the cadet officer training programme in Plymouth because he became a fisherman instead, then signed up for the RNLI. He and his wife, Brigid, then bought a shop in Baltimore.

Cotter was just 24 years old when he served as a lifeboat crewman on the 1979 Fastnet yacht rescue.[2] Six years later, in September 1986, he had just come home from a wedding and gone to bed when he got a phone call to go down to the lifeboat station. Coxswain Christy Collins had been told a yacht had run up on rocks on Mizen Head.

'There was very little information, except that a "Mayday" had been received. It was a mucky night, with poor visibility, and we were on the north side of Mizen when we saw the light; we went into a cove, and we saw a life raft,' Cotter said. 'My brother Liam was on the lifeboat crew at the time, and he put out his hand to Mr Haughey and said, "Congratulations on your sixtieth birthday.'"

The Fianna Fáil leader's 42-foot timber boat *Taurima* was en route from Dingle to Dublin in thick fog when it had a radar malfunction, Charles J. Haughey later told RTÉ News.[3]

'The yacht had gone down very quickly, and Haughey's son Ciaran had got into a dinghy and used the oars to keep the life raft off rocks in a gully below the back of an area known as the Workmen's Quarters at Mizen lighthouse,' Cotter said.

The keepers in the signal station, who had alerted Baltimore lifeboat, climbed down and shone lights to reassure the crew of five that help was on the way. 'The lighthouse men were terrific,' Haughey said. The lifeboat crew were 'on the spot within two hours' and 'we had plenty of craic from there to Baltimore, and cups of tea'.

Haughey sent a guinea to Baltimore lifeboat for its fundraising, and a hamper arrived that Christmas. He would often return to Bushe's Bar in the village – the venue for celebrations after the rescue – and presented a clock from the *Taurima* to Mizen lighthouse ten years later. When asked by a garda on duty outside Leinster House the week after the accident how he escaped from the stricken yacht, Haughey turned and whispered: 'I walked on water.'[4]

Cotter was in or near his shop on the night of 30/31 October 1991 when there was an alert to assist a fishing vessel which had suffered engine failure in storm force winds.

'We were told a Spanish trawler named *Japonica* with fifteen crew on board had broken down 15 miles west of Fastnet around 4.30–5 p.m., when it was just getting dark,' he recalled:

> The weather was pretty extreme, and it took us up to four hours to get there, and then trying to put a tow on was very difficult. The first tow took over an hour. When we were proceeding into Bantry Bay, the tow parted, and we

managed to reconnect it and take it into the safety of the bay where it dropped anchor.

At around 8 a.m., we received a call to assist a sailing vessel, *Atlantis Adventure*, about 20 to 25 miles south of Fastnet. So it was about 7 p.m. when we were back in Baltimore – about 26 hours at sea.

Cotter was conferred with a RNLI bronze medal – one of three bronze and seven silver medals given to Baltimore crew since the station was established in 1919. He was also given the Maud Smith Award for the bravest act of life-saving.

The outcome to a tasking to Mizen Head, Ireland's most southerly point, on the night of 23 November 2000 was less fortuitous. It was around 3 a.m. when an aircraft picked up a distress signal and alerted the Coast Guard. The Shannon Sikorsky S-61, the Baltimore and Castletownbere lifeboats, the navy ship LÉ *Róisín* and the Goleen coast and cliff rescue team were all tasked. The search area was close to the place where Haughey's yacht had been wrecked in August 1986.

'We received a call to say the EPIRB had activated on a vessel called *St Gervaise* 35 to 40 miles south-east of Baltimore,' Cotter said. At that time, it took several satellites to confirm the accuracy of an EPIRB position, he added.

'We made a line from Fastnet to Mizen, and as soon as we got to Mizen, we could smell diesel. By then, the satellites had pinpointed that location. There was no trace of the four crew on board. Just diesel on the water, a few fish boxes and the EPIRB.'

The bodies of two of the crew – Timothy Angland (30) from Mayfield, Cork, and Kieran Harrington (18) from Castletownbere – were found, but the bodies of skipper Gary Kane (30) from Donegal town and Jacques Biger (36) from Brittany, France, had still not been located when the official investigation was published in 2003.

'It has a very sobering effect, even when we might expect it,' Cotter said of the impact on the lifeboat crews. 'When you go out, and communication is not being made with a vessel, you come to the conclusion quite quickly that is serious. And if it is someone you know, and maybe chatted to recently on the pier, that makes it all the worse. During my time on the lifeboat, over fifty people in our area lost their lives.'

On one occasion, in July 2007, when the Baltimore crew responded to a report of a person missing at sea near Mizen Head, the man they were tasked to save managed to get himself ashore, but the crew did pick up an interesting cargo. Cotter recalled:

> It was early afternoon, and as we rounded Mizen into Dunlough Bay we could see these bales in the water, and a helicopter winchman trying to lift them – each weighing about 25 kg. We are trained in retrieving from the water, so we decided to give it a try and got 55 bales of 25 kg each within half an hour or forty-five minutes.
>
> We thought it was cannabis, but it was cocaine. We filled up the lifeboat survivor's cabin with the bales, arrived into Baltimore and we were pulling the boat into the boathouse when we were met by fellas with sub-machine guns and all sorts of stuff … the gardaí and navy. They unloaded bales, took them downstairs, loaded up a van and were ready to leave when someone said, 'What about the bale under the stairs!'
>
> It was something we decided ourselves to do, to retrieve these bales, because if they were left there every criminal in the country would be down. So it was a service to society. I got a phone call from senior RNLI management to say that was not what we were really into, but then the RNLI chief executive wrote to congratulate us for getting drugs off the street …

As for the man we were meant to be looking for, he got ashore, walked 3 or 4 miles to Crookhaven, and travelled by vehicle from there to Rosslare and on the ferry to Wales. A number of years later, he was arrested in Britain.

On the evening of 15 August 2011, Cotter was out on the lifeboat with photographer Nigel Millard, who had been commissioned by the RNLI to take photos of the crew at sea. The Fastnet yacht race was in full swing and some of the crew were keen to watch the contestants sail around the Fastnet lighthouse.

'We were getting ready to get back to Baltimore when we got the call to say a personal bleeper had activated and was registered to the secretary of a company. We proceeded to the area, and couldn't see anything,' Cotter recalled:

Then one of our lads saw a light, and it was a crew on an upturned hull of a maxi yacht, and they had a little flash lamp signalling they were in difficulty. It was quite bright, but they were lucky that it was an LED light that gave out very sharp light.

They told us there were sixteen on the hull and five missing. We were heading into the weather, and no one ever drifts into the weather – so if you are in the water, the chances are you are drifting faster than the boat ...

So we took them off the hull, and we worked with a Baltimore dive company vessel, Aquaventures, which was also in the area.

The lifeboat was then supplied with new information on the drift pattern via Valentia Coast Guard, using software known as SARMAP supplied by Clare-based meteorological company Nowcasting. Cotter continued the story:

Within a very short time, we were able to find five people in the water and take them out. One of the five had been in the US Navy for over twenty years and knew what to do, and knew the chances of being found were greater if all five kept together and tied themselves to each other.

Wendy Touton, partner of the owner of the *Rambler 100*, George David, had been thrown straight into the water when the canting keel snapped. David was with her, and several of the group on the hull joined them to help save them, essentially.

The boat had been doing 20 to 25 knots, and another hour or two in the water and their chances would have been very slim, even though they were wearing personal flotation devices. Wendy was very dehydrated, and very hypothermic, and so the helicopter flew her to Tralee hospital. They thought for a while that she might not make it.

It transpired that the yacht's own satellite beacons did not activate until some ten hours after the capsize, but a personal EPIRB worn by one of the twenty-one crew alerted Scottish and Irish rescue agencies.

Even in a force 10 gale, Cotter never worried when he was on the lifeboat. 'We would travel to Schull from Cape Clear for gas and fuel with my father in a 26-foot [7.9-metre] boat, and coming over the Calves we would have water coming over the rail and I got used to that …' His first posting was the Watson class *Sarah Tilson*, at 14 metres (46 feet) with two engines and an open cockpit aft, whereas the vessel responding to the *Japonica* was the 900-horsepower Tyne class *Hilda Jarrett*, which was completely enclosed and self-righting.

One August night, he thinks it was 2000 or 2001, Cotter got a phone call from a man who told him he was out walking near Baltimore's Napoleonic-era signal tower when he saw a glimmer of a light at sea. Cotter phoned the station and the lifeboat launched to check it out. They found a family of four drifting out to sea, who had used a cigarette lighter to try to get the attention of someone on shore. The mother and daughter subsequently ran a mini marathon to raise funds for the RNLI.

This incident illustrates the 'sea sense' of both the coastal community and the crew, Cotter said – a community which understood perfectly when his shop closed and a notice on the door read 'out on the lifeboat'.[5]

In December 2020 – the year after Baltimore station marked its centenary – Cotter retired from the position of coxswain after forty-five years. Ronnie Carthy, a volunteer for almost thirty years, also retired. In one of many tributes, Baltimore station chairman Declan Tiernan said that 'Kieran Cotter is not only a good leader but also brings luck with him.'

'Improvements in the RNLI vessels are massive, and so you would have great confidence in the boat and in the crew – and we had a particularly great crew in Baltimore, with fishing or merchant navy or sailing experience,' Cotter said. 'Today there are fewer fishermen – historically lifeboat crew were fishermen or small farmers who fished in summer – but the training today compensates for that, and boats now all have the most up-to-date navigational equipment.

'Education is the biggest obstacle to recruiting lifeboat crew, as young people are educated to leave their local area.'

***

Coast Guard winchman Peter Leonard has a number of state marine awards to his name. He was recognised for his role in the helicopter 'near miss' when rescuing the crew of the *Dunboy* fishing vessel off Slyne Head, County Galway in December 1993.[6] With Captain David Courtney and colleagues Mike Shaw and Noel Donnelly, he was also decorated for the rescue of three crew from the French fishing vessel *An-Orient*, some 87 nautical miles west of Loop Head, County Clare in October 2000. And he was recognised for his skill and bravery in saving the life of a man at the top of a 300-foot crane at Limerick docks in March 2005.

One memorable tasking of his was to the Aran island of Inis Oírr on 17 March 1996. Mairéad ní Fhlatharta was in labour with her fourth child. Two nurses travelled with her and her husband Mícheál in the helicopter on the short crossing to the hospital in Galway. Baby Sorcha was born in the back of the helicopter, as Captain Al Lockey flew east. 'We were about halfway across,' Leonard remembered. 'One of the nurses was a midwife, so we just helped out as best we could with towels and things.'

The family didn't want any publicity at the time, but it was the first mission of its type in Irish air-sea rescue. 'The helicopter crew were great, and it was a sort of a distraction,' Mairéad said later. 'I really didn't have time to think about the pain. And I was back home in two days.'[7]

There was an audience – and a large one at that – for another rescue in which Leonard was involved, on the night of 2 February 2002, when an Irish-registered fishing vessel, the *Celestial Dawn*, ran aground while leaving Dingle harbour, County Kerry, in a force 7 south-westerly gale.

The vessel had ten crew on board. Valentia Coast Guard scrambled the Sikorsky S-61 at Shannon, the Valentia lifeboat and the Dingle Coast Guard unit, while local boats also responded.

'It wasn't the heaviest of seas, but there was a big one running,' Captain Derek Nequest, pilot of the Sikorsky tasked to assist, remembered.[8] His co-pilot was Captain Mark Kelly, while John Manning was on the winch with Leonard. As the Sikorsky flew over, the local coast and cliff rescue unit illuminated the area. The crew, some wearing life jackets, could be seen clinging to the portside rails, with waves smashing over the moving wreck.

Journalist Ted Creedon had been among the first to raise the alarm after several red flares were spotted near the eastern entrance to the harbour. He later wrote in his account for *The Kerryman*:

'The first thing that struck us was the stench of diesel fumes on the wind.' He described how he and his daughter Siún, with Dingle fire brigade chief Jimmy Bambury, set out across the cliffs to the lighthouse and spotted the *Celestial Dawn* half submerged and lying to starboard some 15 metres below.[9] Creedon's account continued:

> The vessel was being battered against the rocks on either side of her. Sometimes the swell lifted her high in the air and she bucked like some metal monster, then settled again for a few moments. When this happened the frightened men fought desperately to hold on to the railings. We wondered how long they could survive that.
>
> The approach was too risky for the Dingle Coast Guard rescue boat, and local fishermen, watching from the cliff, feared that the Spanish crew might try something drastic – a situation compounded by noise and language difficulties. Dingle harbourmaster Lieutenant Commander Brian Farrell confirmed that a helicopter was en route.
>
> Valentia lifeboat arrived just after 8 p.m. and her very presence must have brought vital psychological relief and hope to the fishermen below, as it did to those of us who were helpless observers on the cliff above.
>
> There was a whoosh as she fired a flare over the scene. When it burst, an eerie pinkish light lit up the whole area from the lighthouse to the Towereen Bawn on the other side of the harbour's mouth. This allowed the lifeboat crew to appraise the whole situation. Then she switched on her powerful searchlights and trained them on the *Celestial Dawn*.
>
> The trawler's life rafts floated between the vessel and the rocks. There was no escape that way, there was no access to the cliff and she was now sinking deeper into the sea. The men continued to cling to the bucking vessel as the waves broke over them. One man was seen to throw up; he may have swallowed sea water and diesel. We were asked to count

the crew; and when it was certain that there were ten men on board we knew that none had been lost. The lifeboat and the local Coast Guard unit tried to get additional life jackets to the stricken crew but encountered problems.

Creedon described the arrival of the Shannon-based helicopter, with rotors whipping up a 'storm of spray':

After a few minutes, winchman Peter Leonard was lowered towards the trawler. We wondered if he'd make it or would he be battered against the vessel's hull in the wind and waves. We probably forgot for a moment that these rescue crews are highly trained and vastly experienced. Any doubts we had were immediately dispelled because the winchman had no sooner landed safely on the hull than he had securely harnessed one fisherman and both were hoisted to the Sikorsky.

We watched in admiration as he repeated the exercise and one after another the crewmen were lifted to safety while the helicopter remained rock steady in the buffeting winds over the trawler. The roar of her engines drowned out every other sound. I looked along the line of faces on either side of me. All were transfixed by the scene below. I noticed one young girl, perhaps a fisherman's daughter, with both her hands pressed palms together under her chin. The light from the rescue operation reflected on her face. She was praying silently.

One crewman seemed reluctant to leave. He may have been more terrified than the others or perhaps he was too cold to move. The winchman appeared to force the man's hands from the railings before lifting him clear of the vessel. The ten men were rescued in less than 15 minutes. Most of those watching had seen rescue exercises in the past but nothing like this. This was the real thing – a life-and-

death drama being played out before our eyes. It may have
been a routine exercise for the Coast Guard. To those of us
watching from the cliffs, it was a remarkable demonstration
of training, skill, courage and experience …

As the helicopter rose and swung away with her precious
cargo I felt like applauding, my faith in the rescue services
fully affirmed. I told my daughter about the girl I had seen
praying. 'I was praying too, Dad,' she replied. We headed
home across the cliffs as the lights of the Valentia lifeboat
disappeared into the blackness of Dingle Bay.

'I took up one fisherman at a time because of the conditions,'
Leonard said, recalling how one man refused to let go of the guard
rail. 'Myself and one of his colleagues had to prise his hands off
the rail and get the winch strop around him. One of his colleagues
was shouting in Spanish, but he just didn't want to move.'[10] The
helicopter flew the traumatised crew to Kerry Airport.

'There are very few rescues where you can say you have definitely
saved ten lives,' Nequest said. 'It would have been very difficult, if
not impossible, to get them all off by boat in those conditions, and
if there had been an attempt by boat a couple of lives might have
been lost. That's one situation where the helicopter is ideal.'[11]

The Sikorsky captain and crew were awarded a letter of
appreciation for meritorious service at an award ceremony hosted
by the minister for the marine later that year. Peter Leonard was
conferred with the Michael Heffernan silver medal for marine
gallantry, for 'extreme courage' and his willingness to put his own
life at risk to save others.

***

The Celestial Dawn had all but faded from memory when another
fishing vessel ran aground on the south-west coast, prompting one
of the longest search and recovery efforts for several years.

'I do think there's a special code among fishing communities around the coastline, because it is a very difficult kind of life. It's very dangerous. It's a place where people struggle to make a living, because you have to leave home and be gone for a long number of days,' Caitlín Uí Aodha says. 'When you go sea, all you have is the next boat to you, really, for days.'[12]

Uí Aodha's comments come from experience, having qualified as a skipper and become the first woman to be awarded a Bord Iascaigh Mhara grant for a fishing vessel. The Helvick woman continued her career in fishing ashore after she married, while rearing a family of five children.

Her husband, Michael Hayes (52), an experienced skipper, and his four crew were just ten minutes short of tying up in the west Cork harbour of Union Hall on 15 January 2012 when their 21-metre steel-hulled boat ran up on rocks near Adam's Island, at the entrance to Glandore harbour. Hayes and four of his five crew lost their lives – Kevin Kershaw (21) and three Egyptian nationals, Wael Mohamed (35), Attaia Shaban (26) and Saied Ali Eldin (22). The other member of the crew, Wael's brother, Abdelbaky Mohamed (44), was located alive by Toe Head Coast Guard boat in a small cove outside Long Point.

Coast Guard helicopters from Shannon and Waterford, RNLI lifeboats from Baltimore and Courtmacsherry, Coast Guard shore units from Toe Head, Castlefreke and Glandore, Civil Defence teams and hundreds of volunteers from west Cork and beyond took part in the three-week search and recovery operation, along with Naval Service and garda divers.

John Kearney of West Cork Underwater Search and Rescue helped to co-ordinate the civilian diver effort. The search was due to wind down after three weeks, but such was the level of community response – with a marquee for the families at the quay providing refreshments – that it was extended. The body of Michael Hayes was found on the twenty-fifth day and Kearney located Saied Ali Eldin's body two days later, on 10 February.

The subsequent inquest heard harrowing details of how the vessel's VHF radio wasn't working and how Kevin Kershaw made two emergency telephone calls on his mobile phone. However, the two calls were received by two different centres, handled by two different operators, and relayed to Bandon Garda Station and the Irish Coast Guard respectively. A review of the emergency call system by transport minister Leo Varadkar recommended, among a number of changes, that all water-based calls be relayed directly to the Coast Guard.

**

Lifeboat crews on the south Irish coast have a long history of valorous rescues. Several of the Courtmacsherry station's six RNLI medals date back to the early 1840s, when the station was founded. Their 11-metre (37-foot) lifeboat *Kezia Gwilt* participated in the *Lusitania* rescue effort, after it sank in seventeen minutes with the loss of 1,198 lives off the Old Head of Kinsale on 7 May 1915. Second coxswain Daniel O'Dwyer was awarded a bronze medal and his crew's role was acknowledged by the RNLI for rescuing three people from the yacht *Supertaff* in storm-force 10 south-westerly winds on 24 October 1998.

On 24 July 2013, the Courtmacsherry crew joined the Kinsale, Ballycotton and Crosshaven lifeboats when a 42-metre Dutch sail training vessel, the *Astrid*, with thirty young crew on board, ran aground near west Cork's Sovereign islands after losing engine power. The ship had been en route to Cherbourg in France and had joined a flotilla which was heading for Kinsale.

The alert was raised at around midday, and Valentia Coast Guard tasked the Shannon and Waterford rescue helicopters, the four lifeboats and Coast Guard shore teams from Old Head and Oysterhaven. The Kinsale crew of Liam O'Connell, Nick Searls and James Grennan were first on the scene. When the Courtmacsherry lifeboat arrived at 12.35 p.m., all thirty crew and trainees from the

Astrid were in life rafts in a 4-metre swell in force 4–5 southerly winds. Some eighteen of them were taken on board the lifeboat, and twelve were taken on by the locally owned training yacht *Spirit of Oysterhaven*. All were landed safely ashore at Kinsale.

The Cork major emergency plan was activated, and a fleet of five ambulances and medical teams from Cork University Hospital were on the Kinsale quay when the rescued crew and trainees came ashore. Within hours, the *Astrid* had begun to break up and sink in the heavy swell.

On 10 April 2016, Nick Searls was on the helm of the Kinsale lifeboat when it was tasked to assist a 20-metre beam trawler, the *Sean Anthony*, which had lost power when returning from a fishing trip. With three Portuguese fishermen on board, it was forced onto the rocks at Money Point, at the entrance to Kinsale harbour, at about 6 p.m.

Three-metre-high waves were breaking over the fishing vessel's deck when the lifeboat dropped anchor and manoeuvred to within feet of the stricken hull – just seventeen minutes after a 'Mayday' had been issued by the skipper. This allowed the three fishermen, all wearing life jackets, to jump into the water and swim to the lifeboat crew. The community involvement didn't end there, as RNLI volunteers issued an appeal for clothing and shoes for the three crew, who had lost all their personal belongings. The Kinsale station received several offers of accommodation for the men. A few months later, Searls and colleagues Jim Grennan and Matthew Teehan received a state marine award.

On 20 August 2016, Valentia Coast Guard radio requested assistance from Castletownbere lifeboat and a Coast Guard helicopter for an 8-metre yacht in difficulties 45 miles south of Mizen Head in west Cork. A solo sailor in his sixties had left the Azores in early August and had hit severe weather. He had been in regular radio contact with Valentia Coast Guard until his VHF radio was washed overboard. He activated an EPIRB to identify his location, raise the alarm and seek help.

Coxswain Brian O'Driscoll launched at 8 a.m. and located the sailor at 10.40 a.m., some 50 miles south-west of Castletownbere in force 8–9 winds. A 9-metre (30-foot) swell made it extremely hazardous to approach the yacht, which had lost its mast, and take it in tow, but the Castletownbere crew managed to do so. Once the tow was established, the crew became concerned about the sailor's condition and took him on board. It was 8.30 p.m. when the lifeboat returned to port – after twelve and a half hours at sea.

'Only for the lifeboat, things would have ended up very badly today,' the sailor said, paying tribute to the Castletownbere crew.[13]

In October 2018, the Castletownbere station – which was established in 1997 largely through the tireless work and fundraising of Sheila O'Driscoll, Brian's mother – undertook a rescue which earned its crew RNLI awards. A 25-metre fishing vessel, *Clodagh Ó*, with six crew on board, lost all power after its propeller fouled in fishing gear near the Piper Rocks, south-west of the harbour entrance. Coxswain Dean Hegarty launched in a force 9 gale, with driving rain and heavy squalls. It was only Hegarty's second shout as coxswain, having been taken on just five weeks before.

Wisely, he decided to take the vessel in tow, rather than try to take the crew off in such hazardous conditions at night. It took forty-five minutes to steam a quarter of a mile, and two tugboats, close by when the 'Mayday' was issued, escorted them into the harbour.

Hegarty was awarded a bronze medal for gallantry by the RNLI, while framed letters of thanks from the RNLI chairman were issued to lifeboat mechanic Martin O'Donoghue and volunteer crew Seamus Harrington, John Paul Downey and David Fenton, as well as deputy launching authority Michael Martin Sullivan.[14]

***

When Italian-born Lorenzo Cubeddu set out for a short wind-surfing spin off his local beach in north Kerry one November afternoon, he met an angler he knew on the strand and they had a chat about the weather. Farther up the beach, Lorenzo's wife, Amanda, was struck by the image of two experienced men of the sea chatting near the Atlantic shoreline and took a photograph. Some time later, she remarked that this might have been the last photo she had of him alive.

Lorenzo had moved to Ireland from Sardinia in 1998, drawn by his love of sailing, windsurfing and diving. He trained as an RNLI lifeguard, windsurfing and dinghy instructor, and participated in ocean-going sailing. After he met Amanda, they settled in Inch East in Kerry, and he took a job at the SuperValu in Ballybunion.

On that particular day, 11 November 2018, he had spent an hour checking the sea state before heading out from Ballybunion beach around 3 p.m. The wind was steady and constant, with good sunny periods, he remembered. After a while, the wind was on and off, making it difficult to stay upwind – especially with the push of the incoming tide and the chop and swells. The leeway or sideways drifting prevented him from getting back to shore, but he had found himself in these conditions before and was always able to make it back to his point of launching:

> So I kept trying to make ground upwind for a while, only to realise that I had drifted too far from the beach and was facing the cliffs every time I sailed back. I wanted to avoid being crashed onto them by the push of the tide and waves, and to give myself a good, safe distance from the cliffs with time to think about my next move before darkness arrived.[15]

However, the wind then dropped completely, leaving him stranded in the middle of the bay, lying on his board with daylight fading:

> I knew I could not sail back, so I had to make a decision: drop the rig and try to paddle back to land? Or stay with

the board and hopefully drift to safety? Where I was at that moment, with the fading light, the large swells and my distance from land, I was too far to be seen by anyone.

Lorenzo knew that if he panicked, he would not make it at all. He detached the sail, knowing it could have dragged him in the water like an anchor. 'It was a hard decision, but I had no choice, so I lay on my stomach on the board.'

However, the tide was too strong to make headway. Darkness was closing in, and he began to lose his bearings. 'We have a saying in Italy: "If you want to learn to pray, go to sea," and in that moment it made perfect sense to me,' Lorenzo said. 'I keep a very simple but strong faith. So I was praying a lot, and I realised later that everyone I knew – and all of Ballybunion and beyond – was praying for me, which was very humbling.'

Lorenzo 'worked to hold a calm mindset, knew I was in survival mode, and felt very peaceful'. 'It was not natural but supernatural. It was also very sad as I thought of my wife. I did not feel ready to leave her ... I imagined the reaction of the people at my funeral.'

Bioluminescent plankton lights flickered over his board, and he conversed with the tiny organisms as he felt they represented 'life and company ... a little miracle of light in the darkness'. The weather was changing, the wind was picking up and there was a 4-metre swell on the Fenit side of the bay. Still lying on his stomach, with his hands up at the bow and trying not to swallow the sea water which was splashing over his head, he had to close his eyes to protect them from the stinging spray and the rain. Breathing methods he had practised at home began to help.

'After what felt like a long time, I started to feel the cold and the first symptoms of hypothermia kicked in. Even with the help of the neoprene wetsuit, boots and beanie hat, I was freezing.'

Lorenzo knew his position on the board was not helping, as half of his body was in the water, and he was seasick a few times.

'If you think of being in the same position for so many hours, it was not surprising.'

Then, he heard a noise – a distinctive, comforting roar in the sky – and spotted the searchlight of a Coast Guard helicopter. It flew past and disappeared into the distance. He knew he wasn't quite in range for the helicopter's 'Nightsun' light or its thermal imaging camera. Though the crew hadn't seen him, and he knew he was just a tiny speck in a black ocean, he drew great comfort from the knowledge that a search had begun. It gave him 'new strength and hope' and pushed him 'harder to survive'.

Back on shore, Lorenzo's wife, Amanda, had rung him a few times, but got no answer. Normally, they would have a lot of phone contact. She had an unsettled feeling. 'Then I got the phone call that you never want to get, and no one ever wants to make: confirmation from Lorenzo's boss Cormac Cahill in SuperValu that Lorenzo was missing at sea, and a search was underway,' Amanda said.

Amanda fell to the floor in a terrified physical state. Her friends called to the house and picked her up to drive her to the sea to look for her husband. She recalled it was 'excruciating, as all in the car knew they were facing hours of horror'.

The first thing she remembered noticing was how dark it was as she stared out into what seemed like an abyss. She was reassured by the lights of the rescue service trucks and the garda car and knew they would do everything they could to find him. She could hear the Coast Guard helicopter and its large searchlights gave her hope. She remembered how her shock turned to gratitude, as she saw how the cliff was lined with people from Ballybunion. 'There many others also, and I couldn't believe they were there for us – people kneeled to pray, words of firm encouragement, and I felt very humbled,' she said.

Cormac, Lorenzo's boss, offered Angela the sort of support she will never forget, both then and in the days after. 'When my energy was flagging, Cormac kept showing me Lorenzo's details on WhatsApp – it said, "never give up, never surrender". All our friends stood shoulder to shoulder with me, some just far enough away to give me space but close enough so I could read their eyes.'

She said the Garda Síochána also kept a very close eye on her, ensuring she sat in the front of the squad car. She joked with them that this was her first time in custody. Several times, she tried to get out of the car near the edge of the cliffs to call his name, believing he might possibly hear her. One friend said very firmly, 'It will be alright, I'm sure that fella has ended up in Clare!'

Waves of panic alternated with waves of hope, every minute seemed like an hour, and Amanda remembered a sense of being in an unbearable nightmare. At the same time, people who had never met him were now abseiling down cliffs, searching beaches and fields, praying in the local church, and supplying sandwiches and coffee, and she felt sure that Lorenzo could 'feel this outpouring of love on the water'.

At 9.30 p.m., with no word still, Amanda said she decided to 'send him a prayer to rest in peace, in case he needed that from me'. A group of her friends prayed with her for his body to be found. Her thoughts turned to telling his elderly mother, his family in Italy and her own family in Dublin.

As the time passed at sea, Lorenzo fought off exhaustion and found himself saying, 'Okay, if this is it, please God don't make it last too long … make me go to sleep.' But he heard a voice in his head urging him to stay awake. His knew his only chance of survival now was to be 'pushed back to land by the current, chop and swells, hopefully without getting injured or being crashed onto the cliffs', or to make it through the night at sea.

'I felt as though I should have died several times already. So all I could do was to stay calm and strong for as long as I could.'

He suddenly heard a swishing, crashing noise that made him think he was near land or cliffs, and to his delight he was right. Being so near the coast, though, he knew he was in danger of being dashed on rocks. He had to gamble on letting go of the board to try to find his footing:

> I threw the board away with all the force I could, as it could be 'game over' if the board hit me on the head. I took one leap and landed on a ledge! Then I was faced with climbing a jagged cliff, arms nearly giving way with exhaustion. I struggled for handholds to haul myself up. Miraculously, grass at the top held my body weight.

Fortunately, he had some small protection as he was also wearing his neoprene booties for the first time in months – windsurfing is normally better in bare feet. Standing at the top of the cliff in the darkness, he had no idea where he was and there was no sign of life or lights. He was more aware of the cold now and his body was cramping up.

'The first thing I had wanted to do when I landed on the ledge was to find a place to curl up and sleep, but the voice in the back of my head kept saying: "Stay awake!"' He began to wonder if he had been better off in the ocean, as he started to trudge 'robotically between hedges, ditches, climbing over gates and fences. I even received a few shocks from electric fences!' He remembered laughing out loud and exclaiming, 'Really?!'

After a while his eyes adjusted to the dark, and he noticed a little light to his right. It came from a mobile home. A man with blue eyes and a big beard answered his knock, and his first words were a plea – 'Don't rob me!'

The man's terrified gaze then turned to one of puzzlement; he had heard a report on Clare FM radio of a missing man at sea and realised who Lorenzo was. He brought him in, put a coat around him and phoned for help, telling Lorenzo he had not charged his phone in weeks but had done so just the night before. He gave him a cup of tea from his gas fire, telling the windsurfer that he had been a fisherman for many years.

Amanda didn't want to leave the shoreline, but the gardaí wanted her to get some rest and to get warm. Though she felt a sense of guilt about going, she was taken to a friend's house nearby. 'Kindness and support' overflowed there, as well as the cups of tea which she couldn't face. The curtains were closed by a friend to protect her from seeing the heavy rain falling. Friends urged her to remain hopeful. One part of her felt he could survive, another part felt she needed to face facts.

It was shortly after 11 p.m. when two gardaí appeared in the kitchen and the room fell quiet. No one there would forget that moment.

'I presumed at first they were there to tell me that the body had been recovered – instead, they told me that he was alive in County Clare!' Amanda said. 'We were really trying to adjust our minds to what they had just said – "alive in County Clare!?" – and the place just erupted with pure joy, friends danced on the tables and I embraced the gardaí with all my strength and thanked them so much.'

Lorenzo was taken by ambulance to hospital in Limerick and still remembers the noise of the rain on the roof throughout the drive. 'The paramedics told me later that, by the time we arrived at the hospital, my body temperature had stabilised. I was kept in the hospital for three days, mainly to flush out an enzyme from my bloodstream caused by the extreme muscle effort I put in during my long ordeal at sea.'

Amanda had to deal with the media, while Lorenzo learned that the fisherman he had last talked to on Ballybunion beach had raised the alarm and that the extensive search had involved Rescue 115, the RNLI's Fenit and Kilrush lifeboats, the Coast Guard's Ballybunion cliff and sea rescue unit, and the navy vessel LÉ *Niamh*, which was in the area at the time:

> I should have died several times – I had no means of com-
> munication, I could have lost the board, I crossed shipping

lanes, could have broken some bones, or wounded myself, I could have fallen when I was climbing the cliff. Stories like that in Ballybunion don't tend to end so well. Now, I would not go out to sea without a reliable means of calling for help, in my case a personal locator beacon.

In his view, mobile phones were never designed for use in the water as sea safety devices and are not always reliable.

Lorenzo still recalls that sense of calm in the midst of his ordeal, as if nothing else was important. Later, he realised he had been washed up on land at 11 p.m. on the 'eleventh day of the eleventh month of the year'.

15

MIRACLE AT POLL NA bPÉIST

Giovanni and Riccardo Zanon have long been fans of *Father Ted*, the Channel 4 comedy series created by Graham Linehan and Arthur Mathews. In February 2019, the brothers made a short trip to Ireland for 'Tedfest', the festival devoted to the series held annually on the Aran island of Inis Mór, booking a bed and breakfast for the weekend. It was their first trip to the west of Ireland – Giovanni (29), who worked in television, had previously visited the east coast when he drove his DeLorean car over from Italy to attend a festival dedicated to the vehicles in Belfast.

Friday evening on Inis Mór was good fun, with lots of music, and the brothers photographed themselves dressed up as priests. There was nothing official on the programme on Saturday morning, 23 February, so they decided to rent bikes and cycle around the island. They visited Na Seacht dTeampaill – 'the seven churches' – a medieval pilgrimage site, and then felt they would like to have a look at Poll na bPéist – the 'wormhole' – close by, a natural limestone pool at the back of the island.

On a summer's day at low tide, the rectangular pool with its subterranean link to the Atlantic can be approached on foot or viewed from a series of ledges above. The legendary home of a 'serpent', as its name suggests, it appears still, dark, deep and almost tranquil. Swimmers have ventured in on a calm day and sub-aqua teams have explored it. Artist Dorothy Cross was inspired by what she described as the 'exquisite rectangular pool' to create a piece of opera on film in 1999.[1]

However, on storm days, or at high tide, this 'natural theatre' can change dramatically into 'primaeval chaos pitted against fundamental geometry' as author Tim Robinson put it – a boiling cauldron with sheer sides out of which no human could possibly climb.[2]

The site's reputation has grown over recent decades with the advent of online travel guides, augmented by a number of high-profile events that have taken place there. In April 2009, nine-time cliff-diving world champion Orlando Duque completed a double somersault into the pool in a two-second dive from a ledge 27 metres above. Three years later, the limestone plateau was invaded by an army of stewards, scuba divers, paramedics and a senior accident and emergency consultant – along with two helicopters on standby – for the Red Bull drinks company's cliff-diving series. The event organisers renamed it 'The Serpent's Lair', and the first of its dives there in 2012 had an audience of 700. Some of the bolts screwed into the rock still remain. At the time, the island's GP, Dr Marion Broderick, was concerned about the risks of copycat diving by non-professionals and the fact that it would 'become famous for the wrong reasons'.

Broderick was right, in that the site became a magnet even for those who weren't planning to swim there. In April 2015, 21-year-old Apu Gupta from Kolkata, India, was visiting Inis Mór with her parents. She was standing out on a ledge above Poll na bPéist and photographing the Atlantic when a large wave engulfed her, casting her some 10 metres onto rocks below. Fortunately, a Clare-based paramedic, Séamus McCarthy from Cork, and his girlfriend, Fionnuala Quigley, witnessed the incident. With other visitors, McCarthy tied an army jacket to a rucksack and passed it down to the injured girl to hoist her up.

Garda Brian O'Donnell, then based on the Aran islands, was called out to help, and the Rescue 115 helicopter from Shannon was tasked to airlift Apu to hospital in Galway where she was treated for a fractured ankle. McCarthy was subsequently recognised by Water Safety Ireland for his actions, and Garda O'Donnell circulated a video of the incident on YouTube to highlight the risks.

As Riccardo (35) remembered, the brothers had noticed that the wormhole was highlighted as a 'must see' for Aran island visitors on the internet. That Saturday was a cloudy day, marked by typical chilly February weather, with sporadic light rain as they cycled out to find it. They left their bikes where the trail ended, and followed arrows painted on rocks.[3]

As they navigated the rocky shore overlooking the Atlantic, Riccardo remembered seeing a group of people ahead of them, and a couple not too far behind. Eventually, they reached a ledge about 10 metres above the rectangular pool, which is a force of nature at any tide – but particularly on a full tide when the sea is like a cauldron, waves foaming and crashing chaotically against its sheer sides.

The brothers were transfixed by the phenomenon. The sun was shining and the limestone pavement around the wormhole was dry. Riccardo was taking some photos but felt a video might record the full force of Poll na bPéist, so he asked his younger brother to record a clip on his phone.

Although he worked in television, Giovanni wasn't in the habit of making smartphone videos. He began panning from right to left as he moved his screen from Poll na bPéist to the Atlantic just beyond. That image is still frozen in his mind. As if in a scene from a film, the seas magnified on his cellphone screen. Within a second, both he and his brother were whipped off their legs by an enormous force and enveloped in a wave which sucked the air from their lungs and the sight from their eyes.

Giovanni felt himself tumbling at speed, hitting rocks on his way down, convinced that at any second his head would be split open and he would die. Riccardo did not remember feeling the impact as he was hit by a 'big grey wall of sea', whipping him onto the pavement below where his left leg took the full weight of his fall, crushing his pelvis and shattering bones before he collapsed on his back. When he opened his eyes, he was unable to sit up and his left leg was 'floppy' and immobile. At this stage, waves were crashing in against him and he had a sense that he was about to die. He felt a wave of intense disappointment at the idea that his life was coming to a close in 'such a stupid way'.

'I felt this was not an epic way to go. I experienced an extremely fast stream of thoughts in which I suddenly realised that, given the situation I ended up in, I was never going to have a baby with Giulia, my fiancée,' Riccardo recalled. He was calling out for his brother, but the waves had dragged Giovanni about 30 metres across jagged rocks, tearing his arms, hands, legs and knees.

Giovanni tried to grab hold of something as he was swept towards the Atlantic. For the second time, he was sure his life was ending. Somehow, although he had an intense pain in his ankle, he managed to grip a handhold and haul himself back and up, his coat ripped and his body covered in blood. Adrenaline propelled him over to Riccardo, who was lying on the rocks almost motionless. He could see his brother was very pale and losing blood, though he was conscious and 'surprisingly calm'.

They were both in extreme danger, Giovanni realised – exposed to the full might of the ocean. 'All I remember was feeling the intense raw power of nature – the "worm hole" suddenly seemed ten times bigger, the cliffs above enormous, as if higher than a cathedral, and both of us so small and exposed.' He tried to move Riccardo, to drag him to a safer position under the cliff edge. However, the pain was too much and he was forced to stop after a couple of metres. He remembered:

Riccardo was anchored to the ground and could only see the sky, so he really had no sense of how vulnerable we were. I remember strange thoughts going through my head, wondering why they didn't have a ladder … as if there should be such a thing there!

The waves were constantly rising and crashing over, and there was nothing we could do but shout and roar and hope someone could hear us. I had lost my phone and my glasses, and I tried to use my brother's phone but there was no signal.

I didn't really have an idea of how long. But after about twenty minutes of this feeling we were just going to be swept away, I remember my brother telling me that he saw someone. I thought he was dreaming. It was true, someone had seen us.

Riccardo had seen the face of a young man with a slight beard peering over the edge and had called out to him, not sure if he could be heard over the sound of the sea. The man smiled and gestured as if to say all would be 'okay'.

'And then he disappeared, and I really wasn't sure because my own mobile phone was working but it had no signal – I had already tried calling the emergency 112,' Riccardo said:

> So after a while it seemed a bit hopeless, and I was wondering if the guy had understood the gravity of the situation, and maybe his phone also had no signal. And Giovanni was leaning with his back right in against the rock under the ledge, so he had only seen me – because we heard afterwards that the report was about help being needed for one man with a broken leg.
>
> And as I lay there, I had the feeling of my life as an enjoyable movie or TV series that finishes earlier than expected and with quite a disappointing ending – as if the director was in a rush to get the series over.

The helicopter noise was very distinctive and, as Giovanni recalled, 'one of the best sounds I have ever heard in my life'. Riccardo had his head on a rock beside him, shivering with cold and shock, and was beginning to lose consciousness.

'I believed we were just going to die here slowly and so I fell asleep, and then I woke up and saw the underside of the aircraft and the red and white colours, and now I felt we were going to make it after all,' Riccardo said.

Giovanni had already been

triggered by this sound of the approaching helicopter into feeling more positive, feeling maybe we could do it, we could survive.

I could not see without my glasses, but I managed to see the colours of red and white and the writing 'rescue' and knew this was not a leisure helicopter. It was like Jesus to me. We waved our hands because we thought that maybe it wasn't there looking for us …

Never will I be able to find the words to describe the mixture of feelings and wide span of emotions I had in that forty-five-minute event, when I went from desperation to strength and back to desperation. Even now, when I speak of it, it is as if I am describing a movie scene and I am a character but it didn't actually happen to me – perhaps it is the mind's way of dealing with it.

Fortunately for the brothers, the Shannon-based Rescue 115 was already in the air when the alert was relayed from Mill Street Garda Station in Galway to Valentia Coast Guard. It had been tasked to an incident in Doolin, County Clare, and was then stood down – but was still flying when it received the call.

'Then this man was winched down towards us, and I could remember his face so clearly for the next month because he had become the most important person in my life. He asked me a bit about the incident, but I can't remember much then, except that a stretcher was winched down for my brother,' Giovanni said.

Riccardo remembered that winchman Philip Wrenn gave them both an inhaler to help ease the pain they were in. 'And Phil was preparing to put me in a stretcher, but luckily he had not actually done that, when a wave came and hit all three of us and the stretcher ended up in the wormhole – and that could have been with me tied into it.'

'I remember Phil grabbing me and pushing his knee on my brother to weigh him down. At that point, I was not scared anymore, as there was this big man that knew his job. The wave washed the stretcher into the wormhole, and Phil's helmet was knocked off,' Giovanni said.

Aran island-based Garda Gerry Dunne had been alerted by the emergency call, and both he and local Coast Guard unit member Mairtín Ó Flaithearta, along with Rónán Mac Giollapháraic, a member of the RNLI Aran Island lifeboat crew, had rushed to the location. As an islander and guide at the Office of Public Works monument site on Dún Aengus, Mac Giollapháraic was very familiar with sea conditions around Poll na bPéist. The three men witnessed the wave sweeping over Wrenn and the two brothers and saw the stretcher being tossed into Poll na bPéist – realising that if that same wave had hit seconds later, one of the brothers could have been in the stretcher.

Following this, Giovanni recalled:

> The ingenious part of it all was that Phil was trying to improvise as he knew it was too risky and there was no time for another stretcher. He said everyone must hug and we would go up in the winch together. He secured us both and it was exactly what needed to be done – a calculated risk.
>
> So there I am going up in the air and my brother is screaming in pain and this big man is holding on to us both, and I could see the wormhole getting smaller and I felt like I am flying and I am leaving this danger behind, and

I could see the helicopter getting closer. I made one athletic move to get into the aircraft and Ciaran McHugh, who was working with Phil, helped to get my brother on board.

Riccardo did not remember much except the view of Poll na bPéist from above and the sense that the sun was shining as he briefly opened his eyes on the way up. The intense pain he was in had him writhing in agony.

'I don't recall, but maybe I was trying to release myself from the wire, and that would have made it very difficult for Phil,' he said. 'Then I was in the helicopter and Ciaran McHugh put a thermal blanket over me, and I lost consciousness.'

'They cut our clothes apart to check if we had injuries and gave us a thermal cover, because we were cold and we had been virtually in the water and on cold rock for over forty minutes,' Giovanni said:

My first thought then was that they would kill me at work as we were only meant to be away for the weekend … and then I thought perhaps they would forgive me as I had escaped death.

My brother had emergency surgery and was then in intensive care, but after some hours we were side by side in beds in the same ward in Galway. I was kept for two weeks in hospital in Galway and then left in a wheelchair as I had an ankle injury and lots of bruising, but my brother was in for a lot longer and had to have specialised treatment in Tallaght Hospital in Dublin.

I never noticed how cool it was to drive or to play golf or to walk for the first time until I was able to do that again. My brother had very serious injuries. Mine were less physical and more psychological.

After some months, I searched for a name and found Phil and contacted him. He was very surprised because he said he was just doing a job and a lot of the time the helicopter crews don't hear from people afterwards.

Then Darina Clancy contacted us as part of the documentary on the Coast Guard she was working on, and so the film crew flew Phil and Ciaran over to meet us and that was wonderful. What Phil did for us was not in any manual and I wanted to tell him that.

Riccardo had a long road ahead of him. He had to have an Ilizarov external frame installed, a device used by orthopaedic surgeons to lengthen or reshape bone, and had surgery on his tibia to help it grow back. He was still on crutches when the reunion took place with Wrenn and McHugh for the Midas Productions Irish Coast Guard documentary for TG4 television's *Tabú* series.[4]

Riccardo felt forever grateful to all the nursing and medical staff in Ireland and Italy who helped him recover, including orthopaedic consultant Ken Kaar's team at St Finbar's ward in University Hospital, Galway; Professor Brendan O'Daly at Tallaght Hospital in Dublin; and Dr Cosimo Salfi and Dr Corrado D'Antimo of the orthopaedics department at Belluno Hospital.

'The Irish doctors took very good care of me in the first and most critical moments, whereas the Italian doctors had me as a patient for almost two years and performed a complex tibia reconstruction that literally saved my leg,' he said.

In the documentary, broadcast in spring 2020, winch operator McHugh described how the Sikorsky S-92 helicopter crew reacted when Wrenn and the two Zanon brothers were almost washed away. 'We went off into a holding pattern … then we seen this set of waves coming … offshore from about a mile away,' McHugh told *Tabú*. 'It was like you left someone off the side of the road to wait for the bus and then the bus comes and slaps them.'

In 2021, Wrenn was conferred with the Billy Deacon Award. When Wrenn received the award in early 2021, Minister of State for Transport Hildegarde Naughton took the opportunity to congratulate him for his role in the Poll na bPéist rescue. She said Wrenn had demonstrated 'a level of professionalism and commitment that I have no doubt is a great source of pride not alone to his immediate family but to anybody who is involved with search and rescue'. She also noted that the award not only honoured him but also the 'extraordinary work of our Coast Guard'.[5]

'I am kind of glad in a way of the experience, as in how I reacted to it, because the good things about this event are far superior to the bad,' Giovanni observed later. 'Phil won a prize, we were in a documentary, and I feel very differently about life. I wish there was a way for people to change as I did without having to have this type of bad experience, but perhaps it is the actual threat of death that makes us change.'

Some two-and-a-half years after their terrifying experience, the Italian brothers, their parents and Riccardo's girlfriend, Giulia, took a trip to Ireland, and visited Inis Mór with Phil Wrenn. It was an August day with bright sunshine when they returned to Poll na bPéist. The sea was relatively benign, the wormhole was tranquil, and it was hard to imagine how different it had been on that morning in February 2019.

'For a couple of years, I used to think about the accident daily, especially in the shower when I had water on my face or at night or when it rained and a passing car splashed me,' Giovanni said. A musician, he recorded an album with friends during the pandemic, which included a composition he wrote entitled 'Wormhole'.

'I brought the album out on vinyl and CD, and framed the vinyl cover with an artistic image of the Wormhole on my wall. I felt it was a way of turning something deadly into something which makes me happy,' he explained. 'Music is like another language, and the record was dedicated to this wild and beautiful place, and not the incident, which was a force of nature.'

Sitting out on the limestone with his brother and family, he was glad his parents did not have a chance to witness what it had been like on that winter's day. Wrenn pointed out the various locations, and Giovanni was shocked to see how far they had both fallen, in an arc due to the force of the sea, and how far he had been dragged afterwards.

He found a few moments to sit listening to his own composition through headphones above Poll na bPéist. 'It was very special. It helped me to turn the page.'

The brothers also had one unresolved puzzle – who to thank for raising the alarm in the first place. Riccardo was sure he remembered the face that had looked down on him, smiling and giving a thumbs-up sign. However, initial inquiries did not bear fruit, apart from establishing it was not an islander. Garda Dunne had kept the name though, and permission was sought by this author to make contact in spring 2021.

Shaun O'Brien from Strokestown, County Roscommon, had also wondered about what happened after he had raised the alarm. 'I wasn't out on Inis Mór for the Father Ted festival, though I do love the series!' he laughed, when contacted, continuing:

> My girlfriend, Shruti Shukla, originally from India, had never been outside Dublin where we both live. I had been to the Aran islands with my dad, and just really thought it would be somewhere she would see a different Ireland.
>
> We hired bikes that morning, and headed for Poll na bPéist, and almost got lost on the way. We eventually made it and we were at the top of the cliff, but Shruti told me it looked far too dangerous to go down to the lower ledge.
>
> I had seen the Red Bull cliff diving contest at Poll na bPéist online, and just felt we had come this far, and I had to see it. So she stayed up and I went down lower by myself. I could hear someone shouting 'help' as I got closer, and I peered over, saw a man lying there and he told me he had fallen.
>
> I tried my phone but there was no reception, so I went back up to the top of the cliff and dialled the emergency

number. I was only on the phone for a few minutes and they were very efficient. They asked me to go back down and keep an eye on the casualty, which I did, and ten to fifteen minutes later the helicopter came.

The conditions were bad. At first, the casualty – because I saw only one at first – was getting sprayed, but then the sea was insane by the time the helicopter arrived. In the meantime, two guys came on foot from across the cliff and were shouting down to say help was on the way …

I stayed with my girlfriend and we watched as the winchman came down and secured two men, and then this wave came up and over and hit them all. I was thinking the worst, but the winchman managed to hold onto them. I remember one of the two guys took my number – I didn't realise he was a garda – and that was it.[6]

The Italian brothers made contact with O'Brien on their trip back to Ireland; without him, and his decision to ignore his girlfriend's warning, they knew things could have been very different.

16

AMBULANCE WITH WINGS

Picking stones from the ground is never the most stimulating job, but it is a rite of passage for any teenager living on a farm. Glyn O'Connor (15) had done it many times before, chucking rock after rock into a loader attached to a tractor as it moved slowly across the land extending down to the Blackwater river in County Waterford.

The ground was soft and muddy after recent rain. Glyn was working with his cousin Robbie, while an older brother, Cilian, waited in the car to bring him home. He had nearly finished the chore when he stumbled and fell.

His father, Alan, was up at the house in Cappoquin when Robbie rang. Sensing the urgency in his voice, Alan reached the field within two to three minutes – as did Cilian. All Glyn's sister Celyn remembered was hearing that the loader had 'rolled over' her brother's legs.

Glyn was lying on the ground, coughing up blood, when Alan arrived. Cilian remembered how his younger brother tried to stand up immediately after the accident and how he urged him to lie down and keep still. When he learned the full extent of Glyn's injuries – ribs, pelvis, lower spine and femur crushed, lungs punctured – Cilian had no idea where his brother got his strength from, or how he was able to keep talking.

Alan's brother Niall, who was attached to the local fire brigade unit in Cappoquin, was among the emergency responders first at the scene. Niall knew immediately that a helicopter was required and explained his status to the operator at the National Ambulance Service (NAS) emergency operations centre. Within minutes, an AgustaWestland 139 was airborne and flying south-east from the Air Corps Emergency Aeromedical Service (EAS) base in Athlone, County Westmeath.

Captain (now Commandant) Stephen Byrne had a sense that this was an organised response as he and his co-pilot, Captain Eugene Mohan, prepared to land. They spotted a number of garda cars and units of the fire brigade, and someone had erected a post as a navigational guide for the aircraft.

Flying with them were advance paramedic Pat Moran and airman Jamie O'Sullivan, the latter providing technical support. Moran was out of the aircraft and over to the casualty as Byrne and Mohan kept the rotors running. Within minutes, the helicopter was airborne again, with Glyn on a stretcher in the back.

There's little that Pat Moran, from County Roscommon, hasn't witnessed in over twenty years working as a paramedic. His father flew fixed-wing planes and he took out his own rotary helicopter licence in 2007. When the opportunity came to transfer from ground ambulance duty to what was then a pilot Air Corps aeromedical service in June 2012, he jumped at the chance. On that particular day in Cappoquin, he recognised colleagues from the ambulance and fire services as he alighted from the helicopter.

'It was very obvious this was a significant injury, and we were able to take him straight away by stretcher into the helicopter,' Moran said.[1]

Alan O'Connor wanted to travel with his son. Moran had developed a code with his pilots for situations where a relative might want to travel, but where the casualty's condition was critical. 'You never want to refuse, but the safety of the aircraft could be compromised if you find yourself handling both the casualty and the relative,' he explained. 'I would always advise that I had to check with the pilots on fuel levels.'

Alan was taken on board, sitting quietly by Glyn, as both Moran and O'Sullivan worked on his son. The pilots set a course for Cork University Hospital, landing twelve minutes later.

'We landed at a remote site to transfer Glyn by ambulance to hospital – a two-minute trip – and we knew he was deteriorating,' Moran said. A team of fifteen specialist medical staff awaited their arrival in the emergency department.

'We were just through the doors when Glyn went into cardiac arrest,' Moran said.

The hospital team administered CPR, bringing him back, and Moran stayed with them as he knew what drugs had already been administered.

Out in the waiting room, Alan had no idea that his son's heart had stopped beating. Some fifteen minutes after the helicopter arrived, hospital staff asked Alan if he had anyone with him. The family were all back in Cappoquin, he said.

'You need to get them up here,' he was advised and he knew he had better phone his wife, Treasa Gough, since it appeared that Glyn wasn't going to make it. As he waited for her to arrive, he received several further updates and each time it seemed a little more hopeful. Coagulants were working and 'he is still with us', Alan was told.

Glyn's mother, Karen, had died when he was only two years old; now she was being called upon in Alan's many prayers. Treasa had arrived when a doctor came out and told Alan that his son was 'still here'.

After midnight that Saturday, four doctors came out to talk to the couple and explained that they had stemmed the internal bleeding and wanted to transfer Glyn to the Mater Hospital in Dublin the following morning. The couple tried to get some sleep in the waiting room.

In the Mater the next day, Alan and Treasa met the trauma team – Dr Keith Synnott and Dr Frank Lyons – who would operate on

Glyn. It would be one of a series of surgical interventions designed to stabilise his pelvis and lower lumbar spine.

Five days after his horrific accident, Glyn was able to wiggle his toes while in intensive care. He was also talking to his father, who had not left the hospital. It was in the early stages of the Covid-19 pandemic, but Alan could think of nothing except that his son was alive and might even walk again.

At one point, Alan spoke to Jennifer O'Connell of *The Irish Times*, who was in the hospital reporting on the effects of the pandemic. 'Every day this week has been a lottery win for me. The legs were the worry, and suddenly he's moving his toes. Today, he's talking to me,' Alan said.[2]

A week later, Glyn was out of intensive care and having physiotherapy. He was alert and remembered everything. Alan believes that the Covid-19 crisis may have helped save Glyn's life, because there was no delay in the emergency services and no difficulty accessing an intensive care bed. However, as he also realised, it was the helicopter that made the real difference. A regular ambulance would have taken at least ninety minutes to get to Cork.

'When I learned that Glyn had the cardiac arrest, and that this might have happened in an ambulance on the side of a road en route to Cork if he hadn't already been flown there, I knew that we had been so lucky.'

After three weeks in intensive care and high dependency at the Mater, Glyn was transferred back to Cork University Hospital. Several months later, in September, he returned on crutches to Blackwater Community School.

Some seventeen months later, there was a slight bite to the wind as a small group of people gazed at a helicopter preparing to take off from Custume Army Barracks in Athlone. Alan had risen early for the three-hour drive from Cappoquin in County Waterford at the invitation of the Air Corps. With him were his daughter Celyn, now 16, and his two older sons Cilian, now 20, and Glyn, now 17.

There to greet them were the full crew who had flown Glyn to hospital on the day of his accident. They were just about to view the aircraft in its hangar when the crew got the call to respond to an incident somewhere in the midlands.

Glyn was having physiotherapy and had one more operation to go through but had been told that, due to his age, he would make a full recovery. Amid the friendly chat and banter about whether Glyn might join the Air Corps after his Leaving Certificate, there were some sobering exchanges about the details of the incident and how close a call it had been. The Air Corps pilots were unaware that what Alan had been told initially in hospital made him think his son wasn't going to make it.

'So you accept the injuries,' Alan recalled. 'If there was a wheelchair he had to come home in, that would have been fine. You accept anything when you are told your son is dead.'

***

The Cappoquin tasking was one of thousands undertaken by the Air Corps EAS, but, as in search and rescue, aircrews rarely come into contact with those they have assisted after the incident.

'If the alarm goes off, I am going to sprint off and will be in the air in five minutes,' Lieutenant Colonel Phil Bonner said, as he and Commandant Stephen Byrne explained, over a cup of tea in Custume Barracks, how the service was established. It was a temporary measure at first, aimed at easing a political row over a decision by the government in 2011 to close emergency services at Roscommon General Hospital.

A 2003 consultancy study, known as the Hanly report, had advised the closure as part of its recommendations on hospital reorganisation and the centralisation of full accident and emergency services. However, politicians expressed concern about the impact on patients across the west and midlands.

The year after the Hanly report, a separate feasibility study on an all-Ireland emergency medical service had been commissioned: 'Dr Cathal O'Donnell, medical director of the National Ambulance Service, wanted to do a one-year trial of a helicopter emergency medical service to see if it would work from an economic and health benefit point of view,' Bonner explained. The closure of twenty-four-hour services at Roscommon provided the opportunity.

Bonner was part of a team that established the service, working with senior Air Corps officers, including Lieutenant General Seán Clancy, who became Chief of Staff of the Defence Forces in 2021.

'I wrote a food-for-thought paper around 2011 about the capacity that we had to deliver and the need for it, and the situation with Roscommon arose around about the same time,' Clancy explained. 'As part of that, we looked at the gaps in the Monaghan, Cavan, north Mayo area, and the critical time frame to get people by ambulance to an emergency centre, primarily for significant illnesses such as STEMIs.'

STEMI is an acronym for ST-segment elevation myocardial infarction, a term cardiologists use to describe a classic heart attack. Such cases tend to be treated at Percutaneous Coronary Intervention centres, of which there are five operating on a twenty-four-hour basis and one on a nine-to-five basis in the state.

'I was asked to go to a meeting in Naas with the NAS and with Dr Cathal O'Donnell to explore what could be done. Nine months to the day almost, we launched the service,' Clancy said:

> During that period, I spent my time going to Naas, Tullamore, Portarlington, and I had an Air Corps team that included Phil Bonner and Niall Buckley looking at everything from risk assessments and location, to fuel, hangars and basic supports for the aircrews. A forty-five-minute response timeline was key, primarily focused on where ambulances by road couldn't meet that time frame.

It was also clear from the outset that it would have to be an inter-agency effort, with paramedics provided by the HSE who would be trained by the Air Corps.

'So we could bring expertise in command and control, tasking dispatch, and training advance paramedics to crew the helicopter. All the skills, expertise and competence we had we brought to bear,' Clancy said. The Air Corps team also sought advice elsewhere, including the US and Britain. 'It wasn't perfect, but it was part of an embryonic piece, and everyone was apprehensive as it was a one-year pilot scheme,' he added. It was launched by Minister for Health James Reilly and Minister for Justice and Defence Alan Shatter, with Robert Morton, then head of the NAS.

Establishing the EAS service required a degree of innovation for a military organisation that had been involved in air ambulance services since 1964. Whereas air ambulance work is a type of medical evacuation, an EAS service would require developing paramedical capability. In practical terms, Clancy cited as examples a 'health atlas', which involved overlaying the national electricity cable system onto existing maps. The military had not been on the TETRA communications system used by the gardaí and ambulance service, and this also required a degree of integration. When kitting out the aircraft – initially a Eurocopter (EC) 135 – one of Clancy's colleagues designed and built a secure case for holding gases between the seats, which was then certified.

Two weeks after the service began, the EC135 was en route from Athlone to Borrisoleigh, County Tipperary, to bring a patient to a Limerick hospital, when it struck a power line. It was just approaching Borrisoleigh, some twenty minutes after take-off. Wire cutters positioned above the cabin and below the helicopter blades snapped the cable, but the aircraft was forced to land. The Air Corps crew and HSE paramedic on board were not injured and the patient was brought the rest of the way to the hospital by road ambulance.

'Initially, it came as a shock, but that really invigorated and consolidated our motivation in showing this could happen – so we adapted approach procedures and the manner in which we select landing sites,' Clancy said. 'It emerged that it wasn't an established line, in that a farmer had crossed a field to provide power. And the wire cutters did the job, so it was a good outcome,' he added.

After this and several incidents where an aircraft door fell off – again, fortunately, without injury – a decision was taken to upgrade to the AgustaWestland 139.

The EAS was made permanent as a dedicated asset for the NAS in 2015, with funding of 2.2 million euro annually (2021 figures) provided by the Department of Health to the Department of Defence for 480 flying hours and associated costs. Any additional expenditure would be negotiated on a case-by-case basis. The EAS works well with other services, including the Irish Community Rapid Response (ICRR) air ambulance service, which was set up in 2019 to serve the south-east of Ireland on a charity basis and is based in Rathcoole, near Millstreet in County Cork. When the Department of Defence announced that the EAS could not operate for sixteen days between late November 2019 and February 2020 due to staffing and training issues, the ICRR was asked to provide back-up support.

In 2020, the ICRR flew a total of 490 missions across thirteen counties to provide paramedical assistance and transport to hospital for seriously ill patients. One of those missions helped save the life of polocrosse player Shane Harris (31), who was riding his horse near his home in Fethard, County Tipperary in June 2020 when the animal reared up and fell back on top of him.

Harris was knocked unconscious when he hit the ground. His partner, Kim Ronan, who was there with her father and two brothers, raised the alarm. Harris was airlifted to Cork University Hospital and treated for internal bleeding. He had punctured lungs, eight broken ribs and a broken collarbone. He made a full recovery and said he believed the ICRR air ambulance was the difference between him 'surviving and not surviving' the incident.[3]

The EAS took some 'learning' from the Air Corps experience in working with the Garda Síochána on its air support unit. As Bonner explained, there is a clear division of roles between the mission commander, who is the advanced paramedic, and the aviation commander, who is the pilot flying the aircraft.

'The mission commander takes the call and triages it, while I do my own risk assessment based on location, weather and fuel as aviation commander,' he explained. 'It is never a case that the mission commander will say to me that there's a road traffic accident in Limerick and we have to fly there. He will ask, "How are we fixed for Limerick?", and I will do the mental maths. If I say we can't, we stay put, as I am in charge of aircraft safety.'

To ensure a degree of detachment, the aviation commander is not informed of the detail of the incident until well in the air. The team, including the mission commander, will have far more detail as they plan the flight in the operations room.

Agricultural and equestrian incidents, road traffic accidents and severe illness are among the most frequent call-outs, and in the ten years that the service has been in place there is hardly a community in Ireland that has not benefited. The flights are often 'not very technically challenging' compared to search and rescue, Byrne explained. The difference is the immediate environment – 'you are often right in there in someone's home' – which creates a closer relationship with the casualty.

'I remember my first job on this service was to a 72-year-old cardiac arrest, and I thought in terms of 90 kilos of additional weight in the aircraft as I had been so used to flying search and rescue,' Bonner said. 'I was cleaning my sunglasses after we landed, waiting to be heroic, when I saw all the family members arriving and they were distraught, and it really hit me that here I was in this man's back garden and he had passed away. So the emotional connection is different,' he said.

'I've been in Air Corps for twenty-four years – I've done Garda Air Support Unit, military, counterterrorism, VIP, search and rescue: I have instructed and commanded. I am a lieutenant colonel now, but I still volunteer to come down and fly as it has to be the most rewarding thing I have ever done,' Bonner said.

***

In late 2021, Lieutenant General Seán Clancy became the first Air Corps officer to be appointed Chief of Staff of the Defence Forces. After joining the Air Corps in 1984, he undertook border operations from Finner army base in County Donegal, spending up to 120 days a year flying Alouette III helicopters across the border area. He flew search and rescue from 1991, becoming a commander in 1993, and spent a short time in Shannon during the early stages of the Irish Coast Guard before moving to Finner. He knew the four Air Corps helicopter crew who died in Tramore in July 1999 and was instrumental in the instalment of the memorial bench at Finner after the crash.

'Tramore was a terrible shock for the organisation, but also a tragedy from which we had to, and did, learn,' he said. 'You have to learn from an event like this, and that is why it should never be forgotten.'

During his time in search and rescue, he came to know many members of coastal communities, from lifeboat coxswains to lighthouse keepers like Vincent Sweeney at Blacksod in County Mayo. He was the pilot for a tasking after a vessel featured on RTÉ's *Cabin Fever* reality television programme ran aground on rocks off Tory Island, County Donegal in June 2003, helping rescue eleven people.

He was also pilot when a lifeboat volunteer's sheepdog fell from a cliff near Ballyglass in north Mayo and had to be rescued. 'We put our crewman down, and once he got within about two feet of him, the dog made a leap! The winchman just managed to get hold of him, and his knuckles were white. The dog went mad when we landed him in a field – he went tearing off all over the place; just wild!'

One of his more surreal memories is of a medical evacuation from a Norwegian cruise liner off Lough Swilly. A crew member had appendicitis and required an airlift to hospital. As the helicopter performed its 'let down' to approach the ship, he could see there were actually three cruise ships anchored. Night had fallen, the weather was poor, but he could see inside the glass doors of one of the dining rooms on board the ship they were heading for. He saw several guests in dinner jackets enjoying their cigars as they strolled out on deck to watch – almost as if it were part of the night-time entertainment.

Clancy and Air Corps search and rescue colleagues had trained on the Sikorsky S-61 for the Irish Coast Guard's north-west base, relocated to Sligo airport, when a government decision pulled the military out of the service in 2004, despite the fact that Irish Coast Guard director Captain Liam Kirwan had favoured a mix of both state and private operations to prevent a monopoly. Clancy agreed with that approach at the time.

'I often miss the simplicity of it,' Clancy said, recalling how the Dauphin helicopter would be guided into Finner through a gap in the nearby beach by radar, until sight of a strobe light system directed the pilot home to the helipad. He continued:

> Flying the Dauphin at night, you were always on the edge. While winching, if something were to happen to one engine, you knew you were ditching the aircraft if anything went wrong. However, engine failure was a very low risk.
>
> Once you were in the pilot's seat, this was your complete focus, and you had to be on the top of your game. Out and up at 300 feet from Finner, and you were off and you will not see a more beautiful landscape in the world than the Sligo and Donegal coastline.

It is only when you step away from it that you begin to reflect on how beautiful it is, and how lucky you were. That is what you would miss.

He went on to point out:

Almost ten years later, the Air Corps EAS has responded to over 5,000 tasks and been involved in 3,400 as of November 2021 and counting. We know that thousands of lives have had significantly improved outcomes. There hasn't been a community in the state which hasn't been touched by the EAS, and we are very proud of what it has achieved.

It has grown way beyond what was anticipated; it is a primary output of our helicopter fleet, and there is now a review of the service as part of the government's White Paper on Defence.

The Air Corps started the state's air ambulance service in the 1960s; we responded in 1963 to search and rescue; we were the first to bring night-time rescue to a dedicated search and rescue service as a consequence of the campaign run by Joan McGinley [O'Doherty] in Donegal.

So we have a record in pioneering these services. Sometimes the Air Corps can be taken for granted. However, I would never question its enthusiasm, competence and expertise.

17

'WHY AREN'T THEY TURNING ROUND?'

Dawn doesn't always break at sea. The shift into a half-light can be imperceptible as the sun gradually extends its warm glow over a horizon. On this particular morning, there was no horizon, no skyline and no reference point. The only constants were the Atlantic swell, the chilling wind and the damp mist enveloping two figures on a tiny raft.

Sara Feeney and Ellen Glynn could barely make out anything around them, as they struggled to ignore the cold, wearing only swimming togs under their buoyancy aids. The mist thinned as the sun's rays burned it off, allowing them to make out the geography. A low-lying tower painted in black and white to the north was familiar – the lighthouse on the southern tip of Inis Oírr. To the west, a whaleback of limestone running into the sea marked Black Head at the mouth of Galway Bay. To their south, and dangerously close, the Cliffs of Moher and the vast ocean beyond.

For now, their only lifeline was a set of floats attached to fishing gear set several miles south-west of Inis Oírr, which they had managed to grab and secure to their paddleboards. Exhausted after many hours on the water, they scanned the seascape for any movement.

When Sara saw something different, a sense of movement, a hint of a shape, she said nothing to her cousin. 'I thought my mind was playing tricks – I wasn't sure. It was so far away at first, and then it came closer, and so I told Ellen then, and we began waving our paddles.'[1]

The small white dot took a clear form. As it came close, the catamaran cut speed and one of two men on board threw a rope.

Ellen's legs went from under her as she tried to stand up. She fell back and accidentally knocked her cousin off their temporary raft into the sea.

**

It had all begun with a picture postcard of two happy young women setting out for a twenty-minute paddle before dusk on a hot summer's evening. Stand-up paddle boarding had become a popular escape from the Covid-19 pandemic in 2020. As people took to the water in their thousands, equipment providers could barely keep up with the demand. Inflatable paddleboards had a particular appeal. They were on sale for less than €300 in some supermarket chains and could be stored in the boot of a car.

Ellen Glynn had taken to paddleboarding a couple of years previously, after signing up for watersport tuition in Rusheen Bay near her Knocknacarra home. The 17-year-old was the oldest of four girls and was in transition year at Coláiste Iognáid, known as 'the Jez'. One of her younger sisters, Hannah, was also a keen paddleboarder.

Her cousin Sara joined her for the first time in early August, paddling off Silver Strand near their home on the north side of Galway Bay. Sara, an NUI Galway graduate in French and psychology, had been a regular sea swimmer and had done some windsurfing when she was in primary school. An only child, she was several years older than Ellen and they were particularly close.

Mid-August offered ideal weather, with high pressure over an island coming to terms with its sixth month of the pandemic. Lockdown restrictions had eased, but it was what became known as a 'staycation summer', with little or no foreign travel and thousands migrating to the Atlantic seaboard.

On Monday 10 August, the two cousins took to the water off Silver Strand. Ellen's mother, Deirdre, drove them down the narrow isthmus to the beach, where she was joined by her sister, Helen – Sara's mother – with her dog, Otis.

Two days later, they planned another trip after Sara finished work at 7 p.m. in a local health-food shop. Helen offered to take them this time, and in the excitement of transferring the gear from Deirdre's car, Ellen forgot her wet bag which would carry her mobile phone and keep it dry at sea. Deirdre recalled later that Ellen did take a buckle which clipped the boards together.

Ellen's dad arrived home at around 8.30 p.m. as the women were heading off. Johnny Glynn, head of youth development at Galway United Football Club, was a household name – famed for scoring the winning goal in a match against Shamrock Rovers in 1991 that secured a national cup for his club. However, he was in sombre form that evening, as one of his young players had sustained an ankle injury in a match. He had one distraction. Paris Saint-Germain was playing Atalanta in the Champions League, and he was looking forward to catching the second half on television.

Cones and barriers blocked the access road to Silver Strand when Helen and the cousins arrived. They had been erected as part of Covid-19-related public health measures. So they opted for Furbo, a few kilometres farther west, beyond Barna village. The short sandy beach overlooking the Burren in north Clare was busy with swimmers, paddlers and families making the most of the warm evening.

Helen wandered with Otis to the beach's eastern end, picking up a call on her mobile from Sara's dad, Bernard. He had come home to an empty house after a game of golf in County Mayo. She recalled it as one of those evenings during the first 'Covid-19 summer' when people were still 'enjoying the simple pleasures'.

She was leaning back on the rock and laughing as, yet again, Bernard told her he was going to quit golf.

The cousins were also chatting and laughing as they pumped up the two boards. Otis was revelling in the sand and it was, as Helen said later, 'just a blissful evening … that photo moment of just … this is happy'.

Ellen, who normally suffered from poor circulation, remembered she didn't feel cold at all. She realised she had forgotten the wet bag for her phone, but they planned to be on the water for only ten to fifteen minutes. It was now after 9 p.m., and the sun was already setting. Helen checked that they were both wearing buoyancy aids. Ellen had already noted the tide times; high tide was just after midnight.

There was a slight northerly breeze as they set off from the shore, heading out beyond the swimmers. Met Éireann would confirm later that it had been a light north-north-westerly during the early evening, but had backed north-easterly before 8 p.m.

'We had a lovely kind of chat and [were] in good spirits, and the next thing they were just going out,' Helen recalled.[2]

A man with a hurl and a sliotar asked Helen if Otis was able to fetch, and then hit the ball for the dog. Otis fetched it but then dropped the ball in the water and Helen had to paddle out to pick it up. She took a couple of photos of the cousins as they were heading out, around 9.30 p.m.

Otis began playing with another dog as Helen glanced out to sea. She felt a little unsettled but put it down to the fact that she didn't normally take the pair out paddleboarding herself. After a while, as she waited on the beach, she noticed that the cousins seemed far away. Why weren't they turning around?

As each minute passed, they were becoming harder to spot. Helen wondered if she should ring Deirdre. She was afraid she might worry her unduly, so she rang Bernard. He had mentioned that he would call to his father while they were out and had just arrived there when Helen phoned. He said he'd drop over.

Now Helen couldn't see the pair on their boards at all, so she rang Deirdre, who was at home and chatting to a neighbour. Deirdre reassured her that it was all grand. Ellen had a friend living back near Furbo and the pair may have paddled over to say hi, she suggested. She advised Helen to have another look around and ring her back in a few minutes.

Five minutes later, Helen rang again – she definitely couldn't see them.

Deirdre didn't feel unduly anxious but said she would drive out. Her neighbour, Caoimhe Friel, offered to come with her and went back to her house to get her coat. Johnny was upstairs, still watching the match, when he heard his wife leaving and he thought it was unusual she hadn't mentioned where she was going.

Deirdre, for her part, just thought she could nip out to Furbo and would be back home again before anyone noticed. She swung around to Caoimhe's house and was struck by the fact that her neighbour was carrying a big winter coat with her and had been looking for a torch.

Out at Furbo, Helen's anxiety must have shown in her face. Someone asked her if she was alright as she stood on the beach, feeling as if she was frozen to the spot and almost unable to take a full breath. Someone remarked jokingly that perhaps the paddleboarders had 'headed down to Clare'.

A few minutes later, Bernard arrived, followed by Deirdre and Caoimhe.

***

Navigating past swimmers to ensure they had clear water, Sara remembered they had paddled past some rocks close to Furbo beach when they decided to turn. They hadn't realised how far they had travelled.

'Yeah, I remember looking up at the sun on the way out, the sky just looked really nice, and then … I don't know, I can't really grasp how quickly it happened, or what happened,' Ellen recalled later. 'We just turned our heads and we're like, "Oh my God, we're out so far, we better turn back because Helen will start to worry."'

They could feel the wind in their faces as they tried to head into shore, crouching down on their knees on the boards to make some headway – but with little success. As the evening cooled, the land temperatures fell much more quickly than the warm sea, giving energy to the offshore breeze. The northerly to easterly wind was now catching the bows of their air-filled boards and their life jackets as they tried to paddle back to shore.

Each time they tried to point north, the boards swung back by 180 degrees. There were a few fearful moments. Having forgotten the wetbag, they had no mobile phone, no means of communication, other than yelling, roaring, screaming and waving their paddles in the air. Ellen described it later as 'like being in a nightmare and just wanting to wake up'.

The two boards were being pulled apart, so she paddled over to Sara, and admitted she didn't see how they would be able to get back. Their best bet was to lash the boards together and keep paddling. Fortunately, they had the strap for this. Ellen remembered the tide was still in their favour and she knew what time it was going to get dark.

'It was still a lovely evening for a good while, and the water was quite warm. It wasn't till after dark, and the fear sets in, that you realise it's not getting any warmer,' Sara said.

Focused on keeping Furbo beach in their sights, they paddled to maintain a position parallel to shore, kneeling again frequently to reduce wind resistance. It was a neap tide with weak currents, but their temporary raft was like a sail to the wind. They could still see cars on the Furbo to Spiddal road and the bright lights of Padraicíns pub overlooking the beach, but now realised that none of those figures and shapes on shore could see them.

As it got darker, more cars arrived and they spotted the flashing lights of what might have been a garda car. They knew

Helen would have made the phone call and felt reassured by that – but mortified also. Their initial chat was about all the hassle they were probably causing. They hoped their granny, Mary Feeney, wouldn't have heard.

Around that time, Mary was preparing for bed at her home in Upper Cappagh Road in Knocknacarra, when her eldest daughter, Karen, dropped in to borrow a pair of binoculars. Shooting stars were forecast and Karen hoped to catch a good view of them up on the bog near a farm of wind turbines. Shortly afterwards, Mary went to bed.

It was dark when the two paddleboarders saw the first boat, but it was in the distance. They screamed at the top of their lungs, waved their paddles in the air. A second boat appeared, also travelling along the northern shoreline, but was too far away. They were now enveloped in the darkness, with the offshore breeze more like a 20-knot wind. Unbeknownst to them, thunderstorms were building out to sea.

***

'Maybe you had better call,' Caoimhe had said. Helen's hands shook as she pressed the emergency number on her mobile phone. She had never had to ring an ambulance or the fire brigade before, and now a voice was asking her which service she needed.

'The Coast Guard,' Deirdre prompted. Helen gave as many details as she could. She was told to keep her phone on her and the voice on the other end confirmed he had her location.

Deirdre rang her husband, Johnny, and explained what had happened. Along with Bernard, Helen and Caoimhe, she scrambled over rocks at the edge of the beach to see if they could get a clearer view.

It was dark now, and cold. Deirdre and Caoimhe said they would drive back east to Barna pier in case the pair had made landfall there. When they got to Barna, there was no sign and all was dark beyond the short pier. They returned to Furbo to find Johnny had parked the front wheels of his jeep up on the footpath above the beach, with the headlights on, in the hope that the girls could see the beam. Several more Feeney siblings arrived, including Karen, who had been watching the meteor shower over Galway Bay.

Helen struggled to keep her mind focused and calm, but all was 'noise', she remembered. She knew the only sound her mind would register clearly now was that of four particular words for which her heart ached: 'Yes, we have them.'

***

The Coast Guard's marine co-ordination centre on Valentia Island in south Kerry is responsible for a sea area extending from Youghal in east Cork to Slyne Head north of Galway Bay. It had logged that first call from Helen at 10.05 p.m., taking details of two females aged 23 and 17 on white paddleboards.

The station recorded that they had 'no phone, no radios, were wearing life jackets and black wetsuits'. Its duty officer tasked the Galway RNLI inshore lifeboat – a busy, city-based unit that responded to incidents on the River Corrib and had a remit extending out to Black Head in Clare and west to Spiddal. Galway RNLI's duty co-ordinator, Barry Heskin, received the call at 10.09 p.m. and mustered an inshore crew, which headed out to Furbo from Galway docks. Valentia logged that the Galway lifeboat was underway by 10.25 p.m.

Initially, the RIB focused on the north side of the bay, checking the northern shore, along with a cardinal mark at Foudra Rock, directly south of Salthill. The crew also checked several data buoys anchored farther west in the bay to monitor the wave climate. There might just be a chance that the cousins had been carried in this direction. The lifeboat crew lit a white flare to illuminate the sky, but there was no sign, and so the RIB continued on a north-south parallel line search extending from Furbo across the bay to Black Head on the Clare coast. It was joined by the RNLI Aran lifeboat, helmed by coxswain John O'Donnell, which was tasked at 11.19 p.m.

O'Donnell had taken the call from his lifeboat operations manager, and the bleepers to muster crew were sounding as he was leaving the house. He was joined at the Cill Rónáin lifeboat station by mechanic Adam Flynn, navigator Rónán Mac Giollapháraic and crew Daniel O'Connell and Colm Crawford. Expecting a long search, O'Donnell asked one of his fellow coxswains to be prepared to take a relief crew out in the morning.

As it steamed out, the all-weather lifeboat called Valentia to confirm it was heading for Black Head to the south of the Aran islands. Arriving off the Clare headland just before midnight, O'Donnell could see the lights of Shannon's Rescue 115 coming in from the east over Ballyvaughan.

'So we were talking to Galway lifeboat station on the way down, and they informed us that they had given a good search along the area there, the north shore, and there was nothing to be seen,' O'Donnell recalled. 'We decided that we would do a parallel search pattern there from Black Head to Furbo beach, turning west all the time at every leg.'

Back at Furbo beach, Johnny Glynn scrolled through his phone contacts and rang Garda Peadar Ryan, who arrived twenty minutes later. He also rang a friend he knew through soccer – Donie Garrihy, the director of a ferry company running between Doolin and the Aran islands. Garrihy was at home when his phone rang. During the conversation, his wife, Breeda, could see how upset he was, even though his voice sounded calm. He checked his marine traffic app and could see that at least one lifeboat was out. He told Johnny to hang up, keep his phone line free and he would ring him straight back.

Garrihy phoned Thomas Doherty of Doolin Coast Guard and explained the situation:

I told Thomas they needed a helicopter. Thomas asked for Johnny's number and said he'd ring him, which he did after he had talked to Valentia. I rang Johnny back quickly and told him to stay well back now and let them do the work. I had seen the helicopter flying out of Shannon, so I told him it was on the way and would be there in fifteen minutes.

I was trying to sound brave for Johnny, but as soon as I put the phone down, I fell apart. I didn't want him to think that someone he was leaning on was breaking down ... but when I left the pier the wind was very bad, and I just felt anyone on bodyboards or surfboards was going to be taken to sea ... And there was Johnny Glynn's daughter and his niece out in that.

Minutes later, Johnny took the call from Thomas Doherty in Doolin. It was reassuring to know search units were out. Still, in the black, bleak darkness, every minute seemed like an age, every second like an hour as he and his wife and sister-in-law and family strained to hear the sound of a helicopter.

When Deirdre's phone rang around 11.30 p.m., it was her second daughter, Hannah (14), wondering where everyone was. Caoimhe, sitting next to her in her car at this stage, made a walking gesture with her fingers and hand, so Deirdre told Hannah they were 'out for a walk'.

'But it's half eleven,' Hannah replied, incredulous. 'Where's Dad?'

'Maybe he had to nip out and sign something,' Deirdre suggested. At this point, she could hear that Hannah and her youngest sister, Clara (9), were in tears. Alice (12) seemed calmer. Deirdre suggested they all get into their parents' bed to sleep, saying everyone would be 'home soon'.

Almost paralysed with anxiety, the small group of parents, relatives and friends were alert to any signal that the two might have been found. Now they could see helicopter lights. At one point, the aircraft hovered for what seemed like a long time over an area well out into the bay. Deirdre was sure they must have them, but when the aircraft moved again she was worried they had been separated. For a fleeting moment, she wondered if someone might have a phone to video them when they were taken ashore.

Later on, the parents' hopes were raised again when a flare was set off. Each time, they were sure they must have been found and checked with the gardaí present on Furbo beach, but there was no confirmation call.

Johnny remembered the atmosphere on the beach was quiet, tense, subdued, and he was struck by how calm Deirdre seemed to be. Helen remembered being wrapped in coats and jackets by her siblings and hearing words of hope – 'they're going to be okay', and 'they'll be alright' – as she stared, fixated, out into the bay. She switched on the torch on her mobile phone at one point and waved it around, just to let the girls know they were not alone.

'You are just sort of like a little child on the beach,' Helen said later. 'I think there was a time we were just, kinda, standing in a line, and I remember myself and Deirdre were holding hands, and I don't think I can remember the last time since I was a kid, maybe, that we were holding hands.'

By 2 a.m. there was still no sign. During those early hours, Valentia Coast Guard received a call from the gardaí to correct earlier information relayed at 10.05 p.m. – the two women were not wearing wetsuits, only swimming togs. Back at the RNLI station, hearts sank. 'That was not so good news,' station co-ordinator Mike Swan recalled.

By 3 a.m., Bernard had urged everyone to sit in their cars and get out of the rain. By then, the weather had changed, the winds had picked up to around 18 to 21 knots, with gusts of up to 28 knots between 2 a.m. and 6 a.m.[3] With several hours to go before first light, the parents were coming to grips with the awful reality that the two cousins were going to be on the water for the night, if they were still alive. They hoped and prayed silently that they were still together.

Several people from the immediate locality had advised them that if they had managed to reach shore, it was far more likely to be across the bay in Clare, due to the wind direction taking them south-west. However, as Helen recalled later, it was hard to tear herself away from Furbo. She rang the Coast Guard to double check and was told that the likelihood of them coming back to that part of the shore was very remote.

'If they get picked up now, they'll be gone back into the docks or the hospital, or ...' the voice advised.

Helen dropped in briefly to her home in Knocknacarra to change her shoes on the way to Clare with Bernard. Johnny and Deirdre swung into their house nearby. As they approached the back of the house, they could see a light on in Ellen's room. Deirdre had a fleeting sense of relief, followed by a sense of foreboding.

'No one goes into Ellen's room, and I remember my grandmother used to say, "If somebody isn't home when they die, they'll come and knock on the door three times, and that's their soul leaving," so that actually went through my head ... And I went "Oh God," and I was like "no, no, they're fine".'

Hannah had woken up and demanded to know what was going on. Deirdre knew she would have to tell her something but couldn't bear to tell her the whole truth. So she told her that Ellen and Sara had been swept out to sea on the paddleboards, but the helicopters had found them. They had hypothermia, and she and Johnny were on the way to the hospital, and they would all see each other in the morning. It would all be fine.

'And it was like another voice in my head went "and that's the way it's going to be",' she recalled.

One of Deirdre's sisters, Marie, said she would stay at the house with the girls. Rain was lashing the car windscreen with all the ferocity of a winter storm as Deirdre and Johnny drove out towards the Limerick road, down past Oranmore, Clarenbridge and Kilcolgan, turning right for Kinvara and heading towards Ballyvaughan. They pulled off the main road near Newquay to head for the Flaggy Shore. A car pulled up beside them – it was Helen and Bernard, who said they were heading farther west to Black Head.

'The next thing, the whole sky lit up with the lightning, and it was sort of like, "Ahh, what else can you throw at them?"' Helen recalled.

'And you're going, "Oh my God, like, they're out there in bikinis in the middle of the sea",' Deirdre said.

These were lonely drives, every second like an hour, as the couples took every side road. 'And I remember Helen was … she was beside herself. Do you know, she'd just burst out in tears, because she's thinking of the girls out in the water,' Bernard recalled:

> It was an awful night. And so we're driving around, 'cause it's still pitch dark. So there's nothing we can do at that point, and we see a couple of ambulances driving around.
>
> So then of course, myself and Helen put two and two together and get five and think that the ambulances are … going down to collect the girls from somewhere. So we're cat and mouse with these ambulances and, of course, they were there for some other reason, or they certainly weren't there for the girls.

Deirdre, wrapped up in coat, boots and woolly jumper, remembered the physical endeavour involved in fighting off the thoughts in her head about how cold the two young women must be. Johnny felt overwhelmed. 'When I saw the size and how vast the Clare coastline is, it just seemed to make it a lot more difficult to narrow down the possibilities of where they might be … so many inlets … so that made us realise this is a needle in a haystack, this isn't going to be straightforward,' he said later.

The couple saw a figure coming towards them in a high-vis jacket who seemed to know them; at first they didn't recognise

Micheál, a neighbour, who had driven all the way from Galway to walk the Clare shoreline. Johnny broke down. Deirdre struggled to keep it together, remembering 'they had to be somewhere – this is a bay'.

***

Three Coast Guard helicopters swept the inner bay on rotation throughout the night, along with the RNLI Aran and Galway lifeboats, while Doolin Coast Guard worked the Clare coast up to Black Head and the Costelloe unit focused on south Connemara as far east as Furbo and out west to the Aran islands. The helicopters have three-hour fuel ranges and are equipped with a thermal imaging sensor and a powerful 'Nightsun' light. In darkness, however, two people on paddleboards offered what the Coast Guard described later as a 'low profile for detection'.

By 4 a.m., the Shannon-based Rescue 115 had been relieved by Rescue 118 from Sligo. However, when the lightning flashed at around 4.25 a.m., the Sligo aircraft was forced to leave. By 6 a.m., Rescue 115 was back on scene, and it was then relieved by Rescue 117, based in Waterford, at around 9 a.m.

As it continued its parallel search pattern between Black Head and Furbo, the RNLI Aran lifeboat provided shelter to the Galway inshore RIB, about a quarter of a mile behind it on its port side.

'So around about 3 a.m., the rain had started coming down, it was raining heavy, and just around 4 a.m. …well, Rescue 115 left to refuel and Rescue 118 then came down from Sligo … she came in overhead … and she went to Casla Bay and along the shore,' O'Donnell said.

At first he thought the bright flashes of lights were caused by one of the nearby boats shining a searchlight. 'It was lightning that was there all the time … At one point it was so bright I thought it was the helicopter beam hitting the deck. So those girls must have been terrified.'

He explained, 'The way we work, we had two people in the wheelhouse all night, myself and the mechanic in the wheelhouse. There was [*sic*] three lads on the upper stairs position … a searchlight each side, and one fella in the middle with a hand searchlight … so we had three searchlights really.'

O'Donnell remained quietly optimistic. There had been no sighting of boards or paddles, and there was every chance the two women were still alive.

* * *

Air temperatures of around 18 degrees had fallen to 15 degrees during the night. Even though the sea was warm – at around 18 degrees – the estimates for survival at sea in normal clothing would be around twenty hours. The two women weren't aware of this, but they were well aware of their vulnerability in bikinis and life jackets.

Ellen was worried about her own lack of tolerance for cold, but the water had been warm that evening. They kept checking the shore lights, paddling and waiting, and still feeling bad about 'all the hassle we were causing'.

Neither wanted to say what they really thought. Ellen, who was a little stressed, felt an uncontrollable urge to burst into song. She belted out the lyrics of Taylor Swift's 'Exile'. 'At first I'd say Sara thought I was a bit insane,' she said later. 'But she just sorta started singing along … it was a distraction … that was just before the first boat came.'

Sara recalled:

> We definitely knew there was activity and people looking for us. At one point, a boat lit a flare close to us to signal to the helicopter … We thought they would pick up the reflective strips on the boards, or on our buoyancy aids. … Not long after that, we saw the first helicopter. It felt like they were

very close … You get that initial sense of relief and then …
we would scream and roar and no one could hear.

They continued to paddle, all the while straining to identify the
lights on the shore. In the downdraught caused by the helicopters
and the wash from searching vessels, they struggled at times to stay
on the boards. Ellen had fallen off once already, earlier in the night.

Instinctively sensing they needed to keep their spirits up, they
chatted about what they would most like to do when they arrived
back. Ellen said she was really looking forward to a hot shower
and getting into comfy pyjamas. They talked about how lucky they
were to have their life jackets on, how people were looking for
them, how they were going to be found and how everything would
be fine.

Ellen remembered at one point thinking about how cold it
must be for those sleeping out every night with no homes to go
to. She only had to be 'there for one night', she told herself. The
line from 'Exile' about seeing 'this film before' and not liking the
ending kept looping around in her head, and she sent silent mind
messages to her mum, reassuring her that she was okay.

While on the water, they witnessed the meteor shower and
marvelled at bioluminescent light for a time as the seas were lit up
by the chemical reactions of millions of tiny marine organisms.

'So I remember, when we saw the shooting stars, I'd always
wanted to see them, so I thought that was really cool, and then the
plankton in the water,' Ellen said. 'They'd been in the water a year
before that, and I didn't get to see them, so I was kind of thinking
in my head, "Am I getting to see all this stuff now because I'm
going to die?"'

Sara said:

With the meteor shower, between the two of us there was
some amount of wishes made. To be honest, I'd sacrifice a
meteor shower and bioluminescence just to get home safe

> ... We were singing, talking, anything we could to keep our
> moods up. If fear was seeping in, one of us would reassure
> the other ...
>
> It was horrible to be out there and realise everyone would
> be worried sick, and it felt really awful that everyone spent
> so many hours looking for us. I think if we had panicked at
> all, things could have been very different. I know if Ellen
> had panicked, I would have found it very difficult.[4]

The weather deteriorated and the rain was so heavy that it hurt.
They had stopped seeing any lights of vessels, any search activity
now. Their last sight of a helicopter was just before the lightning
storm at around 4.20 a.m. When the aircraft flew off, they knew
they would have to stick it out to first light.

At that point, Sara had a clear memory of being enveloped
in a fear that she could not articulate, knowing the impact any
mention of this might have on her cousin:

> The chances aren't too good for you if the helicopter
> couldn't be out in those conditions ... you know ... because
> the size of the helicopter compared to us and all we have is
> the boards ...
>
> You see the helicopter going in, because of the stormy
> weather, and that didn't bode well for us. We didn't even
> verbalise what might happen, or what we might both be
> thinking.
>
> Ellen probably had total understanding of what was
> going on, but neither of us really communicated that to
> each other ... we didn't really say that out loud at the time.
> If we had started talking like that, it was just another level
> of hopelessness we didn't need.

They lay down on the boards, trying to stay as stable as possible in
waves of up to 2 metres in height, hoping they could just wait the

night out. Ellen thought they were being carried towards Kinvara, though she wasn't sure.

Sara had a sense her cousin might be falling asleep, so she played word games with her to keep her alert and urged her to kick her legs every so often to keep warm.

* * *

The Galway RNLI crew came alongside Barna pier during the night for extra fuel and a crew change. By 5 a.m., local fishing vessels were out.

Back on Cappagh road, the light came on in Mary Feeney's bedroom, waking her and her husband, Tommy. Her eldest, Karen, and youngest, Donal, were at the foot of her bed. They explained that they had some news. Her two granddaughters were missing at sea. As she tried to make sense of the information, Mary remembered giving Karen and Donal a couple of lamps to take back out with them.

Back in Galway lifeboat station, co-ordinator Mike Swan arrived around 6 a.m. to check in with his colleague Barry Heskin, who had been on duty throughout the night. The situation was not looking good, given the night's bad weather on the bay. Some of the lifeboat crew who had been out in the early hours had crashed in chairs or were lying on the pool table to grab some sleep. Breakfast rolls had sustained them during a long night at sea and Swan had organised a box of the same for colleagues on the RNLI Aran lifeboat.

Sailor and yacht chandler Pierce Purcell received an early morning call and set his energies to putting the word out among the sailing clubs, while the family put out posts on social media, appealing for help. Several fishing vessels contacted John O'Donnell on the Aran lifeboat to get advice on where to search.

Ferries serving the Aran islands based in Doolin and in Ros-a-Mhíl also declared they would assist. Several private pilots –

John Kiely and Patrick Curran – joined in with a light plane and helicopter respectively, as did Aer Arann on its routine flights between Indreabhán and the islands.

'We took one of our ferries out from Doolin at 9 a.m. – the *Jack B* – with Captain James Fennell, my nephew Martin Garrihy and myself on board. Island Ferries was also searching in between sailings out of Ros-a-Mhíl, and Bill O'Brien of Doolin Ferries,' Donie Garrihy said. 'We scoured around Inis Oírr and were then told to search between Inis Oírr and Inis Meáin as far down as the lighthouse, and then got a call to double back up from Inis Oírr towards Spiddal.'

The Oranmore-Maree Coastal Search Unit became involved, as did the Marine Institute. The institute had expertise in modelling, combining tide, currents and weather to predict drift patterns on the bay. Over the first daylight hours, there were a number of reported sightings: several kayakers out searching and several objects that turned out to be lobster pots were mistaken for the paddleboarders.

Galway Bay's name belies a sea area as large as the county. As Mike Swan explained later:

> It is like driving from Galway east to Ballinasloe, and then searching from Loughrea in the south-east to Athenry to the north-west … a big area, a load of fields, and then you are looking for two girls and it's night-time.
>
> If there's a wave at all and someone is 100 metres away, there's no way in hell you're gonna see them … you only see them when you're on the top of the wave … and you must remember too that the boat they're in might be on the bottom of the wave. So it is all about searching slowly and methodically …[5]

Friends, relatives and people who didn't know the families drove many miles to join the search, some having left their homes in the middle of the night. Deirdre was aware of her daughter's resilience, and the fact that both young women were, as her sister Helen put it, two smart, sensible girls. She had an inexplicably strong sense of hope and, for some reason, she couldn't get a Taylor Swift song out of her head.

***

They had been 'staring into the abyss' for so long that when the sky changed, it was gradual and almost imperceptible, Sara remembered. Darkness was gradually lifting, but the light was veiled by a sea fog, a thick dislocating blanket that veiled all hints of time of day.

Ellen remembered remarking that it was getting bright at last. Sara replied that her eyes must be adjusting to the darkness.

As the summer sun gradually burned its way through the fog, they could make out shapes. Their last clear view in daylight had been of Furbo beach. Now they had no sense of what they were looking at or where, adding to their sense of bewilderment. When they finally managed to make out the low-lying lighthouse on the southern tip of the Aran island of Inis Oírr, Ellen had a strong sense of wishing it was Galway, or that it could become Galway. Behind them was an inhospitable north Clare coast, marked by the towering, sea-lashed Cliffs of Moher.

It was a terrifying prospect. They were at the mouth of Galway Bay and being carried out into the vast Atlantic, all 5,000 kilometres of it stretching to Newfoundland. Every option was dangerous now, and they felt incredibly alone, with no sound of aircraft searching for them, no sight of any vessels. Perhaps now the search was focused on shore, for bodies. Somehow they had to fight those thoughts and prevent themselves from being swept out 'the gap between Clare and Aran'.

Little did they know that dozens of fishing vessels, small boats and kayaks were now on the water. Social media was alive with appeals to help with the search for the two missing women, with a response from all around the bay.

* * *

Back at her home, Mary Feeney couldn't settle. 'I was like a zombie,' she said later. 'I know I had a blessed candle in the window.'

Her second eldest, Marie, brought her down to her younger sister Breeda's house, close by in Knocknacarra. Breeda's three little boys were a distraction, being innocently oblivious to the seriousness of the situation. Mary's husband, Tommy, phoned anyone he knew who had a boat. He then went down to Furbo beach to help with the search and met a local man who didn't know he was grandfather to the missing women. The man said there was 'no point looking now as their bodies wouldn't come up for three days'.

Other family members were also phoning around, including Marie and her friend Carmel, who contacted her brother, Robert Keane of Boleybeg. Robert phoned the Olivers, knowing the Claddagh-based family had close associations with the RNLI. Robert was friendly with fisherman Patrick Oliver.

Patrick and his son Morgan were due to take a day off after a few busy days on pots in Galway Bay, but Patrick had heard that two girls were missing when his brother Ciaran, one of several relatives attached to the Galway lifeboat, had phoned him earlier that morning.

The Olivers have saltwater in their veins and have participated in many rescues. Back in 2000, Patrick and a friend from the Claddagh had pulled two men from the Corrib – one had jumped in after another man who had fallen in from O'Brien's Bridge. Neither the fire brigade nor the lifeboat could get near them at the time, and Patrick received a state marine award for his efforts. In 2018, Morgan's cousin Sean was among a group of young sea scouts who rescued a man from the River Corrib during the Macnas street parade.

Patrick spoke to his brother Dave, who had been out all night on the Galway lifeboat searching. He then woke Morgan and rang Barry Heskin in the station to check what was going on and where the search was focused. Realising most of the assets were in the inner bay east of Spiddal, father and son then headed straight to their catamaran, the *Johnny Ó*, at Galway docks, and set a course for the Aran islands.

'The boat was full of petrol leaving but I went to the garage to get more,' Patrick recalled. He had his credit card in case he had to go into Inis Oírr to refuel.

Before leaving, Morgan suggested they should bring more 'slack', as in more rope for the anchor. 'I had a funny feeling before leaving that we would be travelling more distances,' Morgan said afterwards. 'I knew that they were like corks on the water.'

***

At 9.30 a.m., the gardaí held a briefing for search volunteers at the Sean Céibh in Spiddal, on the northern shoreline. Cathal Groonell of Cumann Seoltóireachta An Spidéil, the village's sailing club, had been on the way to work in Ros-a-Mhíl when he received a club WhatsApp alert. He turned back to attend the briefing and made several calls to fellow club members to launch the sailing club's two rescue RIBs. There were up to fifty people at the briefing, he recalled. A small blue helicopter landed. The pilot was Patrick Curran from Oughterard, and he then took off and headed out over the bay to help with the search.

'They gave us the channel for the VHF, and they told us to take a line from An Spidéal here to Black Head and search the area east of that, which will be from An Spidéal into Galway,' Groonell said. The two club RIBs followed 100-metre strips of sea, over and back.

'We were all very concerned for the girls and to think that they were out all night on a very bad night,' Groonell said. 'Usually, there would have been some banter on board, but there was none. There was a fair swell out there, there was a good bit of wind and visibility was moderate really with a slight fog, so you really had to be looking very carefully at all times in case you would miss anything.'

Sports psychologist and adventurer Karen Weekes launched her sea kayak from Lynch's pier just beyond Kinvara; she was very familiar with the shoreline from Traught beach to the east to Island Eddy to the north and Deer Island to the west.

Clare fisherman Gerry Sweeney, who launched along with Patsy Mullins, had similar local knowledge, and he still had a vividly clear memory of his own close shave in November 2005:

> I was out fishing and fell overboard near the Flaggy Shore. I was taking in gear, as I did a thousand times before, and thought when I fell overboard I would get back in, no problem.
>
> It was around 1.45 p.m., the radio was going in the boat, and just before my lunch. I drifted with the boat then, hanging onto it for a while, and was in the water for about two and half hours when we drifted close to Deer Island.
>
> I swam onto Deer Island, and it was dark at that stage. It was a south-westerly gale but it was around 8 or 9 degrees. I had a life jacket on, and if I hadn't I would have definitely been gone. When you are in a circumstance like that, survival kicks in and I was out of it for a long time on the island. I still had my oilskins on …
>
> My wife Martina came home and noticed the dinner wasn't eaten and raised the alarm. They were searching from 10.30 p.m., and I heard the helicopter flying over, and thought they hadn't seen me. However, they told me afterwards they had seen me on the first pass, but they had a bird strike, which is a bit of a nightmare for them as there are many gulls and cormorants on the island.

I had put my life jacket back on then at that stage, and they picked up the reflective strips …

The Aran Island and Galway lifeboats trained their lights on the island and that distracted the gulls and cormorants, who flew off. The helicopter flew in then, slow and low, on the fourth pass.

It was Daithí Ó Cearbhalláin who came down on the winch, and I knew him and some of the Coast Guard helicopter Shannon crew – Mark Kelly, Cathal Oakes and Ciarán McHugh – as I had trained with them before.

I never thought I'd be the one who was being lifted! It was around 1.45 a.m. when I got into the helicopter, and I was flown to Shannon where Martina met me.

So on that summer morning of 13 August 2020, Sweeney had a good idea of how cold and disoriented the two women would be, if they had made it through the night alive.

✷✷✷

Sore, aching, muscles cramping, but with all their remaining energy, the cousins tried paddling towards the Aran islands and away from the bay mouth. They made little progress. They discussed other options, like trying to make it to the Clare coast, but decided it was far too hazardous – they risked being dashed against the hostile cliffs and rocky shoreline by the Atlantic swell.

A dolphin broached close to them, providing a temporary welcome distraction.

When they spotted a marker float in the water, north of them and a little east of the southernmost Aran island, they paddled furiously again. It was both physically and mentally draining. They were exhausted and had almost given up, when, as Sara recalled later, they looked back towards the cliffs. As Ellen turned her head to the right, a set of two marker floats bobbed up cheerfully right beside them. The two floats close together were like 'angels from heaven', Ellen said later. With freezing fingers, the cousins grabbed the float leashes and grappled to secure them to the webbing on their paddleboards.

'We knew if we stayed there we would be found, but we also knew if another night fell we would not make it,' Sara said.

They took it in turns to have short naps. One would rest, while the other would watch for waves in case they needed to brace themselves and tighten their grip.

They saw a helicopter circle the Aran islands, but Sara had a sense that perhaps the search pattern had changed. She remembered how terrifying it was to think their family and friends might now think they could not have survived and 'would have assumed a certain outcome at this point'.

'Lots of people don't get the ending that we did in that situation, so that's definitely on your mind the whole time,' she said. She sensed the search would have changed to one of recovering their bodies, if they were lucky enough to be washed up on shore.

For Ellen, alternating between lying down and sitting up, it seemed as if minutes had turned into hours. She had a sense that perhaps it was around 5 p.m. Perhaps they would have to be out one more night, she suggested to Sara. Her cousin's response – that she didn't think she'd last another night – was the first time Ellen began to think that 'we actually might not be okay'.

She lay down to sleep again, and when she opened her eyes, Sara was sitting up, alert.

***

It would have been far too far north for the women to see, but islanders in Inis Oírr had been out looking for them. Paddy Crowe, recently retired manager of the island co-op, Comhar Caomhán Teo, had turned on his radio that morning and heard the news about two women missing 'from the Salthill area'. Living only 100 yards from the shore and having worked previously at sea, he knew how bad the night had been and thought the worst. He switched on the VHF radio to get an idea of the search patterns, having participated in many such call-outs before.

The island's Coast Guard unit was out, and Rescue 117 was flying close to the Aran islands when Crowe's phone rang around 11 a.m. His sister-in-law was out walking with a small child around the back of Inis Oírr near the lighthouse and had seen something. She wasn't sure but knew two women were missing. It was too far away for her to make out clearly and she didn't want to upset the child, she explained. Could Paddy make a call?

Crowe did that, ringing Valentia Coast Guard and relaying all the information he had. Out near the islands on the *Jack B* ferry, Donie Garrihy got a call from Valentia Coast Guard to double back up from Inis Oírr towards Spiddal.

Several other boats picked up a message on the VHF about a 'possible sighting at the south of the Foul Sound between Inis Meáin and Inis Oírr', including the Olivers in the *Johnny Ó* on a diagonal route across the bay. The Olivers were about 4 nautical miles east of the Aran islands at the Killa patch, one of several banks in outer Galway Bay extending from Inis Oírr to Crab Island, when they called the Coast Guard.

'Galway Coast Guard, this is the *Johnny Ó*, *Johnny Ó*, are you getting us there on [channel] 67,' Patrick said.

'Yeah, *Johnny Ó*, Galway Coast Guard, go ahead, over,' was the response.

'Eh, Galway Coast Guard, *Johnny Ó*, yeah, just for your information there, lads, we are just at the Killa patch. We heard there was a possible sighting, is it towards Inis Oírr or was that … was it nothing?' Patrick said.

'Yeah, roger, there was a member of the public there on Inis Oírr reported a possible sighting at the south side of Foul Sound between Inis Oírr and Inis Meáin, over,' the radio officer replied.

'Okay and was anything picked up then, we can head in that direction there, we are about 4 miles away, I just want to check it out and see,' Patrick said.

'Yeah, negative, the 117 [helicopter] is in the area, so if you're there if you could proceed and just give it a look over, that would be much appreciated okay.'

'Yeah, that's no problem, we'll head in that direction there now.'

'So we just took off … we were heading in that direction anyway,' Patrick recalled, all the time watching the fuel gauge to see how much of the 150 litres he had used. He saw Rescue 117 flying through the Foul Sound between the two islands and clearly seeing nothing. He decided to stick to his original plan.

His phone rang. It was Gerry Sweeney, who had been talking to him earlier from Clare.

'Ger was saying "Jeez, I don't know" and I was saying "Ger, they have to be here somewhere like, they have to be" and then I heard Morgan say, "I see them."'

'I was standing on the back of the boat and we've rails on the boat for safety,' Morgan said:

> Up on the back there's what's called a cat catcher. So I was like standing a good few feet above the boat and, eh, I was just like you're in open water so there's not really much to look at like … Inis Oírr and the Cliffs of Moher down to your left … All I saw was like a little black, like, paddle or stick maybe a mile and a half up ahead … instincts kick in and you just ran for the throttle and went as fast as we could. Once I saw it, I knew it was them. There was nothing out there … it was them, thankfully.

Gerry Sweeney had a sense his friend was in luck when he hung up so quickly. 'Before I knew it I heard his voice on RTÉ Radio's Joe Duffy,' Sweeney laughed later.

Sara remembered she was sitting up and looking around, waiting for some 'crazy moment of inspiration' when she spotted the outline of a small vessel. She said nothing to her cousin at first, thinking her tired mind might be playing tricks, especially after so many false alarms the night before. It came closer and closer.

She had to tell Ellen now. 'I think that's a boat out there ...'

Waving their paddles furiously with all the energy they could muster, they extended them as high as they could reach.

***

Helen and Bernard were back in Galway when Helen realised she needed to let Sara's workplace know, so rang several of her friends. Otis needed to get out of the car, so they called over to one of Helen's sisters and found her parents there. When her phone rang, it was her younger brother, Donal, asking if she had heard anything.

'He said, "Okay, don't lose hope now, don't lose hope," but I knew by him that he had obviously heard something, and I was just like, "Oh, phew, this is gonna be all over,"' Helen said.

Shortly after that, Bernard's sister rang her, asking if she had heard anything. It was around 10 a.m. and now she had a sense that perhaps there had been a positive sighting. However, Donal rang back a few minutes later to say, 'It wasn't them.'

Deirdre and Johnny Glynn had also headed back to Galway from Clare, realising they needed to be home for 9 a.m. when their three daughters would be awake. As they came through the city via the Claddagh around 8.30 a.m., they could see there was a lot of search activity.

Johnny said later:

We just happened to stop at the Claddagh, 'cause Deirdre's sister Emer was there, and some other people that we knew. So then we just headed home to tell the girls the news. We didn't want them to be awake and worried, and so that was going to be tough anyway, just trying to explain to them.

And what we didn't realise is that, well, the night before, they knew something was up, which was an awful way for them to be going to bed as well. So yeah, Deirdre did most of the talking in the bedroom, and it was, again, their reaction was, they were, I suppose, in shock and they didn't know what to do initially. And then it was nearly 10 o'clock maybe then, and we had to make plans to try and … I thought the best thing to do was for the kids to actually go out, to be searching.

I didn't want them to be not involved when they were looking back at this and to be asking, 'Well, why weren't we looking and searching?' So we were anxious to leave the house and get out, and then just when we were about to leave, the priest arrived at the house. And that's never a good sign.

Deirdre remembered that Johnny was always the polite one but on this occasion he was edgy. He just wanted to go.

'Deirdre was obviously making him a cup of tea, as she would do, and I was just wanting to go, but Deirdre made the tea anyway, and he was very good,' Johnny said.

The priest sat on the couch with his tea and asked Deirdre if she would like to say a prayer. Her heart missed a beat.

'And I said, "No, no," that I … whatever, we had said a prayer upstairs …'

She explained she had a gut instinct that they were both okay, but asked the priest if, from his experience of this sort of situation, people's gut instincts proved to be right in the end? She remembered the priest looking at her, almost puzzled. She repeated the question.

'And he said, "What you have now is a sliver of hope." And I remember thinking not, definitely not a sliver of hope. I had that image of the kid in *Matilda* that's forced to eat the big, huge chocolate cake.[6] I was like "I have a huge, huge amount of hope. There's no way. It's not a sliver."'

She jumped up and told the priest they had to go and he could pull the door after him. Johnny was already in the car with the three girls. They left for Furbo, passing people on the coastline wearing high-vis vests. Deirdre felt overwhelmed. These people were looking for her child.

When they arrived at Furbo, the sky was cloudy, grey, misty. The pallor of the morning reminded her of the day Ellen was born, and she wondered, for a fleeting second, if it was some sign that this was now the day they were to be separated for ever.

Helen and Bernard headed out to Ros-a-Mhíl and farther west to Carraroe, all the time meeting people out searching. They were not long at Carraroe when Helen's phone rang again. It was Sergeant Barry Donoghue from Clifden Garda Station to say Sara and Ellen had been found alive.

'There was a nice soft sand dune there to catch my fall, and I think Bernard took the phone and he started getting the detail and I was sort of saying "thank you" and broke down,' Helen said. 'We just kinda stood there for a few minutes and held each other and cried after the phone was down, and then it's like, you know, "Let's go, let's go get them quick, let's meet the helicopter."'

Her brother Donal rang a few minutes later to say the two cousins had been able to walk up the pier at Inis Oírr.

✳✳✳

'I'm sorry, I'm sorry, I'm so sorry ...'

Sara reckoned she must have apologised at least fifty times as the two men drew close, threw a rope towards her, and said, 'Okay, we'll take one of ye first.'

'We were thanking them and saying we thought no one was searching and they asked us if we knew how many people were looking for us!' Ellen recalled.[7]

They were 'all over Instagram', the Olivers told them, eliciting a mortified, 'Oh no!' response from the two women.

Ellen remembered asking if it was okay to leave the boards – thinking of the pollution – but the Olivers said they would take them. As she stood up to clamber on to the 7-metre catamaran, her legs went from under her and she accidentally knocked her cousin into the water.

'At that point, we were perfectly safe … I still had my hand on the board,' Sara said later, remembering how distressed her cousin was for her. 'If they had come that far, there was no way they were going to stop that from saving us!'

The two men were hauling the paddleboards onto the deck, when Ellen noticed the paddles were drifting off. 'They had to just literally pull me away 'cause I was going to jump in off the boat and get the paddles,' Ellen said. 'And they put oilskins on us and sat us down at the top of the boat and put jackets over us and jumpers … I was like "Oh my God, thank you so much, we've actually been out here all night … and there's no one looking for us."'

'The two of them were exhausted. I wouldn't say they had much left in them,' Morgan said. 'With every last bit of energy they showed just how grateful they were for us to be there.'

He reckoned they were already hypothermic and in shock. 'We gave them blankets and water and tried to keep the heat in the wheelhouse,' he said.

As they were wrapped in every spare bit of clothing on board, Ellen remembered Morgan suggesting she put her arms up her jumper sleeves for extra heat.

'It was almost like a shutdown at that point,' Sara said:

> My body just knew, 'Okay, you're safe, you can relax now, you're fine, you don't need to be so alert.' When you are out there you are thinking that all of these people are out there looking, and you have it in your head that if they do find you, you are going to be in some sort of trouble … the stress

and everything that you cause people … but they were just so kind, the instant we were on the boat just feeling so safe.

Before Sara curled up and put her head on her knees in case she might burst into tears, Patrick caught a look in her eyes that he believes he will never forget. As he set course north for Inis Oírr pier, he contacted his brother Ciaran. At the lifeboat station, there was one mighty sigh of absolute relief.

***

Mary Feeney was back at home, still unable to settle, all the time tortured by the thought that her granddaughters might have been separated at sea. When her phone rang, it was Donal to say they had been found, but he didn't know if they were alive.

She flopped into a chair and had the phone in her hand when Deirdre rang to say they were still alive. She remembered her sense was of 'joy unconfined'. She went to ring neighbours who had called earlier and she began looking for the priest's phone number, only to see him outside her window.

Johnny Glynn's phone rang on Furbo beach. It was Donie Garrihy. The Clare man remembered being surprised that Johnny sounded so alert when he answered. He knew he had been up all night.

'Hi Donie.'

'Hi Johnny.'

A silence, and then …

'Johnny, if you reared your daughter and your niece, you fuckin' reared them tough.'

'Donie … they're alive?'

'Johnny, they're alive, and we're going up to Inis Oírr … they're being taken ashore there.'

Garrihy could hear his friend crying, calling out to his wife and daughters with sheer joy in his voice as he fell to the ground.

'He left the phone on … I heard everything,' Garrihy said.

The Clare man was in tears himself. 'I could have swam back to Doolin and pulled the ferry after me – there's stuff on days like that which would bring me to my knees, and that morning was one such day.'

Johnny and Deirdre swept their daughter Alice up into their arms.

Irish Independent western correspondent Eavan Murray was close by. 'Family members, friends, volunteers and strangers began cheering, weeping and clapping … The girl's aunt, Breeda Feeney, who had stood at the shore all night, wept with joy,' she wrote.[8]

'We have never been so afraid in all of our lives,' Breeda told Murray. 'At first somebody said there were two bodies recovered, and it sounded very bad, but we were still calm and saying we didn't believe it. And then a guy from the RNLI heard on his radio that they had been found alive.'

'In 13 years of journalism, I have never witnessed anything so wonderful,' Murray posted afterwards on Twitter.

***

Still finding it hard to believe, Bernard Tonge had one abiding memory as he and Helen drove back towards Galway city. They had met so many people, not just friends and relatives, but people they didn't know. He was aware that Helen's sisters had made many calls, that sporting networks had been contacted, including GAA clubs, but there were many others out on shorelines that morning right around the bay:

> If you think about all the people who took time off work that day and time off their own lives to go searching for something … with probably most people thinking, 'there's no chance of finding anything here', and it's so amazing then

that the whole community effort that went into it, and it really opens your eyes to how good people are. Even though a lot of people had no connection to anything, and some people have a small connection or whatever, it was just an amazing, amazing atmosphere.

***

Arms reaching out to take her, Sara Feeney remembered being lifted gently off the *Johnny Ó*.

'There were so many people around, and again you're just not even paying attention to what's happening, you're just kinda moving, floating through everything 'cause you're being carried and lifted and helped everywhere.'

Ellen remembered they had no shoes, as they walked up the pier, and were taken in a van to a waiting Coast Guard helicopter, Rescue 117. They were assessed by the paramedics and offered more fluids and squares of chocolate. As the helicopter took off and flew out towards Galway over the Atlantic, Ellen had a distinctly queasy feeling as she caught a glimpse of the ocean below.

Landing at University Hospital Galway, the cousins spotted the cameras and recognised familiar faces behind the railings – their parents, Ellen's sisters, several of their aunties, some friends. It was 'overwhelming, jarring, strange', Sara remembered, describing the sense of delight and relief, combined with grief, as they were reunited briefly with their parents in the ambulance.

Ellen asked her mother if she got her 'mind messages' and did Deirdre think she was going to die? As they were brought into the hospital emergency department, she remembered being given 'a butter sandwich – and I hate butter …'

Her father Johnny was struck by the fact that his daughter was wearing a cap – one of the hats the Olivers had found to keep the two women warm.

Sara was discharged that night, while her cousin was kept in a couple of days for observation.

***

It 'wasn't rocket science', given the wind direction, Patrick Oliver said afterwards. 'I was basing it on fact they were still on the boards and together. It would have been a totally different story if they were in the water.'

When Aran island fisherman Bertie Donohue heard mention on the radio of the floats which had served as such a lifeline, he knew exactly who owned them. The fisherman from Cill Éinne on Inis Mór catches and processes brown crab. The floats were attached to one of three sets of his crab gear. Donohue had set the three strings of pots close to an area known as 'the Finish' off the southern Aran island that season for the first time. He had planned to move the gear early the previous week, but 'something stopped him'.

'When they got hold of the floats, it was the outer set of gear,' he told this writer. 'If they had missed it, they would be out in the Atlantic.'[9] The hard ground he had selected didn't extend for much farther.

'That is a very exposed location, and I only set the gear there to help another fisherman, who lost 200 pots last October when his boat sank in Inis Oírr. And his boat sank in a north-easterly, the same wind those girls had, which just shows you how tough that weather is,' Donohue added. 'I don't know how they survived that night as there was awful weather, and that north-easterly is cold and makes a very bad chop in the sea when you are away from shore … They are two very tough, very brave girls – and I don't know how they managed to hold on to my fishing gear in that location.'

Their own presence of mind had been key to their survival, and what had happened to them 'could happen to any of us', he remarked.

Donohue lifted the pots several days later and there was a good catch of crab.

***

Many tears had been shed over the years at the Galway RNLI station, close to the harbour office, but these were of a very different kind. There was a sense of disbelief as those present over a long night realised that the two women, wearing only swimming togs under their buoyancy aids, were not only alive, they were also 'chirpy', Patrick Oliver said, and chatting after fifteen hours at sea.

There was a sense of euphoria, and messages of congratulations to all involved arrived from Taoiseach Micheál Martin and Galway West junior minister Hildegarde Naughton. Patrick Oliver spoke to RTÉ Radio's Joe Duffy on his way back in with Morgan to Galway docks.

John Draper, Valentia Marine Rescue Sub-Centre divisional controller, told RTÉ that the cousins were very lucky to have survived in the water for so long without wetsuits. 'They were able to keep afloat on the paddleboards overnight, and that was certainly a factor,' he said. Having life jackets on was also crucial. 'Challenging though they were, the conditions were reasonably warm, the sea water was about 15 degrees – but if they had been submersed in the water, that would have been possibly a different story.'

Later that afternoon, Helen Feeney said that 'paddleboards will never darken our doors again'.[10]

Former rescue pilot David Courtney praised all involved and said that the rescue served to remind us all that there is no substitute for good old-fashioned sea-faring lore and knowledge, as demonstrated by the Olivers, despite the best efforts of the Coast Guard's infrared equipped state-of-the-art helicopters. The Olivers 'headed like a bloodhound straight to the survivors' location,' Courtney observed.[11]

Galway West Independent TD Catherine Connolly tabled several parliamentary questions about the delay in locating the two women. Members of Cumann Seoltóireachta An Spidéil, who participated in the search, shared her concerns. Cathal Groonell, who had been out in one of the search RIBs, had noted that there were 'quite a number of other boats searching the same area, which we thought was a bit of … not a great deployment of the resources. We contacted the Coast Guard on the VHF and they really said just continue doing what you're doing.'

The sailing club wrote to the Coast Guard, explaining its concern about the inadequate deployment of resources and the fact that it believed the search was focused in 'areas of the bay where we feel the casualties were very unlikely to be'. It said it was delighted with the positive outcome and would always be available to assist the Coast Guard, but would 'welcome an annual exercise in which resources such as ourselves could be tasked appropriately and in a way that is helpful to the Coast Guard for training for future events'.

The Coast Guard said it was carrying out its own analysis – which it did, but not for wider publication. It said that it had used SARMAP, a US software programme which was instrumental in Valentia's location of five crew rescued from the *Rambler* yacht which capsized after losing its keel in the 2011 Fastnet yacht race.[12] Using all available data, the software can predict the movement of the drifting survivors and calculate a precise search area.

The Coast Guard emphasised that this search was over a 200-square-mile sea area. If the two women were not falling under the focused spectrum of the 'Nightsun' or FLIR they would be 'difficult to spot', particularly as they had no wetsuits to provide an extra heat source, it said. 'The search was just moving into the south-west of the Inis Oírr sector of the search and rescue box with both aviation and surface assets when the fishing vessel *Johnny Ó* came upon them. It is highly likely they would have been detected within the following one to two hours as it was daylight.'[13]

Water Safety Ireland chief executive John Leech offered his own experienced analysis. Leech, formerly a head of the Naval Service diving team and ship's captain, had participated in many searches and recovered the body of former marine minister Hugh Coveney after he fell down a cliff into the sea while out walking with his dogs in west Cork on 14 March 1998.

The Coast Guard is 'world class', he stressed, and can respond very efficiently if it gets accurate information, but he explained that Ireland's temperate climate means wind and weather conditions could change quite significantly within a very short period of time. On that particular day, calm conditions associated with a hot and balmy evening had transformed overnight, with a northerly wind changing direction and sweeping the two young women offshore. Had they been on solid paddleboards, rather than inflatable craft, they might still have been able to cut through the water and paddle back when the wind picked up, he said.

Leech noted that there were 'quite a few vessels of opportunity there to assist', and 'possibly too many of the vessels were searching on the windward shore' rather than being deployed farther out into the bay. However, the vessels would also have to be suitable for operating in poor visibility and with a strong offshore breeze.

The Coast Guard may have believed the young women were working their way along the northern shore and moving west, Leech suggested, and indicated that the thermal imaging cameras on the helicopters would have been of limited value in the restricted visibility, with an increasing sea state. Existing expertise, such as the tidal-stream modelling employed by the state's Marine Institute, would also have been of limited use in a situation where there were neap tides and negligible tidal influence.

'We had a good fresh breeze going there, so the wind was the main factor, so really what you had to do is figure out what would the wind do and then follow the wind,' he noted. Patrick and Morgan Oliver had done precisely this, he said, and for that reason Water Safety Ireland nominated them for a 'Just in Time Rescue' award.

'They followed their instincts, they know the bay, they looked at the wind, they went after the wind, and they got a bullseye.'

However, the two women were also 'brilliant' – they had worn life jackets and lashed their boards together, he emphasised, keeping each other focused and keeping their hopes up. This was crucial in 'a survival situation where you're spending fifteen hours on a board'.

'We're very lucky to have the Irish Coast Guard that we have,' Leech stressed, but 'obviously it wasn't the rescue that they would like to think back on'.

Valentia divisional controller John Draper confirmed that paddleboards had not been allowed for in its SARMAP technology, which could give projections on drift, taking into account tide and wind factors. For their part, the cousins were just relieved that they were found.

'We were so well looked after, as if them taking time out of their day and deciding to come out and look for us wasn't enough, to meet with that level of kindness and feeling of safety was just incredible,' Sara said:

> These people who go out and take time out of their own lives without hesitating and put their own safety at risk to look for people that they don't know … are heroes … Everyone we met along the way was so kind and helpful … it was lovely.
>
> We are just so grateful to the Irish Coast Guard, RNLI, gardaí, Civil Defence, volunteers, all the people out on the water and on the shore … and we have no words to explain how grateful we are to Patrick and Morgan.[14]

The two women and the father and son were reunited several weeks later, as host Ryan Tubridy's first guests on the first episode of a new season of RTÉ television's *The Late Late Show*. By then, Ellen had taken a sea swim, just to make sure she was not left with a fear of the water.

'A good news story in a world gone mad,' Tubridy said, summarising the impact that the successful rescue had had on a national psyche after six months of the Covid-19 pandemic.

Patrick Oliver explained how, as a father of seven, his own paternal instinct had kicked in when he heard of the missing pair on the Thursday morning. He played down his decision to head for the South Sound, emphasising that many had been out all night searching in difficult weather conditions and that he and Morgan had the advantage of daylight.

Tubridy noted that he wasn't taking credit for saving the cousins.

'We found them, but they saved themselves,' Oliver said.[15]

For weeks afterwards, the local postmen delivered letters with no address other than 'To the Two Luckiest Girls in Galway' and suchlike.

***

After the initial euphoria and relief wore off, the full impact of the ordeal began to hit the two women and their families. Ellen would speak later of how she found it hard to focus at school until she got help.[16] Sara returned to her work, endeavouring to maintain her privacy.

Almost a year after the event, musician Taylor Swift sent Ellen a package, with a three-page handwritten letter and a picture which she had painted of a seascape with a calm sky.

The Olivers received an award from Galway mayor Mike Cubbard in October 2020, and the cousins and their families were also invited. 'Claddagh royalty' was how the mayor described the two men when he presented them with a framed presentation scroll and a bronze model of a currach. 'The rescue highlights the fantastic community spirit which exists in Galway, as hundreds of people across the city and county offered their help with the search operation,' Cubbard said.[17]

The father and son had already been back in the news again, having pulled a man from the River Corrib. They had been preparing to go out fishing when they heard the alert, relayed to Galway RNLI and the Galway Fire Service's 'Swift' rescue unit, involving Patrick's brother Dave. The man was still conscious as they brought him into the quay.

'Part-time fishermen, full-time superheroes!' was one comment on social media.

'We just happened to be in the right place,' Patrick Oliver said, adding 'we just want to go back fishing.'[18]

Several months later, the men's family was hit by tragedy. Father and son fishermen Martin (61) and Tom Oliver (37), close relatives of Patrick and Morgan, died within twenty-four hours of each other after an accident on board their potting vessel on the north side of Galway Bay. Both had been involved in the search for the two paddleboarders. Patrick had a clear memory of Martin ringing him to check where he was going on that morning of 13 August, and he said he was going to the South Sound between Inis Oírr and the Cliffs of Moher.

Galway's Claddagh area came to a standstill on the morning of Friday, 6 November 2020, and winter sun shone brightly, as the funeral cortege left the Dominican church. The silence among hundreds of people lining the route was broken only by the roar of the Corrib and the gentle sound of wind in canvas sails. Three Galway hookers had moored in the Claddagh basin, with musician Sharon Shannon playing soft airs on her accordion on the deck of one as the cortege crossed Wolfe Tone bridge.

Two orange flares were released on the water surface, and members of Galway Bay Sailing Club then lit handheld flares on the dockside. Father and son, who had been inseparable in life, were buried side by side in Rahoon cemetery.

The magnitude of what had occurred only began to hit Ellen and Sara several months later. Speaking a year later, as she prepared for her Leaving Certificate, Ellen said she was more settled with it, and it had become 'a memory rather than a nightmare'. She had been back swimming, but not paddleboarding at that stage.

'I think there's a lot of kinda stages in processing everything that's happened and sometimes I just want to talk it out and I'm so lucky that there's, you know, amazing people around me that I have there to listen and to kinda talk through it with,' Sara said. 'Then other times you just feel like "no, that wasn't me, that never happened", and it's just kinda trying to find the balance and getting back to normal.'

EPILOGUE

World record-holding sea swimmer Nuala Moore from Dingle, County Kerry, comes from a family of fishermen who did not learn to swim – and believed it was almost an impediment to do so. Her county's coastal community has experienced the best and the worst of the Atlantic over centuries – with the writings of Blasket islanders Peig Sayers, Tomás Ó Criomhthain and Muiris Ó Súilleabháin reflecting the harsh reality of island life before developments in communication, transport and air-sea rescue.

It's cool now to be an islander, and cooler still to be a sea swimmer. However, several decades before, Moore and colleagues, such as Donegal's Anne Marie Ward and Henry O'Donnell, were quietly pioneering long distances over open water. The trio were part of a relay team that included Ryan Ward, Tom Watters from Galway and Ian Claxton from Dublin which circumnavigated this coastline in 2006, completing a total of 1,330 kilometres in fifty-six days.

Since then, Moore has set several Guinness world records for her participation in a Bering Strait relay in 2013, and for becoming the first swimmer in history to transit the maritime boundary between the Pacific and Atlantic Oceans (defined on longitude 67°16'W). In that 2018 achievement, she was also the first woman ever to swim off Cape Horn.

Moore, who has always stressed that her feats are a combined effort, with her safety team playing a key role, discussed her swims in detail with her late father Benny. 'He knew every inch of this coastline, and knew the spread of the ocean and how it reacted.

The one thing he always said to me, was to "never take your eyes off the sea, it can take you tomorrow", she said.[1]

Just how cruel the sea can be was demonstrated in February 2022, when twenty-one of a crew of twenty-four on a Spanish fishing vessel lost their lives when their vessel sank on Newfoundland's Grand Banks. One of those who died, Galician fisherman Ricardo Arias Garcia, had been the sole survivor in a highly challenging rescue in Galway Bay by Shannon's Rescue 115 helicopter two decades earlier.[2]

Covid-19 restrictions have helped to redefine the relationship between Irish people and their island rim. This has been reflected in two busy years for Water Safety Ireland lifeguards and RNLI lifeboats, and in the 12 per cent overall increase in Irish Coast Guard call-outs in 2021. Gardaí, Civil Defence members, search and rescue dog teams and mountain rescue volunteers all provide key supports. Often forgotten is the contribution in both fuel and lost fishing time of skippers and crews in every port and harbour, and the many individuals on shore who drop everything to walk cliffs, shorelines and the banks of rivers and lakes.

Water Safety Ireland continues its inspiring work, empowering everyone from pre-school pupils to adults in taking basic steps to make the most of this island's beautiful coastline, while the Irish Coast Guard, RNLI and Met Éireann play their part in issuing regular safety messages.

However, shock waves generated by the death of Doolin Coast Guard volunteer Caitríona Lucas in September 2016 and that of the four Rescue 116 helicopter aircrew in March 2017 are still being felt within the Irish Coast Guard.

Retired search and rescue co-ordinator and radio officer Joe Ryan noted in his bicentenary publication on the organisation that the Irish Coast Guard is 'only in its infancy'.[3] The next such history will reflect the role of drones, equipped with thermal imaging cameras, zoom lenses and powerful spotlights, but there will always be a role for those who know the sea.

APPENDIX
SEARCH AND
RESCUE AWARDS

The **Distinguished Service Medal** (DSM) is awarded to members of the Defence Forces in recognition of individual or associated acts of bravery, courage, leadership, resource or devotion to duty arising out of service during peacetime. Awarded to:

Comdt Barney McMahon, Sgt Alec Dunne and Cpl Michael Brady, for cliff face rescue, Glendalough, Wicklow, 18 March 1970

Capt. Tom Croke, Cpl Terry Kelly and Cpl John Ring, for cliff rescue, Powerscourt, Wicklow, 5 August 1972

Comdt Paddy O'Shea, Sgt Richard Murray and Armn David Byrne, for cliff rescue, Glendalough, 13 May 1977

Comdt Paddy O'Shea, Capt. Donal Loughnane, Sgt Willie Byrne, Armn Owen Sherry and Armn Richard O'Sullivan, for night rescue involving two Alouette III helicopters on Muckish mountain, Donegal

Comdt Jurgen Whyte, Comdt Jim Corby, Sgt Barney Heron and Cpl Daithí Ó Cearbhalláin, for night rescue off the FV *Locative* off Donegal coast, 9 March 1991

Capt. Dave O'Flaherty, Capt. Mick Baker, Sgt Paddy Mooney and Cpl Niall Byrne, for night rescue off Tramore, Waterford, 1 July 1999

Cdr Jim Robinson and Naval Service Gemini crew Mossy Mahon, John McGrath and Terry Brown, for recovery of victims of Air India air crash off Cork coast, June 1985

The **Sir Edward and Maisie Lewis Award** is conferred for rescues at sea by the Shipwrecked Mariners Society. Awarded to:

Comdt Harvey O'Keeffe, Capt. Sean Murphy, Sgt Daithí Ó Cearbhalláin and Cpl Christy Mahady, for night rescue of crew of fish factory vessel *Capitaine Pleven II* off Ballyvaughan, Clare, 5 April 1991

Air Corps No. 3 Operations Wing's search and rescue has received a number of other awards, including the French Fedération Aeronautique Internationale Diplôme d'Honneur for humanitarian service.

The **Billy Deacon Award** is awarded to winchmen and/or winch operators working British and Irish search and rescue regions, named after Billy Deacon, who died during a Maritime and Coastguard Agency search and rescue helicopter mission in 1997. Awarded to:

Coast Guard Rescue 118 winch team member Gary Robertson, for his rescue of
    a fisherman off Arranmore Island, Donegal, April 2016
Coast Guard Rescue 115 winchman Philip Wrenn, for rescuing brothers Giovanni
    and Ricardo Zanon at Poll na bPéist, Inis Mór, Aran islands, February 2019

The Irish state's marine meritorious award scheme initiated in 1999 is one of several award schemes for search, rescue and recovery. Bravery awards are also conferred by Comhairle na Míre Gaile, the Council for the Recognition of Deeds of Bravery, by Water Safety Ireland for individuals and lifeguards, and by the RNLI for its lifeboat crews.

NATIONAL BRAVERY AWARDS – MARINE RECIPIENTS
Gold medal
Michael Heffernan (memorial), Mayo, 9 May 2007
Joseph Barrett, Mayo, 9 May 2007
Peter O'Keeffe (memorial), Cork, 9 May 2007
Jonathan Herlihy (memorial), Cork, 9 May 2007
Caitríona Lucas (memorial), Clare, 20 October 2017

Silver medal
Sarah Courtney, winch crew Rescue 117, Waterford, 12 Nov. 2021

Certificates of Bravery
Rescue 117 crew: Sarah Courtney, Ronan Flanagan, Adrian O'Hara (all Waterford)
and Aaron Hyland (Galway), 12 Nov. 2021

MARINE MERITORIOUS AWARDS
1999, Dublin Castle
The Marine Ministerial Letter of Appreciation for Meritorious Service was awarded to:
Manuel di Lucia, founder and active member of Kilkee Marine Rescue
Carmel Lyons and Peter Leonard, helicopter rescue from FV *Dunboy* off Slyne
    Head, Galway, Dec. 1993

Comdt Donie Scanlan and Air Corps crew, for involvement in FV *Dunboy* rescue in extreme weather, Dec. 1993

Naval Diving Unit, for outstanding contribution to marine search and rescue, particularly the search for two fishermen who lost their lives off Helvick in 1993 and during the *Jenalisa* incident off Dunmore East in 1996

Michael O'Regan, search and recovery of body at Mizen Head, Cork, Jan. 1994

Charlie Cavanagh, search for Greencastle trawler *Carrickatine*, Nov. 1995-Feb. 1996

Billy Dickenson, for rescue of child from car in Wicklow harbour, Nov. 1996

Mattie Shannon, for involvement in a cliff rescue at Cliffs of Moher, Sep. 1997

Pat O'Donnell, Martin O'Donnell, P.J. Walker and crew, and Josie Barrett, for involvement in Belderrig cave rescue, Mayo, Oct. 1997

The Michael Heffernan Gold Medal for Marine Gallantry was awarded to:
Michael Heffernan, who lost his life in the Belderrig cave rescue, Mayo, Oct. 1997

The Michael Heffernan Silver Medal for Marine Gallantry was awarded to:
Capt. Nick Gribble and John McDermott, for contribution to the rescue of five Spanish fishermen from FV *Dunboy*, Dec. 1993

Garda Ciaran Doyle, Sean McHale, for Belderrig cave rescue, Mayo, Oct. 1997

The Michael Heffernan Bronze Medal for Marine Gallantry was awarded to:
Garda David Mulhall, Garda Sean O'Connell, Martin Kavanagh, for Belderrig cave rescue, Mayo, Oct. 1997

15 NOVEMBER 2002, DUBLIN CASTLE

The Marine Ministerial Letter of Appreciation for Meritorious Service was awarded to:
Donie Holland, for contribution and dedication to marine search and rescue over the years

Mr and Mrs Derry O'Donovan, for continuous and outstanding contribution to marine search and rescue

Vincent Sweeney, for contribution and dedication to marine search and rescue over the years

Sean Rodgers, for cliff rescue at Slieve League, July 1998; accepted on behalf of Killybegs Coast Guard unit

Arthur Kee, for outstanding contribution in cliff rescue at Slieve League, Donegal, July 1998

Ballycotton Coast Guard Unit, for search for bodies over duration of weeks from Cork harbour to Carnsore Point, Wexford, May 1999

Richard Grace, for role in rescue of Fergus O'Reilly, Westend, Bundoran, July 1999

Fergus Naughton and Damien McKelvey, for rescue of Shaun Flurey at Tramore beach near Rosbeg, Donegal, Sep. 1999

Vincent Morrissey, for rescue of swimmer, Whitegate area of Cork harbour, 23 Oct. 1999

Jennifer Lewis, for role in rescue of swimmer, Whitegate area of Cork harbour, 23 Oct. 1999

Rescue 115, Capt. Derek Nequest, co-pilot Robert Goodbody and winch operator John Manning, for role in rescue of seventeen crew from FV *Milford Eagle*, Jan. 2000

Lt Neil Ecceshall, for role in locating burning vessel and providing guidance to R115 during rescue of seventeen crew from *Milford Eagle*; accepted on behalf of RAF Nimrod crew

Wing Cmdr A.D. Fryer, for role in locating burning vessel and providing guidance to R115 during rescue of seventeen crew from *Milford Eagle*

Capt. Alfred Pastoriza Garcia, for skilful contribution to rescue of seventeen crew from *Milford Eagle*

Patrick Oliver, for rescue of English tourist who fell from O'Brien's Bridge, Galway, Apr. 2000

Michael Mackay, for role in rescue of English tourist who fell from O'Brien's Bridge

Rescue 115, Capt. Simon Cottrell, Capt. David Courtney and winch operator Eamonn Ó Broin, for heroic search and rescue in extremely dangerous conditions at Cliffs of Moher, Apr. 2000

David Coleman, for role in rescue of Sharon Griffin at Sandycove, Dublin, 6 July 2000

Eamon Noonan, for rescue of young boy from boat that went out of control, Kilkee Bay, Clare, 22 July 2000; accepted on behalf of Kilkee Community Rescue Boat

Costello Bay Coast Guard Unit, for outstanding service in rescue of crew from FV *Arosa*, Oct. 2000

Aran Island RNLI lifeboat crew, for outstanding service in extreme weather conditions over three days in searching and recovering bodies from the FV *Arosa*

Cleggan Coast Guard Unit and crew of Naval Service patrol ship LÉ *Eithne*, for outstanding service in rescue of crew from FV *Arosa*

Naval Service divers, for outstanding service during search for crew from FV *Arosa*

Rescue 115, Capt. David Courtney, Capt. Mike Shaw, winch operator John Manning and winchman Eamonn Ó Broin, for outstanding role in rescue of crew members of FV *Arosa*

Rescue 115, Capt. David Courtney, Capt. Mike Shaw, winch operator Noel Donnelly and winchman Peter Leonard, for role in rescue of crew from FV *An-Orient*, Oct. 2000

Air Corps Capt. Shane Bonner, co-pilot Anne Brogan, winch operator Des Murray and winchman Aidan Thompson, for role in rescue of surfers at Dunluce, Antrim, 19 Feb. 2001

Rescue 115, Capt. David Courtney, co-pilot Cliff Pile, winch operator John Manning and winchman Eamonn Ó Broin, for outstanding service in rescue of crew from FV *Hansa*, Mar. 2001

Ballycotton Coast Guard Unit, for bringing a youth ashore and attending him until medical assistance arrived during rescue at Ballycotton, Cork, 18 Aug. 2001

Peter Cuthbert, for role in rescue of teenage boy pushed into sea by waves at Ballycotton, Cork, 18 Aug. 2001

Ian Fallon, for rescue of young woman at High Rock, Portmarnock, Dublin, 15 Nov. 2001

Rescue 115, Capt. Derek Nequest, Capt. Mark Kelly and winch operator John Manning, for outstanding role in rescue of ten crew from FV *Celestial Dawn*, Feb. 2002

Air Corps Comdt Seán Clancy, Capt. Brendan Jackman, Sgt Daithí Ó Cearbhalláin and Cpl Gavin Playle, for role in extremely dangerous rescue at Slieve Tooey, Donegal, Mar. 2002

The Marine Bronze Medal for Meritorious Service was awarded to:

David Kenneally, for outstanding contribution and commitment to Irish Water Safety

Donal Campbell, for outstanding contribution in cliff rescue at Slieve League, Donegal, July 1998

Aidan McMorrow, for outstanding contribution and unstinting energy during search operation for MV *Lisa Selena*, Oct. 1998

John Ward, for heroic rescue of Ellen Gillespie off Tullan Strand, Bundoran, Donegal, 12 July 1999

Anna Classon, for role in rescue of Shaun Furley at Tramore Beach, Rosbeg, Donegal, Sep. 1999

Martin Shannon, for outstanding service during rescue at the Cliffs of Moher, Apr. 2000

Kevin McDonnell, for role in rescue of English tourist who fell from O'Brien's Bridge, Galway, Apr. 2000

Members of Old Head Kinsale Coast Guard unit, for courage and assistance when a man fell from the cliffs, 7 Jan. 2001

Fergal Walsh, for role in rescue of teenage boy pushed into sea by waves at Ballycotton, Cork, 18 Aug. 2001

The Michael Heffernan Silver Medal for Marine Gallantry was awarded to:

Rescue 115, winch operator Peter Leonard, for his heroic rescue of ten crew from FV *Celestial Dawn*, Feb. 2002

2004, DUBLIN CASTLE

The Marine Ministerial Letter of Appreciation for Meritorious Service was awarded to:

Tory Island Coast Guard Unit and people of Tory Island, for rescue of crew from schooner *Carrie of Camaret* (alias *Cabin Fever I*) off Tory Island, 13 June 2003

John O'Brien, for first-aid skills and commitment to saving a life during rescue of a woman in Dún Laoghaire harbour, 4 June 2002

Air Corps SR110 crew, and John Walsh, for rescue from sea at Portstewart, 24 May 2003

Polish naval helicopter crew, for medevac from *Asgard II*, 16 Aug. 2003

The Michael Heffernan Silver Medal for Marine Gallantry was awarded to:

Staff of the Air Corps, for dedication to duty over a forty-year period

Capt. James Kelly, for tremendous contribution to marine safety

Seamus McLoughlin, for outstanding contribution to protecting the marine environment

Kevin Desmond, for contribution to water safety in Ireland

Frank Nolan, for outstanding contribution to water safety in Ireland

Paul Byrne, for rescue of woman from River Liffey by Dublin Fire Brigade, 28 Sep. 2001

The Michael Heffernan Bronze Medal for Marine Gallantry was awarded to:

Garda Declan Dennehy, for rescue at Wexford bridge, 29 Apr. 2000

Tony Youlten, for rescue of fourteen German students on Lough Corrib, 30 July 2001

Alan Baldock and James Collins, for rescue of a woman from her car in Dún Laoghaire harbour, 4 June 2002

Mary Gill, Helen Mulhall and Ann Hearty, for rescue of mother and two children from the sea at Westport, Mayo, 29 July 2002

Sean Kinsella, for rescue of swimmer in difficulty at Ardamine near Courtown harbour, Wexford, 10 Aug. 2002

Coast Guard winchman Neville Murphy, for rescue of a woman from Hungry Hill, west Cork, 19 Sep. 2002

Rescue 115, Capt. Rob Goodbody, Tony O'Mahony, winch operator Eamonn Ó Broin and winchman Neville Murphy, for medevac of injured crewman from *Princess Eva*, 28 Jan. 2003

Air Corps Cpl Ciarán Smith, for rescue from sea at Portstewart, 24 May 2003

Adrian Moloney and Dermot Spillane, for rescue of young girl swept out to sea at Barley Cove, Cork, 19 July 2003

Winchman Dariusz Szymanski, for medevac from *Asgard II*, 16 Aug. 2003

Vicky Lyons, for rescue of woman from drowning at Dún Laoghaire, Dublin, 19 Mar. 2004

2008 DUBLIN CASTLE

A certificate of participation in a marine gallantry award was awarded to:

Crew of fishing vessel *Suzanna G*, for skill and seamanship during the rescue of six crew of the FV *Darnette* south-east of Dunmore East, Waterford, 13 Sep. 2007

Bantry Community Rescue Boat, for skill and courage during search and recovery operation at Coomhola river flood, 16 Sep. 2007 – Trevor Hughes, Matt Murphy, Nigel Ducker, Aidan O'Mahoney, Maura Keane, Robert McGuinness, Andrew Reynolds, Thomas Power, Martin O'Mahoney and Eugene Cronin

The Marine Ministerial Letter of Appreciation for Meritorious Service was awarded to:

Frank Heidtke, for work as coastal unit advisory group leader which contributed to growing international recognition of the Irish Coast Guard

Kevin Morrin, for prompt response to 'Mayday' call and subsequently saving the lives of three people in Clew Bay, Mayo, 8 Sep. 2004

RNLI Arranmore coxswain Anthony Kavanagh, crew Philip McCauley, Manus O'Donnell, Anthony Proctor, Shaun O'Donnell, Kieran Cox, James Early and Martin Gallagher, for dedication, courage and exceptional seamanship in heading out in storm-force conditions to assist a lone yachtsman in treacherous seas off the north-west coast, 2 July 2005

Capt. Simon Cotterell and Peter Leonard, for skill and bravery in saving the life of a man at the top of a 300-foot crane at Limerick docks, 19 Mar. 2005

Narayan Toolan, for skill and bravery in assisting the rescue of casualty at Easkey pier, Sligo, 12 July 2006

Philip McAvoy, for assisting a member of the public who fell into the water at Creevy pier, Ballyshannon, Donegal, 26 Aug. 2006

Rescue 116, Capt. Ed Shivnen, crew Michael Hennelly, Derek Everitt and Tom Gannon, for skill and courage in rescue of a casualty at Glenmacnass waterfall, Wicklow, 17 Sep. 2006

Dublin/Wicklow Mountain Rescue Team, for skill and courage in rescue of casualty at Glenmacnass waterfall, Wicklow, 17 Sep. 2006

Ardmore, Bonmahon, Carnsore, Curracloe, Dunmore East, Fethard-on-Sea, Helvick, Kilmore Quay, Rosslare and Tramore Coast Guard Units, for dedicated service in search for FV *Père Charles* and FV *Honeydew II*, Jan.–Feb. 2007

Johnny Walsh and crew: for dedicated service in search for FV *Père Charles* and FV *Honeydew II*, Jan.–Feb. 2007

Conor McGuigan, for his courage and commitment in assisting the rescue of three children at Tullan Strand, Donegal, 20 Aug. 2007

Denis Harding, for prompt response to 'Mayday' broadcast and exceptional seamanship and bravery in rescuing six crew members of FV *Darnette*, 13 Nov. 2007

Jarlath Cunnane and crew of *Northabout*, for courage, skill and seamanship in diverting to a distress signal 800 miles east of Barbados and successfully rescuing two French sailors from sailing vessel *Neree*, 9 Dec. 2007

Capt. Hugh Tully and crew, Naval Service, for actions of skill and endurance in saving FV *Shark* and offsetting the threat to the environment in such a sensitive sea area, 19 Jan. 2008

The Michael Heffernan Gold Medal for Marine Gallantry was awarded to:

Liam Kirwan, for professionalism, expertise and dedication in establishing Ireland's future Coast Guard service

Capt. Geoff Livingstone, for professionalism, expertise and dedication in establishing Ireland's future Coast Guard service

Seamus Byrne (RIP), for courage and bravery in attempting to save a life in rough seas at the base of a cliff in Kilkee Bay, Clare, 14 Apr. 2002

Jonathan Herlihy (RIP) and Peter O'Keeffe (RIP), for courage and bravery in saving the lives of a young couple in rough seas off Owenahincha beach, Cork, 3 Sep. 2006

The Michael Heffernan Silver Medal for Marine Gallantry was awarded to:

Colin Williams, for his commitment and dedication as RNLI divisional inspector of lifeboats in Ireland

The Michael Heffernan Bronze Medal for Marine Gallantry was awarded to:

Ryan Kearney, for bravery in entering the water and rescuing a casualty in difficulty, 12 July 2006

Sarah Meehan, for assisting a member of the public who fell into the water at Creevy pier, Ballyshannon, Donegal, 26 Aug. 2006

Jim Griffin, Irish Coast Guard officer in charge, for managing and co-ordinating search for FV *Père Charles* and FV *Honeydew II*, Jan.–Feb. 2007

Garda David Hearne, for bravery, courage and skill in entering the water on two occasions to save a life, 21 Apr. 2007

Anne Kiely, for rescue of child in distress off Beale Beach, Kerry, 30 July 2007

Conor Doherty, for bravery in entering the water and rescuing three children at Tullan Strand, Donegal, 20 Aug. 2007

Ryan Hamill, for courage and commitment in assisting the rescue of three children at Tullan Strand

Oliver Goggin, Shane Begley and Toby Campbell for courage and bravery in assisting a mother and child swept away in a jeep during a flash flood, 16 Sep. 2007

CPO Bartley and firefighting crew, for their actions of skill and endurance in
saving FV *Shark* and offsetting the threat to the environment in such a
sensitive sea area, 19 Jan. 2008

2014 AWARD RECIPIENTS

The Marine Ministerial Letter of Appreciation for Meritorious Service was awarded to:
Union Hall community, for dedicated and heartfelt care and hospitality for the
Tit Bonhomme search and rescue effort above and beyond the call of duty for
any voluntary community-based effort
Bill Deasy, for dedication, professionalism, compassion, humanity and selflessness in providing assistance to search and rescue operation following the
sinking of *Tit Bonhomme* and on many other such occasions in that area
Achill Coast Guard Unit, for saving a man's life in dangerous conditions over an
extended period in Achill, Nov. 2009
Alistair Jones, for bravery and use of skills in a risk-to-life situation involving a
young child at Seapoint, Blackrock, July 2011
Tony and Patrick McNamara, for quick decision-making and acting with skill,
courage and initiative in saving a man's life, Dooagh Bay, Achill, Aug. 2012
Michael O'Regan and the crew of the Goleen Coast Guard Unit, for outstanding
dedication and professionalism in assisting in tragic incident at Ballydehob,
Mar. 2013
Ben Graham, David Grant and Alexander May, for quick actions and selflessness
in helping to save a teenager's life, Balbriggan harbour, June 2013
Jim Griffin, for rescuing seven people cut off by the tide in Tramore Bay, Aug.
2013
Ballyglass Coast Guard Unit and Oliver O'Boyle, for ability to locate and transfer
individual from a mountain on the Bangor Erris Trail, Oct. 2013
Drogheda Coast Guard Unit, for rapid response in darkness and fast-flowing
water to save a woman's life and assist a fellow rescuer, River Boyne, Jan.
2014
Damien Dempsey, for quick thinking and bravery in saving a man's life from the
River Slaney, Enniscorthy, June 2014

The Michael Heffernan Silver Medal for Marine Gallantry was awarded to:
Toe Head Glandore Coast Guard Unit, for risking their lives in atrocious weather
conditions to save a man's life, following the sinking of fishing vessel *Tit
Bonhomme*, Jan. 2012

The Michael Heffernan Bronze Medal for Marine Gallantry was awarded to:
Killybegs Coast Guard Unit, for displaying skill, bravery and courage in effecting
a rescue and saving the life of a man who had fallen down a cliff at Slieve

League, Jan. 2013, in very difficult conditions and for a lengthy period of endurance

Mulroy Coast Guard Unit, for showing bravery and tenacity in mountainous seas and at huge peril to their own safety in an effort to save the life of a casualty at Fanad lighthouse, Aug. 2014

2016 AWARDS

The Marine Ministerial Letter of Appreciation for Meritorious Service was awarded to:
Lifeguard Gavin Byrne, for ability and quick thinking in rescuing three people in two separate dinghy incidents off Morriscastle beach, 31 May 2015

Skerries Coast Guard unit members Vanessa Gaffney, John Ryan, Stephen Gaffney and Christopher Collins, for ability to locate and transfer a young man who was in a critical condition after a fall near Portrane, 20 June 2015

RNLI Lough Swilly crew John McCarter, Mark Barnett and Eunan McConnell, for great character and resilience, professionalism and courage in responding to incident where a car entered the water in Buncrana, 20 Mar. 2016

Coast Guard Rescue 116 crew Richard Desay, Mark Duffy and Ciarán Smith, for ability to locate and transfer individual from cliff side to safe higher ground when rescuing a woman who had fallen 40–50ft from path at Balscadden, Howth, 20 May 2016

Dean Coleman, for ability and bravery in rescuing a swimmer in difficulty at the 40 Foot, Sandycove, 1 June 2016

RNLI Castletownbere coxswain Brian O'Driscoll, Tony O'Sullivan, John Paul Downey and Kyle Cronin, for ability to locate and save a life in challenging conditions over twelve hours when rescuing a lone sailor from an 8-metre yacht 50 miles south-west of Castletownbere, 20 Aug. 2016

RNLI Kinsale crew John O'Gorman, Nick Searls, Jim Grennan and Matthew Teehan, for rapid response, professionalism and skill in saving the three Portuguese crew on board the FV *Sean Anthony* close to the mouth of Kinsale harbour, 10 Apr. 2016

The Michael Heffernan Gold Medal for Marine Gallantry was awarded to:
Davitt Walsh, for showing bravery to risk life at huge peril to his own safety to save the life of a child when a car entered the water in Buncrana, 20 Mar. 2016

Coast Guard Rescue 118 winchman Gary Robertson, for showing bravery at huge risk to himself in the rescue of a fisherman trapped in ropes of a sinking vessel in high waves off Innisinny Island, 9 Apr. 2016

The Michael Heffernan Bronze Medal for Marine Gallantry was awarded to:
Paul Dolan and Dean Treacy, for quick reaction and acute observation in rescuing a boat operator taken ill off Clontarf, 6 Oct. 2012

Sam Nunn, Ruairi Nunn, Brian Kehoe and Niall McGee, for initiative and true heroism in saving nine people from drowning close to Saltee islands, 30 Aug. 2015

Charlie Hennigar, for quick reaction and selfless act in saving three people when the gangway between the Inis Oírr pier and a ferry ditched into the water, 6 June 2016

ENDNOTES

CHAPTER 1

1   *The Irish Times*, 25 August 2018.
2   *The Irish Times*, 15 September 2016. All quotations from the funeral taken from this source.
3   MCIB report into the death of Caitríona Lucas, published 7 December 2018, correspondence 8.4.

CHAPTER 2

1   Failure to find PLBs was identified by Bernard Lucas in his correspondence on the draft Marine Casualty Investigation Board (MCIB) report into the death of Caitríona Lucas.
2   MCIB report into the death of Caitríona Lucas, correspondence.
3   *The Sunday Times*, 17 November 2019.
4   MCIB report into the death of Caitríona Lucas, correspondence.
5   Ibid.
6   Ibid.
7   Ibid.
8   ISO: International Organization for Standardization.
9   *The Irish Times*, 19 December 2018.
10 Ibid.
11 Response to queries by author.
12 Ibid.
13 *The Irish Times*, 18 November 2019.
14 Joint Committee on Transport and Communications Report on Scrutiny of the General Scheme of the Merchant Shipping (Investigation of Marine Casualties) (Amendment) Bill 2020, July 2021.
15 *Sunday Independent*, 31 January 2021.
16 https://afloat.ie/safety/mcib/item/49185-ryan-to-undertake-fundamental-review-of-structures-for-marine-investigations.
17 *Sunday Independent*, 31 January 2021.
18 *The Times* (Ireland), 13 March 2021.
19 *Irish Independent*, 8 August 2021.

20   RTÉ News, 28 October 2021.
21   *The Irish Times*, 9 October 2021.
22   *The Irish Times*, 22 October 2021.
23   *The Irish Times*, 9 October 2021.
24   *The Clare Echo*, 24 November 2021.

CHAPTER 3
1   David Courtney, *Nine Lives* (Mercier Press, 2008), pp. 97–8.
2   Ronan Kelly's Ireland Lockdown Lookback, www.facebook.com/100044139
     624287/videos/537619810549888.

CHAPTER 4
1   Dermot Keyes, *The Munster Express*, 16 November 2009.
2   RTÉ Factual, *Rescue 117*, first broadcast in September 2010.
3   Claire Murphy, Herald.ie, 12 August 2009.
4   Declan Ganley, Twitter, 14 March 2007.
5   *Irish Independent*, 14 March 2020.
6   Lorna Siggins, *Mayday! Mayday! Heroic Air-Sea Rescues in Irish Waters* (Gill &
     Macmillan, 2004), Chapter 15.
7   *The Irish Times*, 3 July 2014.
8   Siggins, *Mayday! Mayday!*, pp. 198–9, 215–16.
9   Air Accident Investigation Unit Ireland: Formal report, Sikorsky S-92A, EI-
     ICR, Black Rock, Co. Mayo, Ireland, 14 March 2017, p. 78.
10   Siggins, *Mayday! Mayday!*, pp. 74, 75–8, 79–80, 91–2, 94.
11   Air Accident Investigation Unit Ireland: Formal report, Sikorsky S-92A, EI-
     ICR, Black Rock, Co Mayo, Ireland, 14 March 2017, pp. 79–92.

CHAPTER 5
1   *Irish Independent*, 14 March 2020.
2   Niamh Fitzpatrick, *Tell Me the Truth About Loss: A Psychologist's Personal Story
     of Loss, Grief and Finding Hope* (Gill Books, 2020).
3   Ibid., pp. 24–5.
4   *Tabú: An Garda Cósta – Ár n-Insint Féin*, first broadcast on TG4, 27 March 2020.
5   Ibid.
6   Siggins, *Mayday! Mayday!*, pp. 124–5.
7   *The Irish Times*, 15 March 2017.
8   Siggins, *Mayday! Mayday!*, Chapters 13 and 14.
9   *Belfast Telegraph*, 15 March 2017.
10   *The Irish Times*, 15 March 2017.
11   Fitzpatrick, *Tell Me the Truth About Loss*, pp. 63–5.

CHAPTER 6
1   RTÉ Radio Documentary on One, *Good Day at Blackrock*, by Cathal Murray
     with Ronan Kelly, broadcast.

2   *The Irish Times*, 16 March 2017.

3   *The Irish Times*, 16 March 2018.

4   Peter Murtagh, *The Irish Times*, 18 March 2017.

5   *The Irish Times*, 2 April 2017.

6   Comharchumann Forbartha Ionad Deirbhile Eachléim Teo.

7   Siggins, *Mayday! Mayday!*, Chapter 11.

8   Details of funeral from *The Irish Times*, 30 March 2017.

9   *The Irish Times*, 29 August 2017.

10   Details on this search from *The Irish Times*, 10 April 2017.

11   Air Accident Investigation Unit preliminary report: Accident, Sikorsky S-92A, EI-ICR, Black Rock, Co Mayo, Ireland, 13 April 2017, Appendix A.

12   *The Irish Times*, 20 April 2017.

13   *The Irish Times*, 23 April 2017

14   *The Irish Times*, 21 April 2017.

CHAPTER 7

1   Details on the memorial service from *The Irish Times*, 20 May 2017.

2   *The Irish Times*, 13 July 2017.

3   RTÉ *Prime Time*, 26 October 2017.

4   Ibid.

5   *The Irish Times*, 14 March 2018.

6   Details of the inquest from *The Irish Times*, 12 April 2018.

CHAPTER 8

1   The AAIU investigation team comprised Paul Farrell (Investigator-in-Charge), Jurgen Whyte (Chief Inspector), Kate Fitzgerald (Inspector – Engineering), Howard Hughes (Inspector – Operations), Leo Murray (Inspector – Operations), John Owens (Inspector – Engineering) and Kevin O'Ceallaigh (Inspector – Operations).

2   *Irish Examiner*, 12 March 2020

3   Air Accident Investigation Unit Ireland, Formal Report Accident, Sikorsky S-92A, EI-ICR Black Rock, Co. Mayo, Ireland, 14 March 2017, published 5 November 2021. Available at: www.aaiu.ie/sites/default/files/report-attachments/Final%20Report.pdf. All following quotes in this section are taken from the report unless otherwise stated.

4   Daniel Kahneman, *Thinking, Fast and Slow* (Macmillan, 2011).

5   *The Irish Times*, 4 November 2021.

6   *The Irish Times*, 5 November 2021.

7   For quotes from IALPA, CHC and the IAA regarding the report see: https://afloat.ie/safety/coastguard/item/52519-rescue-116-final-report-critical-of-management-organisational-systems.

8   RTÉ Radio 1, *Saturday with Katie Hannon*, 6 November 2021.

9   *The Mail on Sunday*, 7 November 2021.

10   Interview with author.

11   For full text of the Dáil Debate on this issue see: www.oireachtas.ie/en/debates/
      debate/dail/2021-11-17/22.
12   www.oireachtas.ie/en/debates/debate/seanad/2021-11-18/11/.

CHAPTER 9

1   All quotes for story of the Greenhaven rescue from *The Donegal Democrat*, 7
      March 1956.
2   *The Irish Independent*, 12 October 2019.
3   *The Irish Times*, 26 October 1956.
4   Quotes in this section from Siggins, *Mayday! Mayday!*, pp. 6–8.
5   Unless otherwise indicated, quotes in this section from Siggins, *Mayday!
      Mayday!*, pp. 10–13.
6   John de Courcy Ireland, *Lifeboats in Dublin Bay: A Review of the Service from
      1803–1997* (RNLI Dún Laoghaire, 1998).
7   More details of the early Coast Guard, and the separate Coast Watch service
      during the Second World War, can be found in Joe Ryan's self-published history,
      Coast Guard: Saving Lives in Ireland for 200 Years (2022); and Dr Michael
      Kennedy, *Guarding Neutral Ireland: The Coastwatching Service and Military
      Intelligence 1939–1945* (Four Courts Press, Dublin, 2008).
8   *The Irish Times*, 26 October 1956.
9   Lieutenant Colonel Michael O'Malley, 'In the beginning', *Irish Air Corps:
      Celebrating 30 Years of Helicopter Operations, 1963–1993* (Air Corps, 1993).
10   Peter Whittle and Michael Borissow, *Angels without Wings* (Angley Book
      Company, 1966).
11   Siggins, *Mayday! Mayday!*, pp. 18.
12   O'Connor and McMahon quotes from Siggins, *Mayday! Mayday!*, pp. 22 and
      24.

CHAPTER 10

1   Siggins, *Mayday! Mayday!*, p. 68.
2   Interview with author.
3   McDermott and Boulden quotes from Siggins, *Mayday! Mayday!*, p. 54.
4   *The Irish Times*, 25 June 1985.
5   *The Irish Times*, 21 June 2000.
6   Interview with author.
7   West Coast Search and Rescue Action Committee Report, 1988, p. 13.
8   The Irish Marine Emergency Service was later renamed the Irish Coast Guard.
9   Air Corps Mission Report: Helicopter Search and Rescue Mission, 9 March
      1990 off the Donegal coast, June 1991.
10   Unless otherwise indicated crew quotes are from Siggins, *Mayday! Mayday!*, pp.
      74–8.
11   Air Corps Mission Report: Helicopter Search and Rescue Mission, 9 March
      1990 off the Donegal coast, June 1991.
12   Ibid.

CHAPTER 11

1   IMES subsequently became the Irish Coast Guard.

2   Unless otherwise indicated, all quotations for this chapter from Siggins, *Mayday! Mayday!*, pp. 103–5.

CHAPTER 12

1   Unless otherwise indicated, all quotes in this section from Siggins, *Mayday! Mayday!*, pp. 142–50.

2   AAIU final report into the Tramore Dauphin crash, July 1999, p. 22.

3   *The Irish Times*, 6 November 2000.

4   *Irish Independent*, 13 November 2000.

5   Findings, Court of Inquiry Dauphin DH248, 30 August 2001, para. 30.

6   Findings, Court of Inquiry Dauphin DH248, 30 August 2001.

7   Siggins, *Mayday! Mayday!*, p. 26.

8   The cause of the 1968 Aer Lingus Viscount crash is still inconclusive.

9   Michael Davies, father of Ros Davies, submitted a list of water safety recommendations to the jury at his son's inquest on 17 October 1995, asking the minister for the marine to act on them.

10   David Carroll, *'Dauntless Courage': Celebrating the History of the RNLI Lifeboats, their Crews and the Maritime Heritage of the Dunmore East Community* (RNLI Waterford, 2020), p. 217.

11   *The Irish Times*, 7 December 2005.

12   Siggins, *Mayday! Mayday!*, Chapter 11.

13   Carroll, *Dauntless Courage*, pp. 234–5.

14   All quotes in this section from Murphy are from interview with author.

15   The details of this story are from Damien Tiernan, *Souls of the Sea: The Tragedy of the Père Charles and Honey Dew II* (Hachette, 2007).

16   See appendix for full list of marine meritorious awards.

17   Unless otherwise indicated, all quotes in this section from Dunne and Murphy from interview with author.

18   *Yachting Monthly*, The Learning Curve, April/May 2021.

19   *RNLI magazine*, October 2018. All quotes concerning the rescue of the Dehler 101 come from this source unless otherwise indicated.

20   www.oireachtas.ie/en/press-centre/press-releases/20211112-ceann-comhairle-presents-25-national-bravery-awards-for-17-acts-of-bravery/.

CHAPTER 13

1   Wallace Clark, *Sailing Round Ireland* (North-West Books, 1976), p. 16.

2   Details on the *Stolwijk* rescue are from https://rnli.org/find-my-nearest/lifeboat-stations/arranmore-lifeboat-station/station-history-arranmore.

3   In 2017, Keith White undertook a round Britain and Ireland voyage in aid of Sailability, aiming to be the first sailor with a disability to complete the circumnavigation of the two islands. RNLI Lowestoft was called to his assistance 27 miles south-east of the port after his sail ripped.

4   All quotes from Ross Classon from interview with author.

5   All quotes from Micheál Conneely from *The Irish Times*, 27 November 2015.

6   *The Irish Times*, 20 January 2015.

7   Unless otherwise indicated, all quotes in this section from citation for Billy Deacon award, 2017.

8   *Irish Independent*, 11 April 2016.

9   All quotes in this section from *The Irish Times*, 6 May 2017.

10   Interview with author.

11   Charlie Cavanagh quotes from interview with author.

12   Adventurer and climbing consultant Mike O'Shea was also part of TAG 07, along with Niall Ferns, then of the Greystones Coast Guard unit, County Wicklow (subsequently promoted to Coast Guard Unit & Support Manager), Frank Heidtke of Dingle, County Kerry, Ray Murphy of Doolin, County Clare, and Vincent Farr of Crosshaven, County Cork.

13   For Walsh quotes see: www.bbc.com/news/uk-northern-ireland-35867593.

CHAPTER 14

1   Quotes from Cotter in this section from interview with author.

2   See Chapter 10.

3   Report by Tom MacSweeney, RTÉ News, 29 September 1985.

4   Ralph Riegel, *Irish Independent*, 15 June 2006.

5   Jackie Keogh, *The Southern Star*, 11 January 2021.

6   See Chapter 11.

7   Siggins, *Mayday! Mayday!*, p. 123.

8   Ibid., p. 206.

9   Ted Creedon, *The Kerryman*, 7 February 2002. All Creedon quotes from this account.

10   Siggins, *Mayday! Mayday!*, p. 209.

11   Ibid.

12   Interview with author.

13   *Practical Boat Owner*, 22 August 2016.

14   RNLI with Nikki Girvan, *Surviving the Storms: Extraordinary Stories of Courage and Compassion at Sea* (HarperCollins, 2020), pp. 237–54.

15   Unless otherwise indicated, all quotes in this section from interview with author.

CHAPTER 15

1   Dorothy Cross, programme, *Chiasm* opera, May 1999.

2   Tim Robinson, *Stones of Aran: Pilgrimage* (Penguin, 1986), p. 63.

3   All quotes from the brothers from interview with author.

4   *Tabú: An Garda Cósta – Ár n-Insint Féin*, first broadcast on TG4, 27 March 2020.

5   Department of Transport press release, 18 March 2021.

6   Interview with author.

CHAPTER 16

1 Unless otherwise indicated, all quotes in this chapter from interview with author.
2 *The Irish Times*, 13 June 2020.
3 *The Irish Times*, 19 February 2021.

CHAPTER 17

1 RTÉ Radio, *Doc on One*, 'Miracle in Galway Bay', by Lorna Siggins and Sarah Blake, first broadcast 1 August 2021. Unless otherwise stated, all quotes in this chapter from this source.
2 RTÉ Radio, *Drivetime*, 13 August 2020.
3 Met Éireann information.
4 RTÉ Radio, *Countrywide*, 22 August 2020.
5 Ibid.
6 Roald Dahl, *Matilda* (Jonathan Cape, 1988).
7 *Irish Examiner*, 14 August 2020.
8 *Irish Independent*, 13 August 2020.
9 Donohue quotes from the *Irish Independent*, 18 August 2020.
10 RTÉ Radio 1 Drivetime, 12 August 2020.
11 *The Sunday Times*, 16 August 2020.
12 See Chapter 14.
13 *The Sunday Times*, 16 August 2020.
14 RTÉ Radio, *Countrywide*, 22 August 2020.
15 RTÉ TV, *The Late Late Show*, 4 September 2020.
16 Interview with Eavan Murray, *Irish Independent*, 11 August 2021.
17 www.galwaydaily.com/news/heroic-fisherman-showed-fantastic-community-spirit-of-galway-with-sea-rescue/.
18 Interview with author.

EPILOGUE

1 Interview with author.
2 For the full story of the original rescue, see Siggins, *Mayday! Mayday!*, pp. 175–6, 178–85.
3 Ryan quotes from: *Coast Guard: Saving Lives in Ireland for 200 Years*.

SELECT BIBLIOGRAPHY

Carroll, David, *Dauntless Courage: Celebrating the History of RNLI Lifeboats, Their Crews and the Maritime Heritage of the Dunmore East Community* (RNLI Waterford, 2020)

Courtney, David, *Nine Lives* (Mercier Press, 2008)

de Courcy Ireland, John, *Lifeboats in Dublin Bay: A Review of the Service from 1803–1997* (RNLI Dún Laoghaire, 1998)

Fitzpatrick, Niamh, *Tell Me the Truth About Loss: A Psychologist's Personal Story of Loss, Grief and Finding Hope* (Gill Books, 2020)

Lankford, Éamon, *Baltimore Lifeboat: A Community Story, 1919–2019* (RNLI Baltimore, 2019)

RNLI Lifeboats with Nikki Girvan, *Surviving the Storms: Extraordinary Stories of Courage and Compassion at Sea* (HarperCollins, 2020)

Ryan, Joe, *Coast Guard: Saving Lives in Ireland for 200 Years* (self-published, 2022)

Siggins, Lorna, *Mayday! Mayday! Heroic Air-Sea Rescues in Irish Waters* (Gill & Macmillan, 2004)

Tiernan, Damien, *Souls of the Sea: The Tragedy of the Père Charles and Honey Dew II* (Hachette Books, 2007)

INDEX